SEMEIA 41

SPEECH ACT THEORY AND BIBLICAL CRITICISM

Editor of this volume:
Hugh C. White

©1988
by the Society of Biblical Literature

Published by
SCHOLARS PRESS
P.O. Box 1608
Decatur, GA 30031-1608

Printed in the United States of America
on acid-free paper

CONTENTS

Acknowledgements v

Contributors vi

Introduction: Speech Act Theory and Literary Criticism
 Hugh C. White 1

I. Speech Act Theory and Narrative Hermeneutics 25

"Performative Utterance, the Word of God, and the Death of the Author"
 Michael Hancher 27

"The Value of Speech Act Theory for Old Testament Hermeneutics"
 Hugh C. White 41

II. Applications of Speech Act Theory to Problems of Biblical Exegesis 65

"(Feminist) Criticism in the Garden: Inferring Genesis 2-3"
 Susan S. Lanser 67

"Speech Act Theory and Biblical Exegesis"
 Daniel Patte 85

"Infelicitous Performances and Ritual Criticism"
 Ronald L. Grimes 103

III. Responses 123

"The Contribution of Speech Act Theory to Biblical Studies"
 Martin J. Buss 125

"Speaking of Believing in Gen. 2-3"
 Robert Detweiler 135

"Philosophy of Language in the Service of Religious Studies"
 Charles E. Jarrett 143

IV. Bibliographies.. 161

Annotated Introductory Bibliography on Speech Act Theory 163

Selected General Bibliography on Speech Act Theory.......... 173

ACKNOWLEDGEMENTS

A special word of thanks is due Michael Hancher who made available to me a comprehensive, unpublished bibliography of works on speech act theory and literary criticism in the early stages of the research which led to this volume. It was of great help both in my research and in compiling the general bibliographies which I have included here. Also I am indebted to both Michael Hancher and Susan Lanser for carefully reading the manuscript of my "Introduction" and offering many valuable criticisms and suggestions. My thanks also to Gerald Larson who collaborated with me on organizing the SBL/AAR sessions where most of these papers and responses were first presented.

A grant from the Faculty Academic Study Program of Rutgers University provided the time needed for the editing of this volume and the composition of the "Introduction."

CONTRIBUTORS TO THIS ISSUE

Prof. Martin Buss
  Department of Religion
  Emory University
  Atlanta, GA 30322

Prof. Robert Detweiler
  Graduate Institute of the Liberal Arts
  Emory University
  Atlanta, Ga 30322

Prof. Ronald Grimes
  Department of Religion and Culture
  Wilfrid Laurier University
  Waterloo, Ontario
  Canada N2L3C5

Prof. Michael Hancher
  Department of English
  University of Minnesota
  Lind Hall
  Minneapolis, MN 55455

Prof. Charles Jarrett
  Department of Philosophy
  Camden College of Arts and Sciences
  Rutgers University
  Camden, NJ 08102

Prof. Susan Sniader Lanser
  Department of English
  Georgetown University
  Washington, DC 20057

Prof. Daniel Patte
  Box 1704 Station B
  Vanderbilt University
  Nashville, TN 37235

Prof. Hugh C. White
　Department of Religion
　Camden College of Arts and Sciences
　Rutgers University
　Camden, NJ 08102

INTRODUCTION: SPEECH ACT THEORY AND LITERARY CRITICISM

Hugh C. White
Camden College of Arts and Sciences
Rutgers University

ABSTRACT

The basic features of the speech act philosophy of J. L. Austin are summarized which are of the most relevance to literary criticism. The ways in which this philosophy has been applied to literary criticism are explained, and suggestions made as to their relevance for Biblical studies. The major forms which the applications have taken are studies of literature which are "about" speech acts, and studies of literature itself as a type of speech act. There is also a parallel but related development which attempts to understand the performative dimension of language as such, which has led to the practice of "deconstruction" in literary criticism. The relation of "Deconstruction" to speech act philosophy is thus examined.

Speech act theory is a philosophical theory of language use which is being applied today to a wide range of phenomena from literary texts to religious rituals, from semantics to law. Its foundations were laid in England during the post-World War II period by the renowned Oxford philosopher of language, John Langshaw Austin, whose untimely death from cancer in 1960 at the age of forty-nine, dealt a major blow to modern philosophy. Though the development of the theory can be seen in his early work in the 1930's and 40's, the book which today is the primary source is the series of lectures that Austin gave as the William James Lectures at Harvard in 1955, unassumingly entitled, *How to do Things With Words* (Austin: 1975). Austin's 'mantle' seems to have passed to one of his former students, the Berkeley philosopher, John R. Searle, whose book, *Speech Acts: An Essay in the Philosophy of Language* (Searle: 1969), systematized and developed the ground-breaking work done by Austin.

This introduction will focus primarily on the various ways in which speech act theory has been appropriated in the field of literary criticism, because the methodological issues that are relevant to Biblical scholarship have been discussed most fully there. The articles in this volume represent most of the various methodological approaches which have developed in this tradition. Their respective positions in the context of this discussion will be indicated at the conclusion.

Literary critics have been attracted to speech act theory for two primary reasons. First, the theory has opened the possibility of a functional approach to literature which is less encumbered with metaphysical presuppositions than previous theories of criticism. As the literary critic Wolfgang Iser says in support of a speech act approach to literature: "the time has surely come to cut the thread altogether and replace ontological arguments with functional arguments, for what is important to readers, critics and authors alike, is what literature *does,* and not what it *means.*" (Iser: 1978)

Secondly, speech act theory offers the means to orient literature away from various formalisms which detach the text from its historical and social matrix, toward its concrete context, without engulfing it once again in the psychological, social and historical conditions of its production. This concern has been fundamental to Mary Louise Pratt's groundbreaking attempt to develop a speech act theory of literature which aims at "supplying the literary speech act with its context, and . . . reintegrating it into the broader schema of our verbal and social activities" (Pratt: 1977).

The possibility of escaping from the "ontological arguments" to which Iser refers was provided by the concept of "performative," or more accurately, "illocutionary" speech. J. L. Austin, in *How to do things With Words,* pointed to a type of language use which had been largely ignored by philosophers, that is the utterance which does not describe anything, but "is, or is a part of, the doing of an action" (Austin 1975: 5). The classic example is the promise. Austin denies that a promise is merely an outer description of an inner spiritual act. Rather, in his view, something *occurs* in the utterance itself: "Accuracy and morality alike are on the plain side of saying, *our word is our bond*" (Austin 1975: 10). Other examples of such words are vows, bets, verdicts, ritual words such as those involved in christening a ship, etc. In many such words, the utterance of the word itself, as with "I promise," coincides with the act. The validity of the promise does not depend on its valid reference to a non-verbal object or state.

Austin's pursuit of this dimension of speech led him ultimately to conclude that even those types of speech such as descriptive statements (which he calls "constative" utterances) whose primary business was to refer, actually communicated effectively only when the force of their utterance was made clear, e.g., that a statement was genuinely descriptive and not ironic, as in the sentence, "Our police department is composed of saints." The meaning of this simple descriptive statement obviously depends upon the nature of the speech act that produced it which determines whether it is to be taken "literally" or ironically. He thus concluded that all utterances were produced by what he called an "illocutionary act", which is "the performance of an act *in* saying something as opposed to the performance of an act *of* saying something" (Austin 1975: 99, 100).

Rather than being dependent upon its correspondence to nonverbal objects, the truth of the illocutionary act of asserting was more fundamentally dependent upon the presence of certain conditions in the social context of its utterance, and sometimes even in the mental disposition of the speakers. Thus, in place of what he called the 'fetish' of the true/false dichotomy central to the verification principle (Austin 1975: 151), Austin spoke with disarming understatement, of contextual "felicity conditions," the conformity or non-conformity to which would make a performative utterance "happy" or "unhappy." For example, a man's utterance of a marriage vow is infelicitous if it is discovered that he is already married, or if it is discovered that the presiding official is not duly authorized to perform weddings (Austin 1975: 14). With this concept the speech act is firmly connected to its social context.

Many illocutions not only constitute acts in their utterance, however, but also produce effects. When these effects are governed by convention, e.g. in a warning being heard and understood ("securing uptake"), in a promise being fulfilled ("inviting a response"), or a naming having the effect of preventing the use of other names ("taking effect"), they are, according to Austin, "bound up with" the illocutionary act (1975: 118). There are other intended and unintended effects of illocutionary acts which are not related to them by convention, however. The illocutionary act of arguing may achieve the effect of persuading or convincing; warning, in addition to having the illocutionary effect of being heard and understood (securing uptake), may also frighten, scare or alarm (Austin, 1975: 117, 118; Searle, 1969: 25). These acts Austin terms "perlocutionary" acts. The fundamental feature of the perlocutionary act is that it refers to an effect upon the receiver (e.g. persuading) achieved *by* an illocutionary act (e.g. arguing), and not to the effect achieved *in* the illocutionary act (e.g. as promising, under the proper conditions, has the effect *in* its performance, of creating a promissory relation between two parties). The definition of some illocutionary verbs, such as requesting, refer necessarily to the perlocutionary act associated with them (the attempt to get a hearer to do something), but others do not (Searle, 1969: 71). It should be noted, however, that some of these distinctions (e.g. between the conventional and non-conventional) were acknowledged by Austin to be less than precise (1975: 119). When examining the application of speech act theory to literature, it is important to bear in mind that there is no single unified theory, but a diverse array of approaches which emphasize and develop different features of Austin's thought. It is to be expected thus that the use of speech act theory in literary criticism will develop in several different quite different directions. The criticisms which exponents of these various approaches direct at each other reflect some of the deeper unresolved philosophical problems in speech act theory which we will note as we examine this internal debate.

* * *

The various ways of appropriating aspects of speech act theory by literary critics might be categorized, for the sake of rhetorical convenience, as "right", "center" and "left" (absolutely no political connotations implied!), to indicate: a sharply circumscribed application which attempts to keep strictly within the terms of the thought of Austin and Searle (right); a use which extends the original theory to deal with certain problems unique to literary theory often utilizing the thought of another major speech act philosopher, Paul Grice (center); and a third approach (left) which emphasizes, more generally, the performative dimension of language as such, and rests largely upon views which arose independent of the work of Austin. All of these approaches will be represented to some extent in this volume.

The key issue which separates these approaches pertains to the choice of proper subject matter for analysis. The question is whether speech act theory is to be applied only to speech acts and their contexts internal to the literary work (right), whether the act of writing itself in its larger social context is to be taken as a type of speech act which has significance for the whole of every literary work (center), or whether the problem must be pushed back even further to the performative function of language as such in the constitution of subjectivity (left). Implicated in these choices are assumptions regarding the extraordinarily difficult problem of the status of the governing conditions, conventions, rules, maxims, etc. (there is no unanimity in the terminology here), which constitute the context of the speech act. At this stage of the discussion, each of these positions has something significant to contribute to our understanding of literature. They will be presented below, not to favor one above another, but to bring out the most important criticisms which each makes of the other. In this way any appropriation of speech act theory for Biblical studies which might be stimulated by this volume may be done from a broad perspective.

We will examine the "centrist" position first and most thoroughly, not only because it represents the earliest kind of application of speech act theory, but also because it has been developed more completely and extensively than either the 'left' or 'right'. The "centrist" position holds that the act of writing a literary work is a particular kind of speech act which illuminates the nature of literature in a global sense. It develops a form of text analysis which utilizes the conventions governing speech acts to analyze speech acts internal to particular literary works. One of the first literary critics to make use of speech act theory, Richard Ohmann, followed the lines of this "centrist" program.

One of Ohmann's central interests was to define more precisely the nature of the 'literary' by using speech act theory to illuminate the distinctive features of the act of composition. Ohmann finds the distinctive characteristic of the act of writing (e.g., in the composition of plays, poems, or novels) to be its imitation of genuine, 'real world,' speech acts. "The writer puts out imitation speech acts *as if* they were being performed by someone" (Ohmann 1973: 98). The literary work then records or implies the conditions which will either make the speech acts it contains "happy" or "unhappy." But this felicity is strictly internal to the literary work, since, in Ohmann's view, mimetic works of literature are "discourses with the usual illocutionary rules suspended, acts without consequences of the usual sort" (Ohmann 1973: 97). This view stems from Austin's characterization of dramatic and literary works as "parasitic" upon real world illocutionary acts, and "'not serious'" (Austin 1962: 104).

This approach to literature might reveal why Biblical narrative seems never completely at home within the category of literature, since the act of writing sacred scripture cannot be understood as mimetic in this sense. Speech acts such as the promise of land, or the Sinai covenant, claim to be real world speech acts, in some sense, and not parasitic.

The major criticisms of this initial attempt to understand the nature of literature with the help of speech act theory, have pertained to the difficulty of separating the literary from the nonliterary, as well as fiction from nonfiction. More recent attempts to develop this aspect of the "centrist" program have attempted to circumvent this problem by breaking down these distinctions, rejecting the concept of mimesis, and defining more precisely the features of the generative speech act which gives rise to these verbal forms.

Mary Louise Pratt, who has been the first to move toward a comprehensive, systematically developed speech act theory of literature, takes Ohmann to task for attempting to distinguish literary discourse from ordinary discourse. Her study of sociolinguistic investigations of "natural narrative" (i.e. narratives told in ordinary discourse), reveal that, "those characteristics of the literary speech situation which Ohmann attributes to a work's being a quasi-speech-act are actually characteristics of the real speech acts that the literary works 'purportedly imitate'" (Pratt 1977: 96).

These similarities, "derive from the fact that at some level of analysis they are utterances of the same type." This similarity is not at the level of narrativity alone, but extends into the depths of the poetic structure, indicating that "most of the features which poeticians believed constituted the 'literariness' of novels are not 'literary' at all. They occur in novels not because they are novels (i.e., literature) but because they are members of some other more general category of speech acts" (Pratt 1977: 69).

The pressing question to which this leads, of course, is what kind of global speech act is a likely candidate to fulfill this large role, if not the act of mimesis? To answer this question Pratt locates the narrative in the context of the author/reader relationship and seeks to understand, in a broad sense, what occurs in an event of narration. In contrast to asserting or representing, a narration involves, "verbally displaying a state of affairs" (Pratt: 136), that is, transmitting a message which has a special relevance to the hearer that exceeds that of simple assertive or representative speech acts. This special relevance requires that the narratives "represent states of affairs that are held to be unusual, contrary to expectation, or otherwise problematic" (Pratt: 136). This endows the narratives with the quality of "tellability," which "characterizes an important subclass of assertive or representative speech acts that includes natural narrative, an enormous proportion of conversation, and many if not all literary works." She terms this subclass of speech acts the "exclamatory assertion" (Pratt: 136).

Such "display texts" evoke the participation of the reader/hearer in quite significant ways: The author invites his addressee(s), "to join him in contemplating it and evaluating it, and responding to it. His point is to produce in his hearers not only belief but also an imaginative and affective involvement in the state of affairs he is representing and an evaluative stance toward it" (Pratt: 136). Ultimately his aim is to elicit an interpretation of a problematic event which is supported by a consensus of himself and his hearer.

Pratt considers this type of verbal activity to be "crucial to our well-being in the world," since "one of the most important ways we have of dealing with the unexpected, uncertain, unintelligible aspects of our lives is to share and interpret them collectively" (Pratt: 140).

But the tellability/non-tellability criterion is not homologous with the fiction/non-fiction categories because, "Our capacity for verbally displaying and evaluating experience and for finding pleasure in such displays applies equally to experience which is claimed to be real as to that which is not" (Pratt: 143).

This linkage of 'literary' speech acts with pre-literary oral discourse corresponds to the way most Biblical scholars today trace much Biblical writing back to an origin in oral tradition. The blurring of the lines between fiction and fact which is characteristic of this type of oral speech also corresponds to the intermixture of legend, myth and history which carried over from the oral to the written stages of the biblical tradition. Pratt's approach would thus suggest that Biblical narrative should be analyzed more in terms of the function served by the telling or 'displaying' of these texts in the religious life of the community, and less attention given to establishing whether they are history, fiction, or some combination of the two.

Having defined the type of global speech act which gives rise to narrative, Pratt proceeds to fill in the conventional literary context shared by authors and readers which makes this type of speech act felicitous. To do this she draws on a variety of sources. They extend from the conventional factors which shape the audience's willingness to enter into a one-way discourse with no opportunity to respond (Pratt: 100), to the assumption created in the reader by the "pre-selection and pre-paration" which the publication process engenders (116), to the "conversational maxims" of speech act philosopher H. P. Grice, which provide a means of analyzing the implications (or "implicatures" in Grice's terminology) of dialogue (152ff.).

Many of these observations regarding the contextual conventions are especially applicable to the context of Biblical writing; for instance, the willingness to give up the privilege of responding takes on religious meaning when the writing is sacred, and the pre-selection process becomes the process of canonization!

With this array of conventions set in place to define the external context of the narrative speech act, Pratt can then turn to the analysis of the speech acts internal to specific narratives.

While indicating that the constituent elements of the natural narrative have their counterparts in the fictional, 'literary' narrative, it is the conversational maxims of Grice's Cooperation Principle which she finds the most fruitful for analyzing the micro-structure of the narrative text.

On the basis of the Cooperative Principle Grice maintains that the coherence and continuity in ordinary dialogue are made possible by the partners' adhering to certain implicit conversational maxims: 1. Quantity—the contribution of each contributor must be informative but not overly informative; 2. Quality—the contribution must be truthful, based on evidence, and not knowingly false; 3. Relation—contributions must be relevant; 4. Manner—contributions must avoid obscurity, ambiguity, unnecessary prolixity, and must be orderly (Pratt: 130). The Cooperative Principle may also be transgressed in ways which Grice has reduced to standard types: unintentional failures, and various knowing transgressions that he terms violations, opting out, clashes, and a type of violation which deliberately "flouts" a maxim in a way that does not actually jeopardize the Cooperative Principle (159, 160).

The concept of tellability generally conforms to the maxim of Relation though it requires going considerably beyond the mere exchange of information (Pratt: 147). But what of the maxim of Quality, which requires truthfulness? Because of the explicit conventions governing the publication of fictional narratives, the non-fulfillment of this maxim does not constitute a violation, as it would in a non-fictional display text, since it is impossible to lie about a manifestly fictional assertion. This maxim would explain why a changing concept of 'truth' in the reading community would lead to serious difficulties in the interpretation of narratives such as those in the Bible, which have no original publication conventions to make clear the nature of their truth claims.

Rather than outright violation of the maxims, the fictional display text "flouts" maxims like that of Quality. "Flouting" is a form of non-fulfillment which, according to Grice, affirms the maxims by 'exploiting' them, and does not seriously endanger the Cooperative Principle (Pratt: 160). Pratt can conclude then that "the literary speech situation is such that at the level of author/reader interaction, all Grice's types of nonfulfillment except flouting either cannot arise or tend to be eliminated in the process of a text's becoming a work of literature" (173). It is because of the implicit observance of the maxims within the real world literary context that they can be flouted so flagrantly and often in the literary work itself.

When the Cooperative Principle is applied to the inner narrative speech acts, one is dealing then, not with the actual author who is communicating through his production of display texts, but with the author implied (or expressly signified as in first person narratives) by the concrete discourse of the text, i.e., the "implied author". This division, which occurs chiefly, according to Pratt, in "imaginative literature," requires her to return to the theory of mimetic speech acts to explain the relation between the speech acts of the implied author (or fictive speaker) and that of the actual author. Various forms of non-fulfillment may occur, but virtually all non-fulfillment of the Cooperative Principle by the actual author takes the form of flouting, whereas the implied author may engage in every form of non-fulfillment (Pratt: 174, 158–200). A sharp difference thus exists between the degree and type of non-fulfillment possible for the actual author, and that permitted to the implied author.

Here again Pratt's analysis illuminates the sharp difference between Biblical writing and at least some types of 'literature' in that the constraints governing the actual author apply as well to the 'implied author' (perhaps because of the important social and religious functions of the Biblical narrative). Thus there is not the extensive "flouting" of the maxims that one finds in many types of "imaginative literature."

Introduction: Speech Act Theory and Literary Criticism

The way in which this approach can illuminate a text can be seen by looking at an analysis Pratt gives of a selection from the beginning of William Faulkner's *The Sound and the Fury*. In this selection, a golf game is recounted by the retarded Benjy, who is the fictive speaker.

> Through the fence, between the curling flower spaces, I could see them hitting. They were coming toward where the flag was and I went along the fence. Luster was hunting in the grass by the flower tree. Then they put the flag back and they went to the table, and he hit and the other hit. Then they went on, and I went along the fence. Luster came away from the flower tree and we went along the fence and they stopped and we stopped and I looked through the fence while Luster was hunting in the grass. "Here, caddie." He hit. They went away across the pasture. I held to the fence and watched them going away.

Pratt points out that, at the level of the fictive narrator, at least two of the maxims of the Cooperation Principle are violated: the maxims of Quantity and Manner. With respect to the maxim of Quantity, Benjy fails to provide a crucial piece of information which furnishes the causal link between the events he describes, namely, the golf ball. The maxim of Manner is violated by the use of vague, indirect wordy descriptions which take six clauses to say what could be said in single brief sentence, "they putted and then teed off at the next hole" (Pratt: 183).

This massive violation of the Cooperative Principle by the fictive narrator can take place without destroying the relation with the reader because, at the level of the actual narrator who is creating a display text, the reader perceives it as an intentional flouting which has significant implied meaning, coming as it does, at the very beginning of the novel: "Faulkner is implicating not that golf is a silly waste of time, but that among other things, the speaker of the story has some cognitive or perceptual impediment, that this fact is relevant to our understanding of what follows, and that he intends us to share, contemplate, and evaluate Benjy's view of the world and contrast it with our own" (Pratt: 183, 184).

While a great many fictive works, especially in the modern period, make use of mimetic violations which cause the fictive author's discourse to deviate from the Cooperative Principle and from the discourse of the actual author, the traditional nineteenth century novel constitutes an unmarked case in which this deviation does not occur. Pratt cites as examples such novels as *Pere Goriot*, *The Mayor of Casterbridge*, *Jane Eyre*, and *Pride and Prejudice*. This may also provide one important reason the Biblical narrative is so often considered to belong to the category of realistic narrative writing.

In interpreting novels of the unmarked variety, there is no secondary level of implied meanings beyond those implied by the discourse of the fictive speaker and the characters. The use of this method to analyze such novels would thus focus upon the speech acts internal to the fictional discourse. Pratt does not provide examples of this type of analysis, but concentrates instead upon the more current examples of deviance.

* * *

Criticism of Pratt's theory has focused upon two primary problems. First, there is unresolved tension between her view of the fictive speech act as a non-mimetic display text at the level of the actual author, and a product of mimesis at the level of the fictive speaker. Second, in describing the "appropriateness conditions" for the external and internal narrative speech acts, she moves from an Austinian/Searlean perspective which places heavy emphasis upon the constitutive nature of the speech act conventions, to a Gricean perspective which proposes only regulative maxims, without making clear the nature of this transition.

Pratt initially rejects Ohmann's attempt to separate literature from real world discourse on the basis of its mimetic character since the world-creating function of the "display text" is not affected by its factuality or fictionality, nonfictional narrative accounts being as world-creating as fictional (Pratt: 95). But since the basic reason for reliance upon the concept of mimesis previously was to account for the fictive content of literary speech acts, her reintroduction of this idea has to have a different genesis, i.e., the need to explain the relation of the speech acts of the fictive speaker to that of the actual author.

Jonathan Culler suggests that this peculiar reversion to the concept of mimesis was occasioned by the desire "to seek in all novels something that resembles a real act by a real person" (Culler 1984: 10). Though Pratt has eliminated the dichotomy between the fictive and the factual internal to literary discourse, she still posits a real, factual author outside of it. Just as the distinction between literary and real world discourse led Ohmann to rely upon the concept of mimesis, so now Pratt's distinction between the actual author and implied author finally forces her to do the same. Culler, however, reflecting Derrida's position, argues that "there is a sense in which all speech acts are imitation speech acts. To perform a speech act is to imitate a model, to take on the role of someone performing this particular speech act" (Culler 1984: 10). If the exclamatory assertion which gives rise to the display text is also an imitation, then the concept of mimesis becomes self-cancelling because ubiquitous, and the focus of the analysis must broaden to include the writing subject. Pratt's positing of a closed, historical subject outside of the discursive process is a sign of what Culler calls a "powerful humanistic ideology," which she assumes but does not question. In his view, Pratt's speech act theory leads the most consistently to the view that, "literary narratives are . . . real world narrative display texts: not fictional speech acts but, if they

Introduction: Speech Act Theory and Literary Criticism 11

must be acts at all, real acts of narration" (Culler 1984: 11). But this would, of course, collapse the distinction between the fictive and the real both with regard to the narrative and to the author.

With respect to the Biblical narrative, where both the actual author and the original situation of communication must be very tentatively reconstructed historically, and where there may be minimal deviation from the maxims, it is easier to eliminate the concept of mimesis as Culler suggests, and to view biblical narratives as "real world narrative display texts."

A second line of criticism of Pratt's work focuses upon the status of the conventions she assembles to serve as the "appropriateness conditions", or "felicity conditions" for both external and internal narrative speech acts. She means by these terms, "rules which users of the language assume to be in force in their verbal dealings with each other" (Pratt: 8). But, as Michael Hancher has pointed out, neither Austin nor Searle used the exact term 'appropriateness condition' to refer to these given assumptions, a slight terminological change that has major implications, as will be seen below. (Hancher 1977: 1086.)[1]

In addition both Austin and Searle distinguish between two fundamental categories of rules.[2] Searle clarifies this distinction by categorizing rules into two types: "constitutive," rules which cannot be violated without causing the total breakdown of the speech act (e.g., rules making up the semantic structure of a language, or the rules of a game), and "regulative," i.e., those which impose a certain order upon actions or utterances which may occur entirely apart from such rules (e.g., etiquette). He sets out to delineate those rules which are "necessary" for the performance of non-defective (i.e., felicitous) speech acts (Searle 1969: 35, 36, 54).

The question with regard to the literary speech act is whether Pratt's "appropriateness conditions" are constitutive rules whose violation would cause a breakdown of an exclamatory assertion, or whether they are merely regulatory. Michael Hancher, in his perceptive critical review of Pratt's book, objects that her appropriateness conditions, such as "tellability", are "loose, merely regulative and customary" and not constitutive (Hancher 1977: 1095).

This criticism points to a deeper problem, however, regarding the role of intentionality vis-à-vis rules and conventions within speech act theory itself. While Pratt bases her work initially on the theoretical base of Austin and Searle, in developing her system of appropriateness conditions she seems far more influenced by Grice, for whom intentionality rather than constitutive rules plays the decisive role. Searle complains, apropos an early paper by Grice, that, "One might say that on Grice's account it would seem that any sentence can be uttered with any meaning whatever, given that the circumstances make possible the appropriate intentions: (Searle 1969: 45). Although Searle gives a prominent place to intention in his speech act theory, he also argues that, "Meaning is more than a matter of intention, it is also at least sometimes a matter of convention" (Searle 1969: 45). Pratt thus seems to have moved from a Searlean viewpoint to a Gricean viewpoint without clearly dealing with the change this implies in the status of constitutive rules. Without rules that are genuinely constitutive and generative of literary speech acts, the appropriateness conditions that Pratt brings together, while descriptively illuminating the social context of literature, lack the rigor to account for internal narratological and semantic structures (see Margolis 1979: 50).

* * *

The status of underlying rules as *constitutive* is both the most powerful and the most problematic, ambivalent concept in speech act theory. On the one hand, Searle holds that these rules can be followed unconsciously, even as phonemic rules operate with little or no conscious awareness or intentionality (Searle 1969: 41, 42). On the other, he insists on the fundamental role played by intentionality in the production of illocutionary force: "In the performance of an illocutionary act in the literal utterance of a sentence, the speaker intends to produce a certain effect by means of getting the hearer to recognize his intention to produce that effect" (Searle 1969: 45).

A certain ambivalence appears in an argument which makes intentionality, which is a conscious factor as Searle uses it here, an integral part of what can be an unconscious constitutive rule. According to E. D. Hirsch this unresolved tension in speech act theory between intentionality and conventionality is simply another manifestation of the perennial conflict between the intuitionist and positivist poles of hermeneutics, which it has failed to overcome (Hirsch 1976: 26).

One must then ask whether constitutive rules, which for Searle (Searle 1969: 51, 52, 186, ftn. 1), and Pratt (1977: 140) virtually define the parameters of human life as we know it, do not have an even deeper function in the formation of human subjectivity. This is a question which speech act theory has not raised, but it is at the root of the ambivalence regarding intentionality and conventionality (or 'constitutivity'). The operation of intentionality requires a "full" subject as a given, which then fills the forms of language with a certain intended meaning. As Frank Lentricchia says (interpreting Paul de Man), "Speech act theory depends upon the metaphysical notion of the subject as the coherent center from which acts are directed" (Lentricia 1980: 317).

The logic of intentionality thus tends to relativize the forms it uses and subordinate them to intentions. The concept of constitutive rules, however, suggests that there are configured acts of speech which produce meaning in their occurrence which transcends and subordinates the

Introduction: Speech Act Theory and Literary Criticism 13

intentions of the language user. To the extent that such acts of speech might be constitutive of human subjectivity itself, intentionality would fall into a fundamentally secondary, derivative position. Any discussion of speech acts at this fundamentally constitutive level would engage the same issues raised in Biblical studies by the concept of "word-event" (*Sprachereignis*) developed by the 'new hermeneutic' (to be discussed in my article below).

This problem is fundamental to the complex relationship that obtains between the actual and implied authors. When speech acts internal to the narrative are conceived as mimetic or pretended acts of speech, they must originate in the intentionality of the actual narrator, whose pretending or imitating activity is necessarily intentional. When narrative speech acts are thereby subordinated to the intentionality of the author, then the rules governing them are also subordinated to the author's intentions, and thus become fundamentally regulative rather than constitutive. It would thus appear that the criticism of Pratt's definition of the literary speech act cannot be overcome without pressing beyond the previous boundaries of speech act theory to seek a more fundamental basis for the conventions which guarantee the felicitous performance of the fictive speech act.

The ambivalence in speech act theory concerning the relationship of the subject to constitutive rules has left open the possibility that the search for the constitutive features of speech acts might move in opposing directions; i.e., toward more formalistic universal definitions of the necessary contextual conditions or underlying structures of linguistic competence (see Saddock: 1975, and Bach and Harnish: 1979), or into the question of the linguistic basis of subjectivity (see below).[3]

* * *

The 'right' pole of the speech act discussion today has arisen in response to the weaknesses of the centrist position, and has turned away, for a variety of reasons, from the attempt to speak at all of a global literary or fictive speech act. Searle influenced this discussion among literary critics with an article entitled, "The Logic of Fictional Discourse." In this article he denies that there are any traits which represent necessary and sufficient conditions for qualifying a work as literature. Rather he thinks that "'literature' is the name of a set of attitudes we take toward a stretch of discourse, not a name of an internal property of the stretch of discourse" (Searle 1979: 59).

He does not reject the distinction between the fictive and the real, however. To illuminate this relation he compares the opening paragraph from a *New York Times* news article by Elizabeth Shanahan with the opening paragraph from a novel by Iris Murdoch. Both have the form of literal assertions, i.e. both are the same type of speech act. The distinction between them which speech act theory can illuminate, is that all of the rules which typically govern the making of assertions (e.g. the need to assert the truth, to provide evidence to support truthfulness, lack of obviousness, sincerity, etc.), are suspended with respect to the fictional paragraph.

The distinction between an assertion which is made in accord with the rules, and one which suspends the rules, is, according to Searle, that the latter is only a pretense: "She is pretending . . . to make an assertion, acting as if she were making an assertion, or going through the motions of making an assertion, or imitating the making of an assertion" (Searle 1979: 64). He does not care which of these terms is used, but prefers "pretend." His position thus appears to be at least in partial agreement with Ohmann's view that there is a mimetic fictional (if not the literary) speech act (a significant difference, of course!).

He goes ahead to make another important distinction however. Most fictive discourse contains some real and not pretended references, e.g., names of places, political events, etc. This requires Searle to make an additional distinction between the composite "work of fiction," which may contain both fictional and genuine assertions, and the more restricted "fictional discourse," internal to the work of fiction in which the illocutionary rules are suspended. The work of fiction thus is a mixture of different sorts of speech acts, and there can be no single literary speech act which unifies the whole (Searle 1979: 73, 74). Such a distinction is not compatible with the separation of the real and implied author commonly made by literary critics today.

The philosopher Joseph Margolis has questioned whether this is a speech act distinction, however. To distinguish between the fictive and the real is not a problem at the level of discourse, but is a conceptual or logical problem of, "accounting for the apparent reference to nonexistent entities" (Margolis 1979: 48).

Similarly, Stanley Fish argues that Searle's distinction between the work of fiction and fictional discourse is not to be found in the work itself, but only at the level of the author's intentions. Thus it does not advance the knowledge of story and novel enough even to enable you to tell the difference between a novel and a laundry list! (Fish 1976: 1017, esp. note 8).

But if you cannot successfully use speech act theory to distinguish between the fictive and the real in terms of the features of the discourse, as Margolis and Fish contend, the last conceptual support for a speech act theory of literature which relies upon the concept of mimetic or pretended speech acts, would seem to have been removed. Fish summarized the situation very well when he wrote that speech act theory, "can't help us to tell the difference between literature and non-literature; it can't distinguish between serious discourse and a work of fiction, and it

Introduction: Speech Act Theory and Literary Criticism   15

cannot, without cheating, separate fiction from fact" (Fish 1976: 1023). He thus is forced to ask, "what can it do well . . . ?" His answer to this question is simply that it can help interpret works which are "about" speech acts. He thinks, for instance, that this is the case with Shakespeare's play *Coriolanus* (Fish 1976: 1024). This is the clearest formulation of the position of the "right" pole of the continuum regarding the application of speech act theory to literature.

This circumscribed role does yield significant new insight into the play. Fish focuses upon the second scene, the antagonists seek to bring about the downfall of the protagonist (Coriolanus) by using his own infelicitous speech act (a request) against him. The constitutive conditions for a request that Searle spells out require that the party requesting must believe that the party of which the request is being made is able to deliver the object requested. For Coriolanus to succeed to the consulship he must request it of the citizens whom he regards with unmitigated disdain. His opponents anticipate that while making his request he will unwittingly convey his belief that the citizens are not qualified to cast their vote for him, and will thus abort the totally conventionalized procedure. In light of this context, the precise significance of his first utterance becomes clear.

> Who deserves greatness
> Deserves your hate; and your affections are
> A sick man's appetite, who desires most that
> Which would increase his evil. He that depends
> Upon your favor swims with fins of lead.
>
> (I.i.177–81)

By judging those who were, by convention, supposed to judge him, Coriolanus "sets aside the conditions governing that ceremony and substitutes for them conditions of quite another kind" (Fish 1976: 1984). In so doing, "He declares himself outside (or, more properly, above) the system of rules by which society fixes its values by refusing to submit to the (speech-act) conditions under which its business is conducted" (Fish 1976: 985). From such an analysis the precise lines of the conflict at the center of the play can be drawn, and a deeper perspective upon its meaning gained.

Michael Hancher, unlike Fish, accepts Searle's distinguishing between fictional speech acts and the broad genre of "fiction" which is less amenable to description (Hancher 1977: 1095). While he distrusts Pratt's attempt to define a global literary or fictive speech act (the centrist concern), he sees a somewhat less circumscribed role for speech act theory in literary criticism than Fish. In his account of humor in Lewis Carrol's *Alice*, he applies recent refinements in pragmatic theory (especially the analysis of "politeness phenomena") to elucidate subtle detail in the dialogue with very fruitful results (Hancher: 1983).

* * *

The 'left' position in this discussion is included here, not because it properly belongs in the tradition of speech act philosophy, which it most clearly does not, but because its representatives share with the philosophy of Austin and Searle a general concern with the problematic of the illocutionary dimension of language, and because most of those who represent this viewpoint show signs of affinity for at least some of the views of Austin, even though highly critical of other aspects of his thought. If the hallmark of the 'right' is its close association of the illocutionary force of language with constitutive rules, and the 'center' ties it more fundamentally to the intentionality of the speaker, the 'left' finds illocutionary force stemming from the constitutive function of language itself independent of either rules or intentionality. This approach has required that the question of the relation of the subject to language be opened and brought into the center of investigation in a way not found in the other two viewpoints. Since some of the most important new insights with respect to this question in the twentieth century have emerged from the fields of linguistics and semiology, those espousing this viewpoint have drawn heavily upon these sources.

One of the most important sources is found in the linguistics of Émile Benveniste who developed an understanding of the 'performative' dimension of language in France independent of Austin. This view of language appeared in Benveniste's work on pronouns—the signs which are the most directly related to the problem of subjectivity. His study led him to the view that the pronouns 'I' and 'you' were not typically representative signs because of their highly unusual reference.

> This is . . . both an original and fundamental fact that these 'pronominal' forms do not refer to 'reality' or to 'objective' positions in space and time, but to the always unique enunciation which contains them and thus reflects their proper use (Benveniste 1971: 252, 253).

Since our only access to the self is through the *I*, such considerations point to a 'performative' function of the *I* in constituting the subject. The subject does not exist outside of or prior to language. The starting point of the 'left' which this analysis of pronouns has provided is thus that humans are located *in* language so that they not only bend language to their purposes, but are also bent by it. Stanley Fish,[4] in his analysis of a seventeenth century English sermon, has eloquently described the most fundamental characteristic of this position.

Introduction: Speech Act Theory and Literary Criticism

> We, no less than the words we speak, are meant, stipulated, uttered by another; in our postures as seekers, after meaning or after Christ (they are of course the same), we place ourselves outside a system and presume to make sense of it, to fit its parts together. What we find is that the parts are already together and that we are one of them, living in the meaning we seek—'in Him we live and move and have our meaning'-not as exegetes but as its bearers (Fish 1976a: 1218).

In contrast to this, both the 'center' and 'right' positions posit a self outside of language, which, in varying degrees, makes language subordinate to the intentionality of the subject. The literary theorist Charles Altieri, speaking from a 'centrist' viewpoint, provides us with a concise comparison of the views of the 'center' and 'right' on this issue. He rejects the notion of constitutive rules in favor of a Gricean concept of nonconventional implicature which is,

> . . . based on intentional properties that entail hermeneutic analysis. Where Austin vacillates, Grice is firm: speaker's meanings are not decoded but interpreted, and interpretation requires correlating in probabilistic terms a particular synthesis of agents' purposes with features of a situation or context (Altieri 1981: 82).

Literary critics such as Wolfgang Iser (1978) and Paul de Man (1979) have incorporated aspects of speech act theory in projects which explore the function of language in the subject. But it is the philosopher Jacques Derrida who has raised the issue of the relation of the subject to language the most forcefully from this perspective, and who has, as well, entered into the most vigorous dialogue with the speech act philosophy of Austin and Searle.

The precise point where Derrida addresses the problematic of the subject is the act of writing where the author/subject engages the text and language. In western philosophical tradition beginning with Plato, writing has, in his view, been relegated at best to an exterior, marginal place not worthy of serious philosophical interest, or at worst, actively denigrated. Speech was valued more highly since it has a more vital and immediate connection with the purity of thought in which the presence of being and truth become manifest. The primary function of speech was "logocentric" since it served to make present (represent) the truth of being through the agency of the logos, whereas, "writing, the letter, the sensible inscription, has always been considered by Western tradition as the body and matter external to the spirit, to breath, to speech, and to the logos" (Derrida 1976: 35, also 43).

Rather than external, however, Derrida sees writing as performing a constitutive function with respect to human subjectivity itself. The point of contact between writing and subjectivity is, perhaps ironically, what he regards as the central feature of writing, i.e. the capacity it gives language of communicating without the presence of the subject:

> Spacing as writing is the becoming-absent and the becoming-unconscious of the subject . . . That becoming or that drift/derivation—does not befall the subject which would choose it or would passively let itself be drawn along by it. As the subject's relationship with its own death, this becoming is the constitution of subjectivity (1976: 69).

Thus by pressing beyond particular texts to the author/subject in the act of writing Derrida uncovers the way in which language functions in the constitution of subjectivity. A way of speaking of the constitutive function of language thus appears which is not based upon contextual rules, but upon the primary constitutive effects of language upon the subject who is *ab origine* in language.

Of course, how he can attribute such an important function to writing is scarcely obvious, and suggests that what he means by writing radically departs from ordinary usage. One of the places where he develops his unique view of writing is, significantly for our purposes, in his lengthy discussion of the philosophy of J. L. Austin in the first issue of the Johns Hopkins journal *Glyph* (1977, also in 1982: 307–330) to which John Searle responds (1977). In *Glyph* 2 (1977a) Derrida gives a lengthy response to Searle. In spite of Derrida's peculiar style of deconstructive *ad hominem* argumentation, especially in the response to Searle, this debate represents a significant encounter of radically opposing poles of the 'left' and 'right' positions regarding speech acts.

What Derrida means by writing is brought into focus by his discussion of "iterability." With this term he is referring to what is intrinsically constitutive of the speech act itself, i.e., the "iterable" or repeatable codes and conventions shared by both parties to a speech act which operate without reference to the intentionality of the author/speaker. It is this capacity which enables written utterances to continue to "speak" when the author is absent or dead (Derrida 1977: 180, 181). But even in oral utterances, it is the iterable codes which accomplish the communication by making each utterance capable of being separated from the presence (and intentionality) of its speaker, as well as divorced from its objects of reference (1977: 183). Stanley Fish explains it this way:

> The moment of production is *itself* a moment of loss, in that its components—including sender, receiver, referents, and message—are never transparently present but must be interpreted or 'read' into being . . . utterances are *only* readable (as opposed to

being deciphered or seen through) even in the supposedly optimal condition of physical proximity (Fish 1982: 703).

The codes, from which we cannot escape, always stand between us and the unmediated presence of the thing we seek to know.

A surprising homology can be seen at this point between Austin's initial use of the performative and constative distinction, and the dichotomy which Derrida develops between writing and logocentric speech. Just as the meaning of constative language arises from its representative aims, so also logocentric speech mirrors or images truth. Just as performative language is distinguished by what it does, so writing is an action which has profound effects. Writing is developed by Derrida, into a very broad concept (as performative speech is expanded by Austin into the more inclusive illocutionary act) which accounts for the constitutive of subjectivity itself; it consequently comes to be more fundamental than the distinction between writing and speech (as the concept of the illocutionary act ultimately displaces the distinction between performative and constative for Austin).

In his study of Austin the approach to literature which Derrida develops also can be seen since he treats philosophical texts as literary texts. He searches both kinds of texts for semantic distinctions such as the "central" and the "marginal," which reveal the particular point at which meanings emerge from the text which escape the logocentric (logical, representational) intentions of the author. In Austin's thought, he found a particularly ironic example. While Austin began, himself, by moving what the logocentric assumptions of western philosophy had previously considered to be marginal, into a position of central importance, his own logocentric assumptions led him to create a marginal category of his own for the various types of literary and dramatic occurrences of speech acts which he considered parasitic or dependent upon 'real world' speech acts. Since this distinction was sustained only by Austin's avoidance of taking up the broader question of the function of language in the subject which is prior to both dramatic and 'real world' speech acts, Derrida's treatment of Austin's discourse involves 'deconstructing' his argument by pointing to the iterable, mimetic, derivative character also of 'real world' speech acts.[5]

Another type of deconstructive criticism focuses upon critical interpretations of major texts. Derrida finds the roots of many differences in the history of the interpretation of a text in the unresolved conflicts and dramas in the text itself. Jonathan Culler describes it in this way:

> Critical disputes about a text can frequently be identified as a displaced reenactment of conflicts dramatized in the texts, so that while the text arrays the consequences and implications of various

forces it contains, critical readings transform the difference into a difference between mutually exclusive positions (Culler 1982: 215).

A continuity is thus established between the tensions within a text and those within the history of that text's interpretation.

* * *

This brief overview of the Derrida's approach to Austin and some types of deconstructive criticism is sufficient to make clear the specific place of disjunction between the "right" and "left" approaches to the phenomenon of illocutionary language, and the appropriation of speech act theory. Michael Hancher's article is poised precisely at this point of disjunction. Speaking from the viewpoint of the "right" pole of this continuum, he finds the identification of self-referentiality and performative speech proposed by French scholars such as Benveniste and Barthes to be an incorrect understanding of Austin, and stresses instead the importance of contextual conditions in defining illocutionary acts. Though he makes a strong case for the performative status of *"Fiat lux"* and other sacramental words, he is still ambivalent about them at the end of his argument, perhaps because of the often problematic character of their contexts.

My article attempts to trace the lines of relation between the understanding of the event character of language in the new hermeneutics and the thought of Roland Barthes, and to show how this tradition of literary criticism can be profitably developed for use in Biblical criticism by deeper engagement with and appropriation of speech act theory. Thus my article, in attempting to relate speech act theory to the perspectives of Barthes and Derrida, suggests the need for some mediation and accommodation between 'left' and 'right' poles of this debate.

Susan Lanser, who considers 'point of view' from a Gricean ('centrist') speech act perspective in her important book *The Narrative Act* (1981), moves in her article toward the second type of deconstructive criticism mentioned above in that she explores the problematic relation of a text to some of its interpretations. With the help of Searle's formula for identifying constitutive factors in the context of speech acts, she analyzes some recent conflicting interpretations of Gen. 2, 3 and finds that the tensions within the text, as analyzed with formal literary methods, have produced mutually exclusive readings in many instances. The use of speech act theory to analyze critical interpretations of texts represents a new way of applying speech act theory by a literary critic.

Daniel Patte, in a programmatic essay, suggests the possibility of a "speech act exegesis" which would supplement both structural and historical exegesis by providing a more suitable way of dealing with the phenomenon of subjectivity than has been previously available. Subjectivity could be approached through the Hjelmslevian method of "catalysis" which aims at disclosing the elliptical elements in a text, combined with the Searlean strategies for reconstructing the inferential reasoning of utterances in terms of rules governing intentionality. From this point of view, it might be possible to establish the distinctive features of religious texts in terms of the intentionality which comes to expression in religious speech acts. This goal of elucidating distinctively religious speech acts and religious texts in terms of their intentionality places Patte's program within the parameters of the "centrist" position.

Ronald Grimes's article arises from the boundary between speech acts and a broader range of conventionally determined symbolic behaviour. He seeks specifically to extend Austin's taxonomy of contextual factors which effect the success or failure of speech acts to include the conditions which determine the success or failure of religious ritual. In so doing he shows the fruitful way in which this type of analysis produces new understanding of a number of important episodes in Biblical narratives which are organized around ritual failure. At the same time he also encounters some perhaps significant deficiencies in the early formulation of speech act theory when it is applied to this range of phenomena.

All three of the positions outlined in this introduction may have important contributions to make to Biblical studies. Many Biblical narratives seem to be 'about' speech acts (prohibitions, promises, covenants, commands, verdicts, blessings, curses, etc.) which might lend themselves fruitfully to the type of strict application of the theories of Austin and Searle advocated by Stanley Fish. The approaches developed by Pratt, Lanser and Ohmann which aim at a broader application of speech act theory to the act of narrative writing, publication and reading, may be capable of shedding light upon a wide range of questions in Biblical studies from the ideology, social position and role of the Biblical narrative writers/editors, and the internal structural dynamics of Biblical narratives, to the canonization of the text and its function in reading communities.

The debate stimulated by the "left" regarding intentionality, conventions and the constitutive function of language (provoked especially by Derrida), raises issues which are central to Biblical and theological hermeneutics. To approach language in terms of its constitutive force may open a way of understanding language which mediates between individual subjectivity and social conventions, between the particularity of historical events and timeless theory and myth, and between 'ordinary language' and occult hermeneutical theory.

At this stage of the investigation the three positions outlined above should not be prematurely viewed as mutually exclusive, in spite of the vigorous rhetoric of the internal polemic between them. The complexity of the issues and the disjoined nature of the present debate suggests that they may share a common ground which has not yet been discovered. We hope that the articles in this volume will encourage further exploration of this possibility.

NOTES

[1] Austin spoke of "necessary conditions," "conventional procedures," (1962: 140) or, more generally, "rules" (1962: 15, 26). Searle uses the term "rule" as the most fundamental general category under which he groups "conventions" (1969: 37, 39) as particular linguistic realizations of sets of more universal rules.

[2] Austin speaks of rules whose violation results in "misfires," i.e. failure to "come off" at all, and rules, the violation of which leads only to "abuses," i.e. some possible uncertainty regarding their meaning or effect (1962: 16).

[3] For a discussion of the mediating role of conventions see Lawrence Manly, "Concepts of Convention and Models of Critical Discourse," *New Literary History* 13 (1981): 32.

[4] Fish is sympathetic with many aspects of the understanding of language found in the 'left' position in his critical work, but does not attempt to integrate them into his way of applying speech act theory. He believes that speech act theory must be utilized as an integral theory and not modified or extended to make it do more than is possible by strictly adhering to its own terms and premises (1976: 1007).

[5] Searle attributes Derrida's concern with the problematic of intentionality to the fundamental mistake, which he shares with classical metaphysics, of searching for the lost foundations of thought (Searle 1983: 78). Though Searle concedes the loss of metaphysical foundations, he does not see this as having any particularly disturbing implications which would require a reformulation of the constitutive function of language in its relation to the self (Searle 1983: 78).

WORKS CONSULTED

Austin, John L.
    1962   *How to do Things With Words*. 3nd ed. Ed. J. O. Urmson and Marina Sbisa. Cambridge, Mass.: Harvard University Press 1962, 1975.
    1979   "Truth." In *Philosophical Papers*, 3rd ed. Ed. J. O. Urmson and G. J. Warnock. Oxford: Clarendon Press.

Bach, Kent and R. M. Harnish
    1979   *Linguistic Communication and Speech Acts*. Cambridge, Mass.: MIT Press, 1979.

Benveniste, Émile
    1971   *Problems in General Linguistics*. Trans. Mary E. Meek. Coral Gables, Fla.: University of Miami Press.

Culler, Jonathan
    1982   *On Deconstruction*. Ithaca, N.Y.: Cornell University Press.
    1984   "Problems in the Theory of Fiction." *Diacritics* (spring): 3–11.

Jacques Derrida
- 1976 *Of Grammatology*. Trans. G. C. Spivak. Baltimore: Johns Hopkins University Press.
- 1977 "Signature Event Context." *Glyph* 1: 172-97.
- 1977a "Limited inc abc . . ." *Glyph* 2: 162-54.

Fish, Stanley
- 1972 *Self-Consuming Artifacts: The Experience of Seventeenth-Century Literature*. Berkeley: University of California Press.
- 1976 "How to do Things with Austin and Searle." *Modern Language Notes* 19: 983–1025.
- 1976a "Structuralist Homiletics." *Modern Language Notes* 9: 1186–1207.
- 1982 "With Complements of the Author: Reflections on Austin and Derrida." *Critical Inquiry* (Summer): 693–721.

Hancher, Michael
- 1977 "Beyond a Speech-Act Theory of Literary Discourse." *Modern Language Notes* 82: 1081–1098.
- 1983 "Pragmatics in Wonderland." Pp. 165–184 in *Rhetoric, Literature, and Interpretation*, a special issue of the *Bucknell Review*, ed. by Steven Mailloux. Lewisburg: Bucknell University Press; London & Toronto: Associated University Presses.

Hirsh, E. D.
- 1976 *The Aims of Interpretation*. Chicago: University of Chicago Press.

Iser, Wolfgang
- 1978 *The Narrative Act: Point of View in Prose Fiction*. Princeton: Princeton University Press.

Lentricchia, Frank
- 1980 *After the New Criticism*. London: The University of Chicago Pres.

Man, Paul de
- 1979 "Semiology and Rhetoric." Pp. 121–140 in *Textual Strategies: Perspectives in Post-Structuralist Criticism*. Ed. by Josue V. Harari. Ithaca, N.Y.: Cornell University Press.

Manley, Lawrence
- 1981 "Concepts of Convention and Models of Critical Discourse." *New Literary History* 13: 31–52.

Margolis, Joseph
- 1979 "Literature and Speech Acts." *Philosophy and Literature* 3: 39–52.

Ohmann, Richard
- 1973 "Literature as Act." Pp. 81–108 in *Approaches to Poetics, Selected Papers from the English Institute*. Ed. by Seymour

Chatman. New York: Columbia University Press.
- 1971 "Speech Acts and the Definition of Literature." *Philosophy and Rhetoric*. Pp. 1–19.

Pratt, Mary Louise
- 1977 *Toward a Speech Act Theory of Literary Discourse*. Bloomington: University of Indiana Press.

Sadock, Jerrold
- 1975 *Toward a Linguistic Theory of Speech Acts*. New York: Academic Press.

Searle, John R.
- 1969 *Speech Acts: An Essay in the Philosophy of Language*. Cambridge: Cambridge University Press.
- 1979 "The Logic of Fictional Discourse." Pp. 58–75 in *Expression and Meaning*. Ed. by John R. Searle. New York, London: Cambridge University Press.
- 1983 "The Word Turned Upside Down." *The New York Review of Books* (Oct. 27): 74–79.

I.

Speech Act Theory and Narrative Hermeneutics

PERFORMATIVE UTTERANCE, THE WORD OF GOD, AND THE DEATH OF THE AUTHOR

Michael Hancher
University of Minnesota

ABSTRACT

The divine utterance *Fiat lux* seems to be the paradigmatic performative, the quintessential declarative speech act, akin to the declarative words of institution in the Eucharist. Yet the concept of performative discourse figures prominently in Barthes's "counter-theological" model of *écriture*. Barthes's appropriation of speech-act theory (as interpreted by Benveniste) is doubly unfortunate: it betrays his project and it betrays the theory. Derrida, too, errs in mystifying the theory. Performative discourse is not essentially mysterious.

I

"*Fiat lux*." "God said, Let there be light: and there was light." No performative could be purer. Saying makes it so (Austin 1962a:7). Granted, "*Fiat lux*" is in the subjunctive mood, not indicative; it does not conform to the standard grammar, "first person singular present indicative active" (66), that Austin tested as a possible criterion for performative utterance in the early chapters of *How to Do Things with Words*. That grammar has become popularly identified with performatives. But the reader who follows Austin into the middle of his argument will find that the criterion failed the test. Performative discourse has no distinctive grammar. What sets it apart is not form but function; the trick is to *do* something with words.

Other verses from the first creation story in Genesis report similar speech acts. "And God said, Let the waters under the heaven be gathered together unto one place, and let the dry land appear: and it was so. . . . And God said, Let the earth bring forth the living creature after his kind, cattle, and creeping thing, and beast of the earth after his kind: and it was so" (Gen. 1.9, 24). God's creation of light may be more striking, more succinct than these other verbal acts—especially "sublime," as Longinus and Boileau called it—but they are all similar utterances, performative utterances.[1]

What *kind* of performative are they? It is correct to call each of them a *fiat* (Skinner 1910:8), but of course that begs the question. What is a fiat in this sense? One commentary, in a single paragraph, refers to *"Fiat lux"* as a *command*, a *charge*, an *injunction* and a *directive* (Cassuto 1961:26). There may be differences to distinguish these terms, but all fall comfortably into the general class of speech acts that John Searle calls *directives*. According to Searle, "the illocutionary point of [directives] consists in the fact that they are attempts . . . by the speaker to get the hearer to do something" (1979:13). *As attempts* they are vulnerable to failure (even if *as directives* they are perfectly executed): the intended perlocutionary effect may evade the illocutionary act. On that count alone divine fiats cannot be directives. Furthermore, directives are supposed to influence the actions of a hearer—and of course there is no hearer present at the beginning of Genesis.

If *"Fiat lux"* looks like a directive but cannot be one, what is it? While outlining his speech-act taxonomy Searle happens to mention this very utterance, which he categorizes as a kind of *declaration* (1979:18). Except for certain aspects (it is supernatural: therefore it does not rely, as usual, on an "extra-linguistic institution") this utterance indeed does epitomize that class. "Declarations bring about some alteration in the status or condition of the referred to object or objects solely in virtue of the fact that the declaration has been successfully performed" (17). By contrast a command, even if successfully performed, may fail in its outcome (it may fail to get the hearer to do something). The main effect of a directive is perlocutionary and contingent. Declarations suffer no such contingency: with them the main effect is illocutionary.

Searle's leading examples of declarations are: "'I resign'; 'You're fired', 'I excommunicate you', 'I christen this ship the battleship Missouri', 'I appoint you chairman', and 'War is hereby declared.'" He alludes to the fact that Austin, at the start, treated just such acts as paradigm cases of performative utterance. Of course Austin went on to dissolve his performative/constative distinction into the general category of illocutionary acts, robbing "performative" acts of their special status. And yet at first glance declarations remain as striking, as arresting—as magical—as the old performatives; they are survivors, performatives *après la lettre*. The most impressive declaration of them all is *"Fiat lux"*: performative of performatives.

Consider some comments on this divine declaration by Bruce Vawter:

> What . . . [lies] behind this particular formulation is the common Semitic conception of the built-in efficacy of the uttered word. In the Old Testament "word" and "deed" are, or frequently are, one and the same: blessings, curses, prophetic pronouncements all obtain their efficacy from their very assertion and from then on lead a life of their own. There is, no doubt, to the modern taste at least some vestige of magic underlying a conception of this kind, though the biblical authors may have been unaware of it. They were, rather, in a society where written documents and instruments were few, testifying to the dynamic effect which perforce had to be attributed to the spoken word. Word is power: the same idea has penetrated the New Testament and is at the base of the Christian conviction of the efficacy of the word in preaching and sacrament. [Vawter 1977:41–42]

These remarks apply not only to the opening of Genesis but also to John's revision of that opening: "In the beginning was the Word, and the Word was with God, and the Word was God." Here is true logocentrism.[2]

"The efficacy of the word in . . . sacrament" has been canvassed by A. P. Martinich, in a speech-act analysis of the seven sacraments (1975). For brevity's sake Martinich does not identify the specific words that effect the Eucharistic consecration (406). In fact the question has a complex history. The early church believed that Christ presented himself throughout the Eucharistic ritual (Maloney 1975:465; Martos 1981:255). But matters were not left so comfortably vague: both Eastern and Western theologians moved to identify in the liturgy a specific moment of consecration. In the West that moment was the priest's recital of Christ's words instituting the sacrament, "'This is my body. . . . this is my blood. . . . Do this . . . in remembrance of me.'" The East preferred a later prayer in the service, the *epiclesis*, which invoked the sacramental intervention of the Holy Spirit (Jungmann 1976:136). Furthermore, in the West the phrasing of the words of institution became less casual, more formulaic. (In the early church celebrants had "quoted the accounts of the Last Supper from memory and as at the moment they were moved to do" [Leitzmann 1979:517].)

Both these tendencies—the conceptual focusing of the Eucharistic ritual, and the specifying of a particular verbal formula—mirror the historical evolution that Austin supposed must have led from primary (or primitive or implicit) performative utterances (such as, "I will . . .") to explicit performative formulae (such as, "I promise I will . . ."; or, "I warn you I will . . ."). Austin pointedly observed that such institutional clarification is "as much a creative act as a discovery or a description. . . . as much a matter of making clear distinctions as of making already existent distinctions clear" (Austin 1962a:71–72).

In the fourth century St. Ambrose analyzed the words of institution in terms suggestive for our purposes:

> Before the consecration the words are those of the priest. He offers praise to God, he prays for the congregation, for the rulers and for all other people. But when he is about to produce the venerable sacrament the priest stops using his own words and starts using the words of Christ. It is therefore the words of Christ which produce this sacrament, *words such as those through which he created all things* [emphasis added]. So if the words of the Lord Jesus are powerful enough to make nonexistent things come into being, how much more effective must they be in changing what already exists into something else![3]

St. Ambrose thus compares the performance of consecration to the divine *"Fiat Lux":* they are similar performative utterances. But who is the performative *agent* in the mass? Christ? or the priest? It is Christ, says Ambrose—anticipating an important Thomistic position (Schillebeeckx 1963:82–89; Brinkman 1975:419). And yet in speaking of the priest's "use" of Christ's words *("utitur sermonibus Christi")*, St. Ambrose inadvertently suggests that the priest *does* things with them— that he too plays a performative role. Viewed in such a light, the celebrant transcends the notorious logical distinction between *use* and *mention* (Searle 1969:73–76; 1977:206). In quoting Christ's words the celebrant does cite or *mention* them; but in reciting them to consecrate the bread and wine he also *uses* them in performative utterance.

Regardless of whether the performative agent is Christ alone or the celebrant also, such liturgical discourse has the absolute efficacy of divine fiat. It succeeds *ex opere operato* ("by the power of rite"), and it constitutes a *"signum efficax gratiae,* a sign which really and actually bestows the grace it signifies" (Schillebeeckx 1963:73; cf. Martinich 1975:293–94). Both these descriptions capture important aspects of performative utterance. As sublime as God's original creative act is the declarative recreation of the substance of the Eucharist—bread and wine—into Christ's body and blood.

If Austin was too discreet to put the Eucharist to such analysis, he did glance more than once at Marriage and Baptism, which supply him with telling and often ludicrous examples of speech-act failure. Canon law, like the common law, may require performative precision. From the sublime to the ridiculous is but a *faux pas.*

II

Some important speech acts are literally sacred, sacramental. In particular, *"Fiat lux"* is the epitome of performative utterance: it lends a theological aura to all performative discourse. Therefore it is strange to find the performative concept at the center of anti-theological argument, which is where Roland Barthes positions it in a famous early essay, "The Death of the Author" (1968). Barthes's burial of the Author recalls Nietzsche's funeral for God ("Gott ist tot"). And the connection is close; for the Author, made in the image of God, could not survive without Him; furthermore, to deny the Author is a way of denying God.

> We know that a text does not consist of a line of words, releasing a single "theological" meaning (the "message" of the Author-God), but is a space of many dimensions, in which are wedded and contested various kinds of writing, no one of which is *original*. . . . Once the Author is gone, the claim to "decipher" a text becomes quite useless. . . . [L]iterature (it would be better, henceforth, to say writing *[écriture]*), by refusing to assign to the text (and to the world as text) a "secret," that is, an ultimate meaning, liberates an activity which we might call counter-theological, properly revolutionary, for to refuse to arrest meaning is finally to refuse God and his hypostases, reason, science, the law. [Barthes 1972:10–11]

These passages, which celebrate the "counter-theological" purpose of *écriture,* directly follow a paragraph in which Barthes identifies *écriture* with performative discourse. That identification requires scrutiny, for it marks the climax of his argument. Furthermore, it inaugurates (in 1968) the appropriation of speech-act theory by literary criticism.

Describing the "modern writer *(scriptor),*" who survives the defunct Author, Barthes asserts that he

> is born simultaneously with his text; he is in no way supplied with a being which precedes or transcends his writing, he is in no way the subject of which his book is the predicate; there is no other time than that of the utterance, and every text is eternally written *here* and *now.* This is because (or: it follows that) *to write* can no longer designate an operation of recording, of observing, of representing, of "painting" (as the Classic writers put it), but rather what the linguisticians, following the vocabulary of the Oxford school, call a performative, a rare verbal form (exclusively given to the first person and to the present), in which utterance has no other content than the act by which it is uttered: something like the *I Command* of kings or the *I Sing* of the early bards. . . . [Barthes 1972:10]

Barthes does not unpack his analogy, but its terms are clear: whereas Classical literature deployed constative discourse in a vain effort to mirror the real world, *écriture* is unashamedly performative, independent, absolute. The irony is that these are sacred, sacramental, qualities. On these terms there is less difference than one would expect to find between *écriture* and Scripture. Barthes's performative metaphor, secretly theological, works to deconstruct his "counter-theological" argument.

It is a fair question how Barthes understands the terms that he invokes. His definition of the performative as "a rare verbal form (exclusively given to the first person and to the present), in which utterance has no other content than the act by which it is uttered," is exceptionable on several counts. There is the mystifying fixation on grammatical criteria, heightened by the admiring adjective "rare." Furthermore, to insist that the performative utterance "has no other content than the act by which it is uttered" is to ignore its illocutionary effect and perlocutionary intention. Barthes's first example, "the *I Command* of kings," is not an example of self-contained or disinterested discourse: such a speech act has immediate social consequences, and ultimately works to change the world.

Barthes's second example, "the *I Sing* of the early bards," has the self-mirroring qualities of *poésie pure*, and seems also a pure fulfillment of the grammatical criterion. Barbara Johnson has followed Barthes in classing such poetic discourse as essentially performative: "When Virgil says 'Arma virumque cano,' is he not doing what he is saying? When Whitman says 'I celebrate myself and sing myself,' is this not a self-referential utterance?" (Johnson 1980:60).[4]

The full answer is: yes, these *are* self-referential utterances—but that is not enough to make them performative utterances. Self-referentiality is not a necessary condition for performative discourse, let alone a sufficient one. Austin noticed that some "indubitable performatives" manage without the self-referential grammar of the first person singular and of the present indicative active. (Some of his examples are: "You are hereby authorized to pay . . . ."; "Passengers are warned to cross the track by the bridge only"; "Notice is hereby given that trespassers will be prosecuted" [Austin 1962a:57].) *"Fiat lux,"* too, is performative but not self-referential. The notion that self-referentiality is essential to performative discourse is not Austin's notion but Émile Benveniste's.

When Barthes wrote "The Death of the Author" he had not read anything by Austin; hardly anything was available in French. But he had read and reviewed Émile Benveniste's *Problems in General Linguistics* (1966, 1971; cf. Barthes 1966); there he encountered the mysteries of performative discourse.

Some of those mysteries are heresies. Benveniste was an unhappy reader of Austin's synoptic lecture "Performatif—Constatif" (1962b), because in that lecture Austin colonized a linguistic territory that Benveniste had independently discovered (Benveniste 1971:234). He regretted that Austin gave up the grammatical criterion for performative discourse, and also (worse yet) that he collapsed the very distinction between performative and constative. Benveniste's commitment to formalism made him deny that imperatives are performatives ("I order you to shut the door," he held to be a legitimate performative; but not, "Shut the door" [237]). It led him to insist on the grammatical criterion as the hallmark of authentic performative utterance. (The only deviation he allowed was the substitution of "hereby" in certain official utterances in the second or third persons.) And the grammatical criterion fostered his exaggerated sense of the self-referentiality of performative discourse.[5]

There is a moment in his discussion when Benveniste sets formalism aside, in favor of a contextualist understanding of the way that performatives work:

> . . . acts of authority are first and always utterances made by those to whom the right to utter them belongs. This condition of validity, related to the person making the utterance and to the circumstances of the utterance, must always be considered met when one deals with the performative. The criterion is here and not in the choice of verbs.

But immediately Benveniste succumbs to the lure of grammar:

> Any verb of speaking, even the most common of all, the very *say*, is capable of forming a performative utterance if the formula, *I say that* . . . , uttered under the appropriate conditions, creates a new situation. That is the rule of the game. [236]

Here, in this formulaic rendering of a "verb of speaking," is the prototype for Barthes's and Johnson's examples, "the *I Sing* of the early bards," Virgil's "*Arma virumque cano*," and Whitman's "I celebrate myself and sing myself." These are amply self-reflexive utterances, but they are not performative except by metaphorical courtesy. The fault is contextual. Though singing—poetry—may normally respond to certain circumstances, and flourish on conventional occasions, it permits too much contextual variation to qualify as a performative act. Several efforts to define poetry as a particular kind of illocutionary act have necessarily failed (Ohmann 1971; Levin 1976; cf. Searle 1979:63-64). Barthes called "I Sing" a performative not because of its conditions of utterance but because of its canonical grammar—and because of the allure of self-reflexivity.

A parallel case may dispel that allure. If I said "I whisper this to you," and if, for good measure, in saying it I actually whispered it, I would be performing a conspicuously self-referential act, and deploying the canonical grammatical construction in the approved way; but nobody would be tempted to call the act a performative utterance. Searle offers a way of explaining the difference: such verbs as "whisper" and "sing" identify the *manner* in which a speech act is performed, rather than the *kind* of speech act. For example,

> One may announce orders, promises and reports, but announcing is not on all fours with ordering, promising and reporting. Announcing . . . is not the name of a type of illocutionary act, but of the way in which some illocutionary act is performed. An announcement is never just an announcement. It must also be a statement, order, etc.
>
> . . . .
>
> Both "insist" and "suggest" are used to mark the degree of intensity with which the illocutionary point is presented. They do not mark a separate illocutionary point at all. Similarly, "announce," "hint," and "confide," do not mark separate illocutionary points but rather the style or manner of performance of an illocutionary act. [Searle 1979:9, 28]

"Whisper" is in the same category, and so is "sing," in both its literal and figurative senses. These verbs foreground ways or styles of performance; they do not mark distinctive kinds of speech act.

So Barthes's appropriation of speech-act theory is doubly unfortunate: it betrays his project, by importing a theological trope into a counter-theological argument; and it betrays the theory, by fetishizing the performative/constative distinction, and also by taking the theory of performative utterance too narrowly (the grammatical criterion) and then applying it too broadly (the example of *"I Sing"*). Barthes learned most of these mistakes from Benveniste; one wishes that he had read Austin for himself.

But would that have helped? Later French readings of Austin do not inspire confidence. When Gilles Lane translated *How to Do Things with Words*, and came to gloss the title, he ignored its relation to the traditional opposition of *words* to *deeds,* and instead cast a knowing glance in the direction of Dale Carnegie's self-help handbook, *How to Win Friends and Influence People*.[6] When Austin discussed "the use of language in poetry," he gave as an example the line (from Donne), "Go and catch a falling star" (104). Failing to recognize that Austin was quoting from a poem, Lane laboriously "explained" the supposed idiomatic meaning of the phrase—something like, "Get out of my sight!"[7] Austin early set to one side the "peculiar" and atypical speech-act anomalies of poetic discourse, because they resulted from "a sea-change in special circumstances" (22): Lane creatively translated "sea-change" as *revirement* (55; figuratively, "sudden change," but originally a nautical term, meaning "tacking-about"), instead of tracing the word to Ariel's threnody in *The Tempest:*

> Full fathom five thy father lies;
> Of his bones are coral made;
> Those are pearls that were his eyes;
> Nothing of him that doth fade
> But doth suffer a sea change
> Into something rich and strange.

To read Barthes, Benveniste, Johnson and Lane is to recognize Austin's own right to such an epitaph.

The sea change continues, even in this paper. At the outset I mystified speech-act theory by sanctifying it, by identifying performative discourse with the word of God. I am not the first to burden human speech acts with the aegis of divine authority. The aspect of speech-act theory that most offended Jacques Derrida (aside from John Searle's know-it-all style of debate) was the transcendental omniscience that the theory seemed to presuppose for any speaker. Derrida took it as axiomatic that a speaker, on Austin's theory, must have exhaustive knowledge of the total context of action, as well as "the conscious presence of the intention of the speaking subject in the totality of his speech act," and a "free consciousness present to the totality of the operation, and . . . absolutely meaningful speech *[vouloir-dire]* master of itself: the teleological jurisdiction of an entire field whose organizing center remains *intention*" (Derrida 1977:187–88, 192). He pressed this supposed axiom to reduce the theory to absurdity, since obviously no human ever has the privilege of such transcendental consciousness. The only person who has such a consciousness is God.

That would be a sound objection, if the theory did depend upon such an axiom; but it does not. The axiom is Derrida's invention, not Austin's.

It is true that Austin does mention more than once the need to take into account "the total speech act in the total situation" (1962a:147; quoted by Derrida 1977:196n.6); but "total" here lacks the cosmic reach that Derrida criticizes. Austin uses this rhetoric mainly as a corrective—that is, he uses it to defeat the old habit of discussing statements ("constatives") with reference to their prepositional content only and without reference to the (crucial) circumstances in which they are uttered (52). He also once uses the phrase "the total speech act" to denote the co-occurrence of the locutionary act and the illocutionary act (147). Neither use of the word "total" commits Austin to the idea that omniscience is a precondition for performative utterance. Indeed, such an idea would jar with the rest of his work. In another connection Soshana Felman, a disciple of Derrida who is not always a reliable expounder of Austin, correctly observes that "intention, for Austin, is scarcely present to itself, scarcely *conscious*" (1983:100).[8] The divine omniscience that Derrida finds at the heart of Austin's theory is the product of his own exaggeration.

I confess to a similar exaggeration. *"Fiat lux"* is the supreme performative, but it is also exceptional. Sacramental speech acts are sacred, but they are not typical. Austin does not care whether the thing being christened is a baby or a boat, nor whether the marriage ceremony is conducted by a priest or a naval captain. Of course such paired examples could be used to argue that secular speech acts are degraded versions of sacred ones, and that may be true in some cases. But that is not the only possible history. It may be that sacred speech acts are heightened or idealized versions of the ordinary performative discourse that people have always encountered in everyday life.

NOTES

[1] After praising passages in the *Iliad* "which represent divinity as genuinely unsoiled and great and pure," Longinus commented:

> Similarly, the lawgiver of the Jews, no ordinary man—for he understood and expressed God's power in accordance with its worth—writes at the beginning of his *Laws:* "God said"—now what?—"'Let there be light,' and there was light; 'Let there be earth,' and there was earth." [Longinus 1965:11–12]

Boileau added, "ce tour extraordinaire d'expression, qui marque si bien l'obéissance de la créature aux ordres du créateur, est véritablement sublime, et a quelque chose de devin" (Boileau 1837: 286; cf. 242, 246).

[2] Derrida characterizes the purest form of logocentrism (a limit case, a utopian impossibility) as the case in which "the thing, the 'referent,' is . . . immediately related to the logos of a creator God where it began by being the spoken/thought sense" (1976: 14–15).

[3] Martos 1981: 256, freely paraphrasing *On the Sacraments* 4:4.13–15; cf. Ambrose 1955: 51–52, 1963: 301–02.

[4] As the interrogatives suggest, Johnson is only provisionally committed to such a classification. She has deconstructive doubts about the criterion of self-referentiality—which she correctly assigns to Émile Benveniste (discussed below), rather than to Austin or to Barthes. But her examples of poetic performatives match Barthes's example and share its weaknesses.

[5] In several respects Benveniste's formalist account anticipates the "higher-performative-clause analysis" advocated by Ross (1970) and Sadock (1974). Effective objections to the Ptolemaic over-complexity of such an analysis, lodged by Searle (1979: 163–172) and Bach and Harnish (1979: 220–25), have an indirect bearing on Benveniste also.

While this essay was in press I encountered an article by Catherine Kerbrat-Orecchioni (1984), which judiciously and sympathetically interprets Benveniste's response to Austin.

[6] "Le titre original: *How to do Things with Words*, qui signifie littéralement: 'Comment faire des choses avec des mots,' n'est pas dépourvu d'humour. Il se réfère ironiquement à la tradition

anglo-américaine des livres de conseils pratiques (du genre: *How to make Friends*, 'Comment se faire des amis')." (Austin 1970a: 6)

[7] After rendering the line as "Va-t'en donc attraper une étoile filante," Lane offered the following apology:

> Nous donnons ici la traduction littérale d'une expression anglaise dont l'équivalent français serait difficile à trouver. Le sens (la "valeur") de l'énonciation anglaise serait à peu près le suivant: va faire ce que tu voudras (des choses ridicules ou impossibles, peu m'importe); tout ce que je désire, c'est que tu me débarrasses de ta présence. Le contexte indique, justement, qu'il serait difficile de percevoir tout ce qui entre en jeu dans l'expression d'une telle énonciation. [Austin 1970a: 116, 176]

[8] Like his account of truth, Austin's account of intention builds in a large tolerance for leeway and approximation:

> Although we have this notion of my idea of what I'm doing [viz., my "intention"]—and indeed we have as a general rule such an idea, as it were a miner's lamp on our forehead which illuminates always just so far ahead as we go along—it is not to be supposed that there are any precise rules about the extent and degree of illumination it sheds. The only general rule is that the illumination is always *limited*, and that in several ways. It will never extend indefinitely far ahead. Of course, all that is to follow, or to be done thereafter, is not what I am intending to do, but perhaps consequences or results or effects thereof. Moreover, it does not illuminate *all* of my surroundings. Whatever I am doing is being done and to be done amidst a background of *circumstances* (including of course activities by other agents). This is what necessitates *care*, to ward off impingements, upsets, accidents. Furthermore, the doing of it will involve *incidentally* all kinds of minutiae of, at the least, bodily movements, and often many other things besides. These will be below the level of any intention, *however* detailed (and it need not of course be detailed at all), that I may have formed. [Austin 1970b: 284–85]

WORKS CONSULTED

Ambrose, Saint
  1955   *Sancti Ambrosii Opera*, 7. Trans. Otto Faller. *Corpus Scriptorum Ecclesiasticorum Latinorum*, 73. Vienna: Hoelder.
  1963.   *Theological and Dogmatic Works*. Trans. Roy J. Deferrari. Fathers of the Church, 44. Washington, DC: Catholic University of America Press.

Austin, J. L.
  1962a   *How to Do Things with Words*. Rpt. New York: Oxford University Press, 1965.
  1962b   "Performatif—constatif." *La philosophie analytique*. Cahiers de Royaumont, Philosophie, 4: 271–81.
  1970a   *Quand dire, c'est faire*. Trans. Gilles Lane. Paris: Seuil.
  1970b   "Three Ways of Spilling Ink." Pp. 272–87 in *Philosophical Papers*. 2nd ed. London: Oxford University Press.

Bach, Kent, and Robert M. Harnish
    1979   *Linguistic Communication and Speech Acts.* Cambridge: MIT Press.

Barthes, Roland
    1966   "Situation du linguiste" (review of Émile Benveniste, *Problèmes de linguistique générale*). *La Quinzaine littéraire,* 15 May 1966: 20.
    1968   "La mort de l'Auteur." *Manteia* 5: 12–17.
    1972   "The Death of the Author." Trans. Richard Howard. Pp. 7–12 in *The Discontinuous Universe.* Ed. Sallie Sears. New York: Basic.

Benveniste, Émile
    1966   *Problèmes de linguistique générale.* Bibliothèque des sciences humaines. Paris: Gallimard.
    1971   *Problems in General Linguistics.* Trans. Mary Elizabeth Meek. Miami Linguistics Series, 8. Coral Gables, FL: University of Miami Press.

Boileau, Nicolas
    1837   *Oeuvres complètes,* 3. Paris: Philippe.

Brinkman, B. R.
    1975   "'Sacramental Man' and Speech Acts Again." *Heythrop Journal* 16: 418–20.

Cassuto, U.
    1961   *A Commentary on the Book of Genesis.* Trans. Israel Abrahams. Jerusalem: Magnes.

Derrida, Jacques
    1976   *Of Grammatology.* Trans. Gayatri Chakravorty Spivak. Baltimore: Johns Hopkins University Press.
    1977   "Signature Event Context." Trans. Samuel Weber and Jeffrey Mehlman. *Glyph* 1: 172–197.

Felman, Shoshana
    1983   *The Literary Speech Act: Don Juan with J. L. Austin, or Seduction in Two Languages.* Trans. Catherine Porter. Ithaca: Cornell University Press.

Johnson, Barbara
    1980   "Poetry and Performative Language: Mallarmé and Austin." Pp. 52–66 in *The Critical Difference: Essays in the Contemporary Rhetoric of Reading.* Baltimore: Johns Hopkins University Press.

Jungmann, Josef A.
    1976   *The Mass: An Historical, Theological and Pastoral Survey.* Collegeville, MN: Liturgical Press.

Kerbrat-Orecchioni, Catherine
    1984   "La pragmatique du langage: Benveniste et Austin." E. Benveniste aujourd'hui: Actes du Colloque international du C.N.R.S. Ed. Guy Serbat. Bibliothèque de l'Information grammaticale, 1. Louvain: Peeters.

Leitzmann, Hans
    1979   Mass and Lord's Supper: A Study in the History of the Liturgy. Trans. Dorothea H. G. Reeve. Ed. Robert Douglas Richardson. Leiden: Brill.

Levin, Samuel R.
    1976   "Concerning What Kind of Speech Act a Poem Is." Pp. 141–60 in Pragmatics of Language and Literature. Ed. Teun A. van Dijk. Amsterdam: North-Holland.

Longinus
    1965   On Sublimity. Trans. D.A. Russell. Oxford: Clarendon.

Maloney, G. A.
    1967   "Epiclesis." New Catholic Encyclopedia 5: 464–66. New York: McGraw.

Martinich, A. P.
    1975   "Sacraments and Speech Acts." Heythrop Journal 16: 289–303, 405–417.

Martos, Joseph
    1981   Doors to the Sacred: A Historical Introduction to Sacraments in the Catholic Church. Garden City, NY: Doubleday.

Ohmann, Richard
    1971   "Speech Acts and the Definition of Literature." Philosophy and Rhetoric 4: 1–19.

Ross, John Robert
    1970   "On Declarative Sentences." Readings in English Transformational Grammar. Ed. Roderick A. Jacobs and Peter S. Rosenbaum. Waltham, MA: Ginn.

Sadock, Jerrold M.
    1974   Toward a Linguistic Theory of Speech Acts. New York: Academic.

Schillebeeckx, E.
    1963   Christ the Sacrament of the Encounter with God. New York: Sheed and Ward.

Searle, John R.
    1969   Speech Acts: An Essay in the Philosophy of Language. Cambridge: Cambridge University Press.
    1977   "Reiterating the Differences: A Reply to Derrida." Glyph 1: 198–208.

1979 *Expression and Meaning: Studies in the Theory of Speech Acts.* Cambridge: Cambridge University Press.

Skinner, John
1910 *A Critical and Exegetical Commentary on Genesis.* International Critical Commentary, 1. New York: Scribner's.

Vawter, Bruce
1977 *On Genesis: A New Reading.* Garden City, NY: Doubleday.

THE VALUE OF SPEECH ACT THEORY FOR OLD TESTAMENT HERMENEUTICS

Hugh C. White
Camden College of Arts and Sciences
Rutgers University

ABSTRACT

The relationship of the concept of word-event *(Sprachereignis)* in the new hermeneutic and the concept of "writing" in Roland Barthes and Jacques Derrida is discussed, and the more functional and conventional view of truth as "felicity" espoused by speech act philosophy is introduced as a mediating position between the two. Such a view might serve as the basis for a type of narrative hermeneutics in which literary and historical criticism could be more satisfactorily integrated than is presently the case.

The work of Rudolph Bultmann has exerted a major influence on modern Biblical studies primarily because he faced, and responded rigorously and imaginatively to the two horns of the twentieth century hermeneutical dilemma. He embraced the disciplines of the historical-critical method as a means of dealing with the text as an artifact of the past, and he imaginatively drew upon the philosophy of Martin Heidegger to provide an existential analysis in terms of which the message of the New Testament could be made understandable to human beings in the cultural framework of the twentieth century. In so doing, however, he bequeathed to the subsequent generation a bifurcation between collective, objective history *(Historie)* and individual, existential history *(Geschichte)*, which, in spite of numerous efforts, has not yet been overcome (Nations: 1983).

This problem was first addressed in the 1950's by the leaders of the "new hermeneutics" movement, Gerhard Ebeling and Ernst Fuchs, both of whom were former students of Bultmann (Robinson: 1964). In the early 60's it led in this country to a series of consultations at Drew University which brought together leading figures in both the German and American hermeneutical discussions (Robinson and Cobb; Robinson, ed.: 1964). Robert Funk, speaking from the viewpoint of a New Testament critic involved in this discussion, poses the crucial question when he asks: "can historical criticism be taken up into the theological task in such a way that it does not lose its independent critical powers but nevertheless functions positively in the service of theology?" (Robinson and Cobb: 165).

The answer offered by the "new hermeneutics" to this dilemma involved breaking down the barrier between the objective and subjective dimensions of history on the basis of an understanding of the linguisticality of existence. As Gerhard Ebeling said in shifting away from the Bultmannian type of existential analysis, "existence is existence through word and in word" (1964: 109). The language that served as the basis of human existence was not propositional language, however, but language understood as an intersubjective event: "Word is therefore rightly understood only when it is viewed as an event which—like love—involves at least two. The basic structure of word is therefore not statement—that is an abstract variety of the word event—but appraisal, certainly not in the colorless sense of information, but in the pregnant sense of participation and communication" (1964: 103). He characterizes this type of communication event as "promise": "As communication word is promise" (1974: 104). The purpose of historical criticism is then to enable the original speech events of scripture to occur again in the present (1964: 94).

The hermeneutical issues posed by the work of Bultmann were as important for Old Testament studies as they were for New Testament. This can be seen not only from the contribution of Bultmann to the ground-breaking collection of essays on Old Testament Hermeneutics edited by Claus Westermann (1960), but also by a subsequent volume of essays on the relation of the Old and New Testaments edited by Bernhard Anderson (1964) for which Bultmann provides the lead essay. Claus Westermann in the first volume posed the hermeneutical issue for O. T. scholarship very sharply: "The period of Orthodoxy thought the Word of God in the Old Testament was available without any concern for history . . . The exact opposite happened in the period of theological work which began with the Enlightenment . . . 'God's Word' became dependent upon historical thinking . . . The time for these two extremes is over, and now begins the laborious task of asking step by step what actually the Old Testament itself is saying in its texts about the relation between the Word of God and history" (1960: 48–49).

Though language in the Hebrew Bible, with its promises, covenants and prophetic judgements, provides ample justification for the type of language analysis developed by Ebeling, it is perhaps symptomatic that the only essay in these two volumes which attempts to make such an analysis of Old Testament materials was written by James Robinson, a New Testament scholar (1963a). Although there is recognition of the importance of the question of language on the part of the Old Testament scholars writing for these volumes (e.g., Wright 1960: 196), the question is not approached theoretically. Rather, the typical attitude seems to be that expressed by Alfred Jepsen who makes a firm distinction between the reconstruction of the objective history of Israel on the basis of scientific methods, and the interpretation of ancient Israel's religious or theological view of history, and sees no serious conflict between them: "The relationship between depiction of history *(Geschichtsbild)* and the view of history *(Geschichtsanschauung)* is analogous. The Old Testament has a very definite view of history, of the actual history of mankind and of Israel. Its view of this history revolves about the belief that God is the Lord and the guide of just such a concrete history . . . But this view of history remains valid even though in many, indeed very many, of its details the depiction of history may be in error. For this assertion is an assertion of faith, which can indeed be stated as such, but which cannot be objectified" (1960: 268, 269). One of the most popular theological views of history was provided by the promise/fulfillment schema (Zimmerli 1960: 89–122; Westermann 1964: 200–224), and another was found in a revitalized typological interpretation (von Rad 1960: 17–39; Wolf 1960: 344 n. 14). In general these interpretations of ancient Israel's view of history conform to G. Ernest Wright's opinion that the theology of the Old Testament should be built up from the concrete language of the scriptures, and not from the language of twentieth century philosophy: "This essay suggests that a theology is possible which is based more on a study of the creative symbols and the language appropriate to them than on existentialism which rests its theological case on a language abstracted from a study of the psyche" (1963: 196).

In New Testament studies, however, this type of accommodation of historical criticism and theological interpretation was made more difficult by some individual events such as the resurrection, which could not be so easily given up without presenting serious problems for a theological *Geschichtsanschauung*. In addition the primary locus of New Testament interpretation was clearly the twentieth century, whereas the chief hermeneutical problem among Old Testament scholars in these volumes was primarily the relation of the Hebrew scriptures to the New Testament, and only secondarily to the contemporary world. This clearly makes it much easier to remain within the language world of the Bible in developing a hermeneutical perspective.

The developments of the last twenty years have shown that the possibility of developing a satisfactory *Geschichtsanschauung* of the Hebrew scriptures has not been realized and no longer seems viable. But the need for a theory of language, which the new hermeneutic attempted to develop, to mediate between the poles of historical criticism and theological interpretation is still with us in the form of the tension between the new structural and literary approaches to the text and traditional historical criticism. The continuing centrality of language to this problem led Robert Culley to say in a recent survey of the new developments in narrative study: "There is no reason why biblical scholars should not examine the language dimension of the biblical text with all its complex structures, including the literary structures produced by the imagination, with the same intensity and thoroughness that scholars have devoted to the study of the links texts have with their settings, their historical dimensions" (1985: 190).

There is a tendency for the preoccupations and obsessions of each new development in the history of research to ignore or reject the insights and concerns of the previous phase, as, for instance, modern architecture rejected the eclecticism of victorian architecture, and in turn has seen its own passion for purity of form rejected by the new eclecticism of post-modern architecture. It is important that continuity be maintained between the present post-modern hermeneutical development which is now influencing Biblical studies, and the new hermeneutics. Deconstruction itself, as espoused by Jacques Derrida, represents, in part, a sharp reaction against Heidegger whose later thought was very influential upon the new hermeneutics, and as the shortcomings of deconstruction become more visible, a premature rejection of the central concerns of deconstruction is easily envisaged.

This article will not attempt to resurrect what many will regard as the dead past, nor to survey the complex development of Old Testament hermeneutics (see Kraus: 1982; Buss: 1974; 1979; Polzin: 1977; Stuhlmacher: 1977; Culley: 1985; Coats: 1985) or hermeneutical theory over the past two decades (see Hoy: 1982), but simply to pick up the threads of the earlier discussion regarding language, and particularly the central issue of the speech-event *(Sprachereignis)*, which have not been given sufficient attention in the discussion of Biblical hermeneutics in recent years, and relate them to some relevant new developments in philosophy and literary hermeneutics. The specific proposal to be presented here is that new possibilities for the resolution of some of the problems upon which the earlier discussion seemed to run aground, and which deconstruction also presents for Biblical studies, may be offered by J. L. Austin's speech act philosophy. The specific point of contact between these two approaches to language is found in Ebeling's characterization of scriptural communication as "promise." Before discussing speech act theory, however, attention must be given to developments within literary criticism which provide important points of contact with the concept of language event within the new hermeneutic. It is from the vantage point gained by this correlation that the contribution of speech act theory to the resolution of the hermeneutical problem may be seen more clearly.

* * *

The general hermeneutical problem might be stated in simple terms: Historical criticism detaches the past from present concerns in order to prevent the distinctive, unique, and even alien features of previous historical periods from being ignored or distorted by the passion to make the past relevant to present circumstances. But the gap that is left between the present and past becomes so immense that the significance of both is threatened by the sea of relativity. Theology, on the other hand, tends to seek within the transitory events of the past either eternal truths, or *Geschichtsanchauungen*, or significance for the present in some other form, to the extent that the historical uniqueness of the past is eroded and some transhistorical truth is imposed on the living and changing present.

This hermeneutical dilemma arose in literary studies beginning with the so-called "new criticism" in this country during the twenties and thirties which sought to interpret poetic texts in terms of their own immanent, verbal features rather than in terms of the psychology and history of the author. As David Daiches says, the purpose of the "new criticism" was "the rescuing of the work of literary art from biography and history and the discovery of its uniqueness" (Spiller 1962: 97). In the 50's and early 60's a French "nouvelle critique" developed embodying some of these same concerns, but based on a much broader theoretical foundation in Russian formalism, Saussurian linguistics, and neo-Freudian psychoanalysis. This debate follows the same contours as that within Biblical studies. The central hermeneutical problem was posed in its most radical form by a leading voice of the "nouvelle critique," Roland Barthes.

For Barthes the literary work is primarily a system of signs whose meaning is fundamentally a product of semiotic processes immanent to the work itself. The importance of his analytic work for our purposes here, however, was his attempt to find, in the final form of the work, traces of the process of writing which had produced it, i.e., he was seeking in the literary work traces of a seminal historic occurrence, but the type of historic event he was seeking had a linguistic rather than a political, social or psychological character. When the process of literary creation is examined, the importance of biographical, and psychological history to the work becomes much less self-evident. The power of language to shape the subjectivity of the author, and the insubstantiality of the author's own self, apart from language, then begins to appear. So Barthes can describe the actual situation of the author in this way: ". . . the subjective is not an individual 'fullness', which one has the right to empty into speech or not (according to the literary genre), but, on the contrary, an emptiness which encircles the author with words so that each manner of writing, which does not lie, signifies not the inner attribute of the subject, but his absence (Lacan)" (1969: 82).

Thus for Barthes, when one returns to the primal situation of the literary work, one does not find a factual, cultural situation which can be objectively reconstructed by the historian, but the inner semiotic process of the subject vis-a-vis language. How then can one speak of the original meaning, or the original intention of the author?

For both the critic and the author, there is an irreducible linguisticality at the basis of their subjectivity. Barthes asks, "who is this I that exists before my speech? How can I experience my language as an attribute of my person? How can one believe that when I speak, it happens because I am? Literature does not permit this illusion because in literature I experience my I as being given by language" (1969: 44).

When the author comes to write, s/he enters into a different type of historical moment, i.e., not an historical circumstance which has objective, empirical form, but one which is at the very center of the historic process itself, i.e., the moment of writing. Barthes describes language and style as "blind forces," the former a horizon of social familiarity, and the latter a force which arises from one's biological nature (1970: 14). Writing, however, he describes as a "pact which binds the writer to society", an "act of historical solidarity," a "relationship between creation and society" (1970: 12, 14). It is in the tension between the givenness of language and tradition, on the one hand, and biological necessity, on the other, that the act of writing as limited freedom and choice occurs: "Writing as Freedom is . . . a mere moment. But this moment is one of the most explicit in History, since History is always and above all a choice and the limits of this choice" (1970: 17). While Barthes diminishes the significance of objective history for literary understanding, he sees the act of writing as reaching into, "the deeper layers of History" (1970: 17).

This deeper engagement with language cannot always be accommodated within the comfortable dialectic of reason. It is in his discussion of modern poetry that Barthes describes a primal form of the encounter with language which the poet makes available to his reader. In contrast to "classical speech," which is characterized by the careful articulation of logical and syntactic connections and by a reference to a final meaning, "in modern poetry, connections are only an extension of the word, it is the Word which is 'the dwelling place', it is rooted like a *fons et origo* in the prosody of functions, which are perceived but unreal. Here, connections only fascinate, and it is the Word which gratifies and fulfills like the sudden revelation of a truth . . . Fixed connections being abolished, the word is left only with a vertical project, it is like a monolith, or a pillar which plunges into a totality of meanings, reflexes and recollections: it is a sign which stands. The poetic word is here an act without immediate past, without environment, and which holds forth only the dense shadow of reflexes from all sources which are associated with it (1970: 47).

Barthes here is thus pointing to an encounter with language which transcends the manipulation of words. Language is being depicted as an event, a force, which stands over against both the poet and his reader as a generative power which transcends grammar and syntax: "The word here has a generic form; it is a category. Each poetic word is thus an unexpected object, a Pandora's box from which fly out all the potentialities of language; it is therefore produced and consumed with a peculiar curiosity, a kind of sacred relish. The Hunger of the Word, common to the whole of modern poetry, makes poetic speech terrible and inhuman" (1970: 48).

Thus at the root of the writing process is this primal encounter with language, or the Word, which, in some sense, stands over against historical and cultural conditions as it stands over against the writer. It is in the tension between the intrusion of the Word, and the givenness of linguistic tradition that the limited freedom of the writer is exercised, and that the act of writing itself acquires its historicality. Barthes has thus come to find the primary historic dimension of the text not in the objective conditions of the author's life and circumstances, but in the specific acts of textual production. In these acts the literary process and the sequential events of time are no longer distinguishable. Similarly all that is important from the psychology of the author is absorbed into the textual product itself, and is manifested in linguistic form.

* * *

This movement by Barthes toward giving a certain primacy to language represents an implicit rejection of the individualistic existentialism of Sartre. A corresponding movement was taking place in Germany in the thought of Heidegger and in the discussion of the New Hermeneutic. Unlike Sartre, Heidegger's thought in the late 1930's underwent a major shift away from the vestiges of subjective individualism still residing in his earlier analytic conceptual mode of thought *(Being and Time)*, and toward an understanding of thinking in which the initiative lay with language or being. As James Robinson described it, "Prior to the turn, thinking is conceived as basically derived from *Dasein's* initiative; after the turn, thinking is envisaged as given to *Dasein* by the initiative of being" (1963: 19).

Connected with this "turn" in Heidegger's thought was a thoroughgoing critique of traditional, metaphysical language. The truth of being cannot be reduced to conceptual language, the validity of which is based upon a theory of correspondence between language and its object *(adaequatio rei ad intellectum)*. Rather Heidegger returns to the 'soil' out of which metaphysical thought has grown, i.e., the primal tension between the unthought and the thought, the unspoken and the spoken, and begins to speak of being as an event of disclosure to thought prior to the formulation of traditional metaphysical systems. As he writes: "the being-there of the historical man is the breach through which the being embodied in the essent can open. As such it is an *in-cident* (*Zwischen-fall*, a fall-between), the incident in which suddenly the unbound powers of being come forth and are accomplished as history" (Heidegger 1959: 137). This event of the manifestation of being coincides with an occurrence of language: "In accordance with its historical, history-disclosing essence, being-human is *logos*, the gathering and apprehending of the being of the essent . . . simultaneously with man's departure into being he finds himself in the word, in language" (1959: 143). This historic departure into language/being is not the result of reflective deliberation, but of being overpowered *by* language. He considers poetic language the purest and most potent form in which being manifested itself (1959: 144).

It is from this "later Heidegger" then that the students of Bultmann who initiated the discussion of the "new hermeneutic" took their point of departure (Robinson 1964: 48, 49). They sought to move beyond the Bultmannian program, inspired by the "early Heidegger", of interpreting Christian literature in light of the open questions posed by the human existential situation *(dasein)*, to a deeper understanding of the role of language in the shaping of consciousness and faith. As Fuchs writes, "The responsibility for speaking resides already in language, not outside it. That is my *thesis*. He who notices recognizes that language 'grants.' Language is not the abbreviation of thinking but thinking is an abbreviation of language. Language is gift" (Robinson 1964: 55).

This move toward the understanding of the self and consciousness not as the subject of language, but rather as the product of language becomes a theological premise for Ebeling: "His (i.e., human) existence is, rightly understood, a word event which has its origin in the word of God and, in response to that word, makes openings by a right and salutary use of words. Therein man is the image of God" (1964: 104). Language is here understood not instrumentally, but as a divine power which manifests itself in linguistic events, i.e., speech events. These events bestow upon the creature his humanity, and simultaneously his divine likeness. Echoing the "turn" of the later Heidegger, Ebeling then redefines the existentialist approach to the interpretation of texts to give priority in the human situation to language: ". . . existence is existence through word and in word. Then existentialist interpretation would mean *interpretation of the text with regard to the word event*" (1964: 109). It is the task of scriptural interpretation then to discern the primal events of speech which gave rise to it, and to allow those events to occur again in the present through the interpreter.

Here a correspondence becomes evident between Roland Barthes' movement away from Sartrean existentialism toward an understanding of the creative act which accords a primary role to language, and the "turn" in the later thought of Heidegger (and the theologians who were influenced by him). For both, language comes to be understood as a power, a force which occurs in the consciousness of the poet. Historic consequences flow from this language occurrence.

For Heidegger, however, this occurrence of language was integrally tied to "being" as the voice of being, whereas for Barthes there is no explicit translinguistic referent or metaphorical allusion to such. It is in the thought of Jacques Derrida that the ultimate distinction between Barthes' understanding of "writing," and Heidegger's view of language as the voice of being, is extended and fully elucidated. Derrida replaces the Heideggarian use of the term "being" with the term "trace", i.e., pure difference which is at the root of all dualisms of interior/exterior, presence/absence, body/soul, nature/culture, signifier/signified, etc. (1977: 70). With this term he attempts to free writing completely from subordination to metaphysics. Though he goes much further than Barthes in his anti-metaphysical polemic, it is clear that for both there is a decisive turn toward language as the horizon of consciousness which leads away from the questions and terminology of traditional metaphysics toward those of linguistics and semiotics.

This turn toward language and semiotics took place on a broad front in France in the post-war period due largely to the influence of Russian emigrés such as Roman Jakobson, who brought the insights of Russian formalism, and the Swiss linguist, Ferdinand de Saussure. From the anthropologist Lévi-Straus's study of Amer-Indian myths to the neo-Freudian psychoanalysis of Jacques Lacan, the new focal point of the most serious reflective thought was the structure and production of texts. Many tensions existed within these rich traditions of scholarship, however, and the approaches to the analysis of texts which emerged took a variety of forms.

The watershed which brought about the most fundamental division between approaches to texts was de Saussure's distinction between the two aspects of language: *La parole* or the event of speech production, and *la langue* or language as a closed system of mutually defining features. In Saussure's view (at least as disseminated in the early posthumous publication of his 1906–11 lectures [1966]), language must be understood essentially as an unchanging system rather than a sequence of speech events caught up in the relativities of the non-verbal material and temporal flux. This distinction within linguistics is homologous, on the philosophical level, with the distinction already encountered in Heidegger between the objective language of concepts (dependent upon a view of truth as *adaequatio rei intellectus*), and language as historic occurrence. Literary criticism which has emerged from this linguistic discussion has thus tended to take either a more objective, formalistic approach to texts which minimized or totally excluded the semantic importance of the event of text production (the approach taken by Lévi-Strauss, Greimas, and others), or has sought to understand the structure of texts from the viewpoint of the language occurrence in the act of writing, i.e., from the viewpoint of the event of text production (the approach taken by Barthes, Kristeva, Derrida, and their followers). It is thus in the latter tradition that one finds the concern of the later Heidegger and the new hermeneutic group to develop an approach to texts which is founded upon the primary language occurrences which give rise to texts, and is expressed in non-objectifying language.

* * *

It is at this juncture then that it is possible to begin to see more clearly the dilemma of the present situation with regard to Biblical hermeneutics, and the role which the language philosophy of J. L. Austin might play in resolving it.

At the root of the hermeneutical problem lies the practice of historical criticism which attempted to sever the text from the presuppositions and ideology of the critic in order to grant the text its right to historical uniqueness. This method viewed the language of the text as signifying ideas and facts that were peculiar to the world and time of its authorship, and its truth or meaning could only be established through reestablishing the connections between the language of the texts and these referents, i.e., through reconstructing the extra-textual historical milieu that provides the referential context which discloses the original meaning of the text and the intentions of the author.

On the other extreme, reflecting the turn away from history toward the epistemological primacy of language in text analysis, are the formalist approaches which assume that the meaning of the text arises from the internal linguistic/semantic structure of the text itself. Here the view of truth and meaning of the text is the same as in the historical approach; it is the referential content of the text's language which determines its meaning. But now the reference is strictly to the logical structure of its semantic content rather than to extra-textual, historical/cultural objects of reference. The reconstruction is of the semantic micro-universe of the text itself, rather than of the biography of the author and his historical world. This leaves again a cleavage between history and text.

Intermediate between these two extremes are those approaches taken by Barthes and Heidegger (and their disciples) which attempt to deal with the historicality of the text by analyzing the event of its production, and with the linguisticality of the text by depicting that event as an occurrence of language. The problem encountered by the Barthesian approach is that the language event tends to become so inward and subjective, so momentary and experiential, that it can only be juxtaposed against all referential reconstructions, whether historical or semantic. This means that the continuity of the text, whether diachronically or synchronically conceived, is described as a closure which suppresses and disguises the open, creative language occurrences which produced it, and which constitute its fundamental semiotic structure. The critic who is attuned to the process of writing must then disassemble or "deconstruct" the closed network (often defined with assistance of linguistic or semiological categories) which provides the historical consistency and logical continuity of the text in order to reveal the open process of writing which produced it.

The guarantee of this openness for Barthes, however, finally becomes a negativity, the "infinite paradigm of difference", the foundation of *la langue* (Saussure) and consciousness (Lacan) which sets itself against all positive universal paradigms of which the text would always be only a "Copy" (1974: 3). Barthes's "difference" corresponds to Derrida's "trace," also a pure negativity. The almost mystical depiction of the function of the "Word" in Barthes's early writing thus undergoes reduction to the rigorous, negative purity of "difference" in his later work. The avoidance of all metaphysical and ontological langauge has led to an inability to speak of the event of language in a positive sense.

The new hermeneutic discussion stemming from Heidegger in Germany led to a different problem. Heidegger's depiction of being as word-event was infused with profound positive meaning for the human subject: "The question of how it stands with being proves to be the question of how it stands with our being-there in history, the question of whether we *stand* in history or merely stagger" (1959: 169). When this view of being was appropriated by theologians of the new hermeneutic such as Gerhard Ebeling, Heidegger's view of being provided a way of reconceiving the primal language events of scripture which seemed to escape the objectifying effect of traditional metaphysics. Within a theological context, language events thus became even more unequivocally positive. This suggested to Ebeling the possibility for a kind of theological linguistics, i.e., a recasting of theology so as to give primacy to the process of language through which revelation occurred and scripture was formed. This possibility was realized with his book, *Introduction to a Theological Theory of Language* (1973).

In this interesting work, Ebeling dealt with most of the basic theoretical problems which are taken up in linguistics and language philosophy, such as the relation between the structure of particular languages and universal structures, language as a synchronic system vs. language as diachronic acts, the relation of the speaking/writing subject to language, the problem of reference, and the conditions which make for effective speech acts (1973: 96, 132, 100, 122, 123, 205). He does not, however, appropriate the valuable work of modern linguistics and language philosophy, but rather relies on the tradition of theological reflection over language, and his own insight.[1] The result is a book rich in suggestive thought, but one which does not produce a thorough, linguistically grounded method for text analysis. It is often difficult to distinguish between a purely linguistic feature and a theological point, and many times what he places in the latter category belongs in the former.

More recently Carl Raschke has forcefully brought the later Heidegger's understanding of the event character of language once again to the hermeneutical discussion precipitated by Derrida. While Raschke is sympathetic with Derrida's deconstruction of the sign, he sees the need for retaining Heidegger's more positive view of the Word as a "presencing presence." Heidegger's eschatological view of meaning as an occurrence at the end of the process of hermeneutical discussion rather than at the beginning, escapes Derrida's critique of the representational sign. But Raschke is critical of the solitariness and monological character of the type of speech which Heidegger seems to posit as the norm for the human condition, and seeks to complement Heidegger's thought with the more concrete dialogical perspective of Martin Buber.

In spite of his desire for concreteness, however, he cannot see linguistics and semiotics as offering anything but the objectification and closure of representational language (1979: 55). He would most likely say the same regarding ordinary language philosophy. Thus he is able to make an eloquent appeal for theology to entrust itself to the manifestation of the Word "de novo from out of the event of confrontation and address between persons who have arrived at an ontological relation of I and Thou" (91), but does not relate such an appeal to the detailed work of textual analysis which these more analytical approaches to language might make possible. Meaning for Raschke is finally produced by the naked and inexplicable occurrence of the poetic Word beyond all qualifying contextual conditions.

Thus neither the major French, American, nor German works we have surveyed which place primary emphasis upon the act of speech have developed an approach to text analysis which finds a way of speaking positively of the content of the language occurrence itself while, at the same time, appropriating the system and insights of modern linguistics or language philosophy. The rejection of metaphysics by the Barthes school brings about the reduction of the language of the speech act itself to a semantically empty act of writing, or trace (which ultimately must rely upon neo-Freudian theory for its meaning), while the German new hermeneutic school leaves its positive theological interpretation of the language of the speech act unrelated to the modern linguistic discussion with the insights it affords regarding the structure of texts. As a consequence it remains suspended between metaphysical closure and some form of mystical ontology.

* * *

The need thus is for an approach to the text which can, on the one hand, provide a theoretical basis for speech acts without falling prey to metaphysics, mysticism, or individual subjectivism, and, on the other, make use of insights afforded by linguistics and language philosophy without having the subjective dimension of the speech event negated by atemporal synchronism or empiricism. Hermeneutical philosophy which gave rise to the "new hermeneutics" has not led to a satisfactory way of dealing with narrative texts, as Raschke's recent work in this tradition illustrates.[2] The insights of linguistics and language philosophy need to be incorporated if the capability of detailed text analysis is to be developed. Without such capability, text analysis will ultimately remain the province of historical criticism with the seemingly unresolvable conflicts mentioned above. The developing 'literary' approaches to the Biblical text have generally not carried forward the concern of the new hermeneutic with language and history, but have relied on various 'new critical' and formalist methods which perpetuate the theoretical cleavage between the historical and aesthetic dimensions of the text.[3] The various speech act centered structural approaches which have both theoretical depth and a capacity to produce a detailed text analysis are so averse to metaphysics that they have failed to develop a theory which will provide a basis for a positive understanding of the speech acts, and of the continuity of the narrative structures which unfold from them.

* * *

What contribution can speech act theory then make to the resolution of these problems of Biblical hermeneutics? Austin's concepts of illocutionary force and felicity (see the "Introduction" above) provide the starting points for a nonmetaphysical theory of language, and a view of truth which escapes the limits of the correspondence theory. By focusing upon the inter-subjective function of language and the conventions which support it, Austin has developed a perspective which links the individual subject's experience of language with a general system which is both linguistic and social. This makes possible a functional view of truth which is non-metaphysical without being enshrouded in the ontological mysticism of the later Heidegger or the individual relativity and semantic negativity of deconstruction.

In addition it opens the possibility of a systematic approach to language which is rooted in the social concreteness of ordinary language usage rather than synchronic-universal, logical, or mechanistic patterns.

With respect to literature, this orientation toward ordinary language provides categories with which the diachronic surface features and form of the text can be seriously analyzed, and a practical method of text analysis developed. It thus offers the possibility of overcoming the division which characterized the new hermeneutic, between hermeneutical philosophy, which espouses an ontological view of language, and historical-critical methods of text analysis which presuppose the correspondence theory of truth.

The results of Austin's investigation seem particularly suited to Biblical, and especially Hebrew narrative hermeneutics since the most prominent linguistic features of the Hebrew narrative are the central word events which have the form of Austin's classic examples, i.e., promises, commands, warnings, verdicts, and the like. But perhaps more important, because of the importance of felicity conditions, a speech act theory of literature would have to place Biblical literature in its social and even historical context, thereby bringing together the literary and historical perspectives. By treating language itself as an act, the dichotomy between literary word and historical fact is eliminated at the theoretical level. The meaning of language is understood neither in terms of a logical (or existential) system, nor its correspondence to empirical fact, but in terms of the conditions which govern its use. The division between word and event, between the theoretical and factual, is thus overcome in principle.

The appropriation of the language theories of J. L. Austin for religious studies is not a novel proposal. The philosopher of religion, Ninian Smart, wrote his doctoral dissertation under Austin (1958). Of more interest to research in Hebrew narrative is the work of another student of Austin, Donald Evans. His book, *The Logic of Self-Involvement* (1963), published only one year after *How to do Things With Words,* was written in response to the absence of a theory of language, particularly in the theology of Rudolph Bultmann, to support his existential analysis of Biblical texts, i.e., he was responding to the same deficiency in Bultmann which prompted the new hermeneutic, although he does not seem to have been familiar with this movement. Bultmann, he argues, "Like other biblical theologians . . . does not provide an adequate account of how any language can involve a speaker logically in something more than a mere assent to a fact" (11). His proposal involves developing a new "logic of self involvement" on the basis of Austin's theory of performative language. Why is a new logic needed? He claims that, "Older logics deal with propositions (statements, assertions); that is, they deal with relations between propositions and relations between terms of propositions. Modern biblical theory, however, emphasizes *non-propositional* language, both in its account of divine revelation (God's 'word' to man) and in its account of human religious language (man's word to God). In each case the language or 'word' is not (or is not merely) propositional; it is primarily a *self-involving activity,* divine or human. God does not (or does not merely) provide supernatural information concerning Himself, expressed in flat statements of fact; He 'addresses' man in an 'event' or 'deed' which commits Him to man and which expresses His inner Self" (14).

The starting point of this 'logic' is not an ontological understanding of language events, such as is provided by the later Heidegger, but the use of the concrete, "ordinary," language of the Bible itself, a starting point very compatible with the inclinations of Biblical theologians such as G. Ernest Wright noted above. After developing this mode of logic in the first part of the book, in the last half he applies it to the Biblical language about God as Creator.

While this approach is very suggestive for the work of Biblical scholarship, it is directed toward issues relating to the philosophy of religion, and not to textual or narrative analysis.[4] Several important lines of influence upon theological and Biblical studies have flowed from it, however. Robert Jenson utilized this perspective to deal with the question of the verifiability of religious language, but relied upon the 'new hermeneutic' to deal with the issue of word-events in Biblical narration (1969; see also Mananzan: 1974). A. C. Thistelton, about the same time, proposed that the concept of language event, put forward by Ernest Fuchs in connection with the interpretation of New Testament parables, could be strengthened in important ways by the incorporation of insights from Austin and Wittgenstein (1970). G. B. Caird's more recent work, *The Language and Imagery of the Bible* (1980), also owes much to Evans and to Austinian thought generally.

Of direct relevance to the hermeneutical concerns here is the influence Austin and Evans have had upon Paul Ricoeur.[5] In an autobiographical statement of the evolution of his thought in 1973, Ricoeur concludes by indicating a turn in his thought toward Austin, Evans, and ordinary language philosophy generally. He makes a programmatic proposal to 'graft' linguistic analysis to phenomenology, seeing in their unification, mutual benefit for both, as well as for hermeneutics. His reasons for this proposal are important: "What happens in the more intricate cases of text-interpretation and what constitutes the key problem of hermeneutics is already foreshadowed in the interpretive process as it occurs in ordinary language. Thus the whole problem of text-interpretation could be renewed by the recognition of its roots in the functioning of ordinary language itself" (1973: 96).

This turn toward ordinary language philosophy is already visible in an earlier article where he proposes "the methodology of text interpretation as a paradigm for interpretation in general in the field of the human sciences" (1971). Here he suggests that actions themselves be understood in terms of speech act theory: "The different classes of performative acts of discourse described by Austin at the end of *How to do Things with Words* may be taken as paradigms not only for the speech acts themselves, but for the actions which fulfill the corresponding speech acts. A typology of action, following the model of illocutionary acts, is therefore possible. Not only a typology, but a criteriology, inasmuch as each type implies *rules*, more precisely 'constitutive rules' which, according to Searle in *Speech Acts*, allow the construction of 'ideal models' similar to the *Ideal types* of Max Weber." This intriguing theoretical suggestion would go far toward breaking down the barrier between historical narrative and historical events which is at the center of the hermeneutical problem being discussed here. It corresponds closely also to Claus Westermann's assertion regarding events in the sacred history of ancient Israel ". . . the only basis for a creed is this: that a *factum* is recognized as a *dictum* (1960: 48).

Though speech act theory was not pursued in Ricoeur's volumes on biblical hermeneutics (1975; 1980), it does appear again in his work on metaphor. There he argues that new meaning emerges in ordinary discourse (sometimes through metaphor) as an occurrence of language at the intersection of the opposing tensions of sense and reference. This tension between the old and the new lends "historicity" to the power of signifying which occurs in the instance of speech. He sees speech act theory (especially as developed by the early work of Ladrière), as providing an important element in this understanding of meaning in terms of the semantic dynamism of the act of speech in ordinary language. (1979: 297, 298). He has extended this in his understanding of the New Testament parable as the "metaphorization of a discourse" (1982: 355).

The French theologian Jean Ladrière, drawing heavily upon Evans, has recently published the most wide-ranging treatment of the Christian faith thus far, from an Austinian perspective (1984). No attempt can be made here to summarize his lengthy analysis of so many diverse aspects of religious life, from liturgical rites to theological discourse and cosmology. One particularly novel use of speech act theory which should be lifted out, however, is his treatment of the performativity of the gospel narrative as a whole in light of its liturgical use in the life of the church: ". . . to the extent that it is not considered as a mere historical document, but as an always living presence itself of a word which is offered for our ratification, the gospel narrative has this singular virtue of making us enter by its own force into this that it renders manifest. But it is through the performativity characteristic of its ecclesiastical usage that it is received always as a living word" (II.:39). The concept of performative language, for Ladrière, bridges the gap between the word-events within the scripture, and the use of scripture as sacred canon in the life of the church. Such a perspective may be able to shed new light upon the central concerns of the recent discussion of canon/canonical criticism.

The Austinian concept of performative language has also been given a centrally important role by Timothy Polk in his recent thorough-going and illuminating study of the confessions of Jeremiah (1984). Utilizing Donald Evans' early work on Austin in a very general way, Polk argues for the self-involving and self-constituting nature of much of the language of the confessions (e.g., 136). This work is very suggestive of the type of fruitful insights which a speech act approach to the literature of the Hebrew Bible offers.

* * *

The missing element in all of these early efforts to appropriate speech act theory is the development of a method of literary analysis capable of illuminating the specific topography of the Biblical narrative. The lack of this development may be due in part to the fact that most of the previous work in the field of religious studies has been done by philosophers of religion and theologians rather than Biblical scholars who must deal in more detail with a body of sacred literature. What progress has been made toward applying speech theory to the problems of literary analysis which might be useful in analyzing Biblical literature? A comprehensive speech act theory of literature would have to treat the semantic level, the pragmatic level, and the syntactic level. Such an inclusive theory does not yet exist, and there are currently many debates especially in philosophy and literary studies about the implications of this theory at each of these levels. (See "Introduction")

At the semantic level we encounter the issue which arose above in the thought of Heidegger and Barthes regarding the status of the Word or Logos as a generative power which can be distinguished from the multiplicity of words. The recognition of language as an historic force in both hermeneutic philosophy and Bathesian semiotics has brought to light some features of language which appear also (though in a much more restrained form) in Austin's theory of illocutionary force, but speech act philosophers have not shown any inclination to search for common ground with these investigations (and are not likely to do so in the future). Such a development would require the reexamination of the assumptions of speech act theory regarding the relation of language and subjectivity, as the fascinating debate between Searle and Derrida (discussed in the "Introduction") has shown. It is, of course, at this level as well that the controversial question of the linguistic status of the divine Word (discussed also in Michael Hancher's article in this volume) would have to be determined as a central element in any speech act theory of Biblical literature.

At the pragmatic level of intersubjective communication, more work has been done in the field of literature to utilize speech act theory, as discussed in the "Introduction" to this volume. The type of analysis developed by Mary Louise Pratt may be particularly suited to the Biblical narrative. At the outset it resolves the question about the "literariness" of Biblical writing by breaking down the boundaries between literature and ordinary discourse (see also Nohrenberg 1974: 21–24). But perhaps more importantly, it provides widely applicable categories for systematically analyzing the layers of embedded speech acts which are so characteristic of Biblical narratives. It is at this level of dialogical interplay between the characters and the resulting intersubjective dynamic which sets the plot in motion, that the kind of theological insights into the speech-events of scripture produced by Gerhard Ebeling, are refined and enriched by this enlarged context of language analysis.

Finally, the analysis of syntax also has an important place in Pratt's method of analysis. The effect of syntax upon the reader often is the most powerful force in determining the response of the reader, and the meaning which s/he derives from reading. The theoretical integration of this level into the foundations of speech act theory is still weak, but it is clear that much profitable work can be done on this problem.

* * *

The new hermeneutic failed to carry Biblical studies beyond historical exegesis because it was unable to develop an adequate means of applying its central understanding of the event character of language to the analysis of longer Biblical narratives. It consequently was forced to work too much within the methods and conclusions of historical criticism. When new methods of narrative analysis appeared they were brought by the structuralist movement which found little meaning or importance in the event of speech production, and sought to explicate the text in terms of logical, synchronic models. The semiological approach to literature which has flowed from the influence of Roland Barthes, combined a central emphasis upon aspects of the event character of language with a deep, complex appropriation of the insights into language of modern linguistics and psychoanalysis. But the various forms of continuities within literary texts which were brought to light with great subtlety and sophistication, were perceived ultimately as forms of closure imposed upon the open, acts of speech/writing. This has led to the 'deconstructive' approach to narrative today seen in the works of Jacques Derrida.

Speech act theory offers to Biblical critics a framework within which some accommodation between the two poles of this discussion may at least be attempted. The basis of this accommodation might be a functionalist understanding of truth (in terms of Illocutionary Force) which is at least potentially open to the view of the Word as event espoused by the new hermeneutic, and yet able to deal positively with narrative continuities and complex textual development without subsuming them beneath a closed, synchronic, semantic system. With its emphasis upon language as act, and upon the meaning of concrete speech conventions, it offers as well the possibility of achieving some form of integration with historical criticism.

Of course, speech act theory is itself a varied field of investigation, with many internal schools of thought not all of which would lend themselves to the type of development I am suggesting. But this is a debate which, I believe, would be profitable for Biblical critics to enter.

NOTES

[1] For a critique of the view of language espoused by the later Heidegger and Ebeling from the viewpoint of J. L. Austin and the English analytic school, see Zuck (1972), and also Verhaar (1969: 17), who points out Ebeling's "total lack of a theory of language" (which was not satisfactorily remedied by this later book).

[2] The search by hermeneutical theology during the 1970's for a non-objectifying mode of theological discourse found it in such forms of speech as *poesis* (Hopper 1974: 31), metaphor (Ricoeur: 1975) and aphorism (Miller: 1970). Although all of these possess what might be generally described as a performative dimension, a detailed discussion of them cannot be undertaken here. The general difficulty which they present is that their strategies of contemporization leave behind the primary word events and their contexts (see McKnight on Ricoeur: 213), and are much more adept at dealing with shorter poetic, parabolic, and aphoristic modes of expression than with narratives. Some of the same problems have arisen in the newer deconstructive theologies which reflect the same hermeneutic concerns, e.g. Charles Winquist's search for a deconstructive theology brings writing and metaphor into the center of theology conceived as a hermeneutical "word-event," and a "work": "It is the work and not its content that is the first-order theological achievement. It is the work that lives in the dialectic between force and meaning" (1986: 55, 56). His way of relating these insights to text analysis follows Derrida very closely and suffers from the same inability to deal with textual/narrative structures except as forms of repression (59, 60). See the "Introduction" above.

[3] Geoffrey Hartman comments regarding Robert Alter's *The Art of Biblical Poetry* that "Alter is finally the latest and the best flowering of the New Criticism," and also that "The objection to Alter's project is not that he reduces the Bible to art . . . but rather that he fails to provide an adequate understanding of art itself. He interprets Scripture only in a single, irreversible direction; the referential one, in which all musical qualities are translated into meanings, or else regretfully put aside" (Hartman: 1986). Meier Sternberg, in his recent work on the poetics of Biblical narrative, pursues the formalist aim (among others) of defining the "literariness" of the Biblical narrative (1985: 43).

[4] Robert W. Funk, one of the leading exponents of the new hermeneutic in the U.S., discussed briefly the relation of Austin's philosophy to the concept of *Sprachereignis*, but did not develop it [1966: 28]. Subsequent important contributions from philosophical theology are Morse (1979) and Thiemann (1985) which were not obtained in time for analysis in this essay (see Annotated Bibliography for comment).

[5] For a concise summary of Ricoeur's contribution to the study of the Hebrew Bible see Culley (1985: 179, 180).

WORKS CONSULTED

Anderson, Bernhard W., ed.
    1963   *The Old Testament and Christian Faith: A Theological Discussion.* New York: Harper & Row.
    1974   "The New Crisis in Biblical Theology." Pp. 159–174 in Courtney (1974).

Barthes, Roland
    1969   *Literatur oder Geschichte.* Frankfort am Main: Suhrkamp Verlag.
    1970   *Writing Degree Zero.* Boston: Beacon Press.
    1974   *S/Z.* Trans. by R. Miller. New York: Hill and Wang.

Buss, Martin
    1974   "The Study of Forms." Pp. 1–56 in *Old Testament Form Criticism.* Ed. by John H. Hayes. San Antonio: Trinity University Press.
    1979   "Understanding Communication." Pp. 3–44 in *Encounters with the Text: Form and History in the Hebrew Bible.* Ed. by Martin J. Buss. Philadelphia: Fortress Press; Missoula: Scholars Press.

Caird, G. B.
    1980   *The Language and Imagery of the Bible.* Philadelphia: Westminster Press.

Coats, George W.
    1980   "Theology of the Hebrew Bible." Pp. 239–262 in Knight (1985).

Courtney, Charles, Olin M. Ivey, and Gordon E. Michalson, eds.
    1974   *Hermeneutics and the Worldliness of Faith: A Festschrift in Memory of Carl Michalson.* Drew Gateway 45.

Culley, Robert C.
    1985   "Exploring New Directions." Pp. 167–200 in Knight (1985).

Derrida, Jacques
    1977   *Of Grammatology.* Trans. G. C. Spivak. Baltimore: Johns Hopkins University Press.

Ebeling, Gerhard
    1964   "The Word of God and Hermeneutic." Pp. 78–110 in Robinson, ed. (1964).
    1973   *Introduction to a Theological Theory of Language.* Trans. R. A. Wilson. Philadelphia: Fortress Press.

Evans, Donald D.
    1963   *The Logic of Self-Involvement: A Philosophical Study of Everyday Language with Special Reference to the Christian Use of Language about God as Creator.* London: SCM Press.

Heidegger, Martin
    1959   *An Introduction to Metaphysics.* Garden City, N.Y.: Doubleday.

Hopper, Stanley Romaine
    1974   "Theology, Culture, and the 'Thirteen Ways of Looking at a Blackbird'." Pp. 15–36 in Courtney (1974).

Hartman, Geoffrey
    1986   "Meaning and Music," a review of *The Art of Biblical Poetry* by Robert Alter. *The New Republic* (April 28): 25–30.

Hoy, David Cousins
    1982   *The Critical Circle: Literature, History and Philosophical Hermeneutics.* Berkeley: University of California Press.

Jepsen, Alfred
    1960   "The Scientific Study of the Old Testament." Pp. 246–284 in Westermann.

Jenson, Robert W.
    1969   *The Knowledge of Things Hoped For: The Sense of Theological Discourse.* New York: Oxford University Press.

Kraus, Hans-Joachim
    1969   *Geschichte der historisch-kritischen Erforschung des Alten Testaments von der Reformation bis zur Gegenwart.* 2nd ed. Neukirchen Kreis Moers: Verlag der Buchhandlung des Erziehungsvereins.

Knight, Douglas A. and Gene M. Tucker, eds.
    1985   *The Hebrew Bible and its Modern Interpreters.* Philadelphia: Fortress Press.

Ladrière, Jean
    1984   *L'Articulation du Sens.* Vol. I "Discours scientifique et parole de la foi;" vol. II "Les langages de foi." Paris: Les Éditions du Cerf.

Mananzan, Sr. Mary-John, OSB
    1974   *The "Language Game" of Confessing One's Belief: A Wittgensteinian-Austinian Approach to the Linguistic Analysis of Creedal Statements.* Lingustischen Arbeiten 16. Tübingen: Max Niemeyer Verlag.

McKnight, Edgar V.
    1978   *Meaning In Texts: The Historical Shaping of a Narrative Hermeneutics.* Philadelphia: Fortress Press.

Miller, David
    1970   *Gods and Games: Toward a Theology of Play.* New York: The World Publishing Co.

Nations, Archie L.
    1963   "Historical Criticism and the Current Methodological Crisis." *Scottish Journal of Theology* 36: 59–71.

Nohrenberg, James
   1974   "On Literature and the Bible," *Centrum*, 2, 2: 5–43.

Polk, Timothy
   1984   *The Prophetic Persona: Jeremiah and the Language of the Self.* Journal for the Study of the Old Testament: Supplement Series 32. Sheffield, England: JSOT Press.

Polzin, Robert M.
   1977   *Biblical Structuralism*. Philadelphia: Fortress Press; Missoula: Scholars Press.

Rad, Gerhard von
   1960   "Typological Interpretation of the Old Testament." Pp. 17–39 in Westermann (1960).

Raschke, Carl A.
   1979   *The Alchemy of the Word*. AAR Studies in Religion 20. Missoula: Scholars Press.

Ricoeur, Paul
   1971   "The Model of the Text: Meaningful Action Considered as a Text." *Social Research* 36: 529–562.
   1973   "From Existentialism to the Philosophy of Language." *Philosophy Today* 17: 88–96; also pp. 315–322 (Appendix) in Ricoeur (1979).
   1975   "Biblical Hermeneutics." *Semeia* 4: 29–148.
   1979   *The Rule of Metaphor: Multi-disciplinary studies of the creation of meaning in language*. Trans. by R. Czerny with K. McLaughlin and J. Costello. Toronto: University of Toronto Press.
   1980   *Essays on Biblical Hermeneutics*. Edited with an introduction by Lewis S. Mudge. Philadelphia: Fortress Press.
   1982   "La Bible et l'imagination." *Revue d'Histoire et de Philosophie Religieuses* 42: 339–360.

Robinson, James M.
   1963   "The Historicality of Biblical Language." Pp. 124–158 in Anderson (1963).
   1964   "Hermeneutic since Barth." Pp. 1–77 in Robinson, ed. (1964).

Robinson, James M. and John B. Cobb, Jr.
   1963   *The Later Heidegger and Theology*. New York: Harper and Row.
   1964   *The New Hermeneutic*. New York: Harper and Row.

Saussure, Ferdinand de
   1966   *Course in General Linguistics*. Ed. by C. Bally, & A. Sechehaye, trans. by W. Baskin. New York: McGraw Hill.

Smart, Ninian
   1958   *Reasons and Faiths*. London: Routledge and Kegan Paul.

Spiller, Robert Ernest, ed.
  1962 *A Time of Harvest*. New York: Hill and Wang, 1962.
Sternberg, Meir
  1985 *The Poetics of Biblical Narrative: Ideological Literature and the Drama of Reading*. Bloomington: Indiana University Press.
Stuhlmacher, Peter
  1977 *Historical Criticism and Theological Interpretation of Scripture*. Trans. by Roy A. Harrisville. Philadelphia: Fortress Press.
Thistelton, A. C.
  1970 "The Parables as Language-Event: Some Comments on Fuchs's Hermeneutics in the Light of Linguistic Philosophy." *Scottish Journal of Theology* 25: 437–468.
Westermann, Claus, ed.
  1960 *Essays on Old Testament Hermeneutics*. Trans. by J. L. Mays. Richmond: John Knox Press.
Winquist, Charles E.
  1986 *Epiphanies of Darkness: Deconstruction in Theology*. Philadelphia: Fortress Press.
Wolff, Hans Walter
  1960 "The Understanding of History in the Old Testament Prophets." Pp. 336–356 in Westermann (1960).
Wright, G. Ernest
  1963 "History and Reality: The Importance of Israel's 'Historical' Symbols for the Christian Faith." Pp. 176–199 in Anderson (1963).
Zimmerli, Walther
  1959 "Die Weisung des Alten Testamentes zum Geschäft der Sprache." Pp. 1–20 in *Das Problem der Sprache in Theologie und Kirche*. Ed. by Wilhelm Schneemelcher. Berlin: Alfred Toepelmann Verlag.
  1960 "Promise and Fulfillment." Pp. 89–122 in Westermann (1960).

II.

*Applications of Speech Act Theory
to Problems of Biblical Exegesis*

(FEMINIST) CRITICISM IN THE GARDEN: INFERRING GENESIS 2–3

Susan S. Lanser
Georgetown University

ABSTRACT

Taking as its point of departure two revisionist readings of Genesis 2–3, this essay explores differences in interpretation that may emerge from different understandings of language itself. Biblical scholar Phyllis Trible and narratologist Mieke Bal both seek to demonstrate that Genesis 2-3 inscribes sexual equality rather than male supremacy. They are able to refute standard interpretations because they assume a theory of language as formal code, in which meaning is a function of surface propositions and their semantic and grammatical properties. The more traditional rendering of Genesis 2–3, on the other hand, is consistent with the model of communication proposed by speech act theory, whereby meaning always depends on specific contexts of language use in which the process of inference plays a powerful role. By exploring the implications of these two linguistic models for reading Genesis 2–3, the essay raises issues central to the interpretation both of biblical narrative and of discourse in general. Finally, I suggest that a deeper understanding of gender relations in Genesis 2–3 might be revealed by the tensions between the text's formal structures and its structures of inference.

In the "The Function of Criticism at the Present Time," the essay that furnishes the epigraph for Geoffrey Hartman's *Criticism in the Wilderness*, Matthew Arnold uses a biblical metaphor to imagine critics of his generation as wandering Israelites able perhaps to glimpse but not yet to reach the Promised Land. In a conflation fitting for a poststructuralist for whom reading can have no final resting point, Geoffrey Hartman suggests that perhaps the wilderness *is* the Promised Land (15), the terrain of a wild, Romantic freedom to read other-wise. Elaine

Showalter allows both possibilities when, in "Feminist Criticism in the Wilderness," she envisions the feminist critic as a theoretical pioneer. For reasons that are more than playful, I would like to give this image yet another turn by positing a critical garden alongside the critical wilderness. I mean each landscape to map a particular set of assumptions about "literary" interpretation in general, about biblical interpretation in particular, and finally about language itself.

I want to explore these assumptions by looking at two feminist readings of Genesis 2–3. If no mythical garden has been as consequential as Eden for human history, no critical garden has been so consequential either: surely there is no narrative in the Hebrew Bible whose interpretations and misinterpretations have had wider and more powerful effects. On women these effects have of course been particularly insidious: from the *Malleus Maleficarum*'s justifications for the persecution of women as witches to the continued debarring of women from the Catholic priesthood to the advertising slogans for Eve's Cigarettes, the Genesis 2–3 story, as justification for misogyny, has pervaded and invaded women's lives. Feminist criticism has also been in the garden for at least half a millennium, since Isotta Nogarola published in 1453 an epistolary debate between herself and her friend Ludovico Foscarini on the relative guilt of Adam and Eve.[1] Centuries of mis/readings of "Adam and Eve" present contemporary scholars with a formidable legacy. But precisely because it is so overdetermined a text, Genesis 2–3 stands as both challenge and sign—a challenge to the clarity of our interpretive processes, a sign that interpretation and hence theories of interpretation count, that how we read does make a difference.

It is in the spirit of both understanding the past and changing the present that feminists have returned to Genesis 2–3. Their scholarship has taken two main forms. Most contemporary feminist critics, while recognizing centuries of misogynist misreadings of the text, nonetheless contend that by any reading Genesis 2–3 portrays man as primary and woman as subordinate.[2] But a few feminist critics, in a gesture of recuperation, read Genesis 2–3 as an egalitarian text. It is these readings that motivate my inquiry, which originated in the desire to discover what different hermeneutical principles might lead to such divergent feminist readings of a single text.

The primary examples of the revisionist reading come from biblical scholar Phyllis Trible and narratologist Mieke Bal.[3] They write for different purposes: Trible is committed to a recuperation of the Bible as liberating Word; Bal sees in the Genesis story the "semiotization of the female" (319) and the origins of literary characters. But their textual approaches are similar; indeed, Trible's reading is the basis for Bal's. Since their work shares with much contemporary biblical scholarship an explicit grounding in "literary" methodologies, it also provides a way to explore important questions about the nature of (biblical) interpretation and about the theories of language that underlie both narrative and interpretive acts (or, as I have been putting it, what it might mean to situate interpretation in a garden or a wilderness).

The focus for my inquiry, then, is not so much the *content* of these feminist readings as the *contexts* they bring to bear on their interpretation of the text. In order to explore this question, I want to isolate and in fact overemphasize one of the major patterns in Bal and Trible's recuperative strategy: the ways in which they imagine language to operate. Since I am interested less in the arguments themselves than in the procedures of reading that make them possible, I will omit or relegate to footnotes those matters in which this question of language is not at stake. I should also caution that I will be ignoring some of the differences between Bal and Trible when these are not relevant to my own inquiry.[4]

Trible's and Bal's analyses of the status of woman in Genesis 2–3 concentrate on two textual moments: the creation of woman (2:18–24) and the pronouncement of the consequences for eating the fruit (3:16–19).[5] Trible's highly detailed account of every verse, and Bal's briefer and more theoretical essay (which unlike Trible's has literary purposes beyond the reading of Genesis) share the following arguments, though sometimes on different premises: that man and woman were created not sequentially but simultaneously, from a sexually undifferentiated being; that woman is not secondary, dependent or derivative, but is in fact the "culmination" of creation (Trible 102); that the woman is treated less severely than the man for disobeying; and that inequality between the woman and the man enters only after 3:16 as a consequence of disobedience, not as a punishment and by no means (at least for Trible) as part of a divine plan. Both Trible and Bal thus read Genesis 2–3 as a linear text and the relationship of man and woman as changed by the act of disobedience. In this way they differ from scholars like Phillips and Claude Westermann, who argue that there is no change in the state of male/female relations after the "Fall," despite what Westermann acknowledges as a "profound tension" (262) between 2:18/23 and 3:16. Bal, but not Trible, reads Genesis as a continuous narrative[6] and hence draws on Genesis 1 to support interpretations of Genesis 2–3.

As a point of entry let me look closely at the premise that anchors both readings: the argument that the "earth-creature" *ʾādām* as created in 2:7, has no gender at all, that *hāʾādām* is not "the first man" but an "it." Gender comes into being only with the creation of woman in 2:22, which entails the sexual differentiation expressed in 2:23, the verse that first uses the word *ish* to rename the earth-creature as "man."[7] Man and woman are hence created at the same moment, and man's sexual identity depends upon woman's as much as hers depends upon his.[8] One cannot, therefore, say that woman was created for man or that she was taken from man; Bal even jokes about man as the "leftover" (324) after the creation of woman.

Scholars well trained in the decoding of linguistic signs, Trible and Bal are certainly correct to assert that *hāʾādām* designates not a male person but simply a particular creature formed of dust whose name is linked at least homonymically to a word for soil or earth. They are equally correct to assert that the masculinity of the word *hāʾādām* and of its attendant pronouns is a matter of grammatical gender and not necessarily of sexual identity. The traditional reading of *hāʾādām* as the male person then becomes a centuries-old mistake, for Bal a failure of reading worthy of some contempt:

> What makes readers assume this creature is male? What, by another equally strange twist, makes them assume that this mistaken priority implies superiority? Unable to read an unfulfilled character, they supply the lacking features. (322)

Bal is exactly right in suggesting that readers assume and mimeticize. But what is for her a "strange twist" might also represent another way of conceiving communication itself. As Sperber and Wilson would put it, Trible and Bal's reading derives from a theory of language as a code or system of signs, in which meaning is a function of semantic, grammatical, and phonological or orthographical properties and communication a process of encoding and decoding sentences. But there is another model of communication that would explain the traditional reading of *hāʾādām* as male: the speech-act model developed by philosophers like J. L. Austin, H. P. Grice and John R. Searle.

As speech act theory understands language, the basic unit of communication "is not, as has generally been supposed, the symbol, word or sentence," but rather "the production or issuance of the symbol or word or sentence in the performance of a speech act" (Searle 16). Meaning is therefore a function of the *context* in which linguistic communication is performed. When people speak, they are assuming a complex system of what Searle calls "constitutive" rules—rules that do not simply govern but actually create the meaning of a particular utterance. Searle phrases this understanding in the formula "x counts as y in context c;" (35): "under certain conditions" a particular utterance has a particular meaning.

This understanding of language implies that meaning is created not only by decoding signs but by drawing on contextual assumptions to make inferences. That is, every act of understanding relies (unconsciously and sometimes also consciously) on complex rules and assumptions about social and cultural behavior and language use. Put somewhat differently, discourse is not "a set of signs with a fixed meaning" but rather "a dynamic system of communicational 'instructors' with a variable meaning-potential which is defined by specifying co-texts and contexts" (Schmidt 401). Within such a framework communication is a function not only of signifiers but of silences; meaning is not coextensive with words-on-a-page but is constituted by the performance of the text in a context which teems with culture-specific linguistic rules that are almost never articulated.[9] Understanding is a (mostly automatic) process of selecting among possible meanings "so as to achieve as much intelligibility as possible," thereby creating what Wendell Harris calls an "ecology"—note the aptness of the garden here—that is, a "consistency between contexts," that will "make the expression work" (123).

The following exchange constitutes a classic example of the way in which inference may supplement or supplant formal meaning even in a brief exchange:

Alan: I have a headache.
Joan: I have an aspirin.

By the rules of inference, or what H. P. Grice discusses in terms of "implicature," Alan has every right to take Joan's statement, which *as code* is merely an assertion that she possesses aspirin, as an offer to give him the drug. It is not that Joan is hedging; she is simply responding to a linguistic ecology whereby "I have an aspirin" is sufficient, in the context created by Alan's own utterance, to constitute an offer. This is so because sentences embody not only propositional but also what Austin called illocutionary acts—social actions performed in the process of uttering propositions. A sentence like "I have an aspirin," which in a different context might count as mere statement of fact (i.e., an "expositive" illocution), here functions as a "commissive," i.e., an illocutionary commitment "to a certain course of action" (Austin 157). One could say, then, that the *meaning* of Joan's sentence is constituted by the sentence that precedes it.

These unspoken conventions are no more or less external to the text than are the denotations of words or the rules of formal grammar; they are carried within or evoked by the text. The distinction between a formal theory of language and a theory of language use is not, then, a distinction between text and extra-text. My reading of Genesis 2–3 works as closely with the text as Trible's and Bal's. But while Bal and Trible might have recourse to a grammar or a dictionary, there is not, as yet, much of a "grammar" or "dictionary" of inference. Both approaches rely on knowledge about language; the study of inference relies largely on knowledge that has not yet been codified[10]—not because it is impossible, I submit, but because it has been considered either insignificant or self-evident.

Obviously literary texts are far more complex than everyday conversation, and different kinds of texts bring different forms of inference to bear. Indeed, the idea of literature, like the specific idea of Biblical narrative, is itself a constitutive context, and "the way people produce and understand literary works depends enormously on unspoken culturally shared knowledge of the rules, conventions and expectations that are in play when language is used in that context" (Pratt 86). I will come back to the question of how the processes of decoding and inference operate in the reading of literary texts. But a fairly standard process of inference is at work, I would argue, in the conventional reading of *hāʾādām*'s maleness in Genesis 2. Let me postulate that when a being assumed to be human is introduced into a narrative, that being is also assumed to have sexual as well as grammatical gender. The masculine form of *hāʾādām* and its associated pronouns will, by inference, define *hāʾādām* as male. I am not suggesting that one *cannot* read *hāʾādām* as a sex-neutral figure; I am saying that readers *will* not ordinarily read Genesis 2 in this way. Gendered humans are the unmarked case; it is not *hāʾādām*'s maleness that would have to be marked but the *absence* of maleness. In this instance, indeed, what Rickheit et al. describe (33) as two reinforcing systems of inference are at work: the inference brought, a priori, *to* the reading of Genesis 2:7 that a living creature named with masculine pronouns will be male, and the inference drawn, a posteriori, *from* the reading that since the creature being created as a helper is "woman," then the creature for and from whom she has been created is already "man." As far as I can determine, this process of inference operates as fully in Biblical Hebrew as, say, in modern French, which is also a language of dual gender.

Indeed, Trible and Bal's argument does not explain why, if *hāʾādām* has become a new being, *hāʾîš*, the text continues to use *adam*, rather than *ʾîš*, to designate the creature supposedly transformed by the creation of women into man. Trible does acknowledge that "the basic word for humanity before sexual differentiation, *hāʾādām*, now becomes a sexual reference so that it is used frequently, though not exclusively, for the male" (98).[11] But the text provides no marking, no context, to lead readers to make a new inference about the meaning of *ʾādām*. If, as Trible suggests, the narrative now shifts between two meanings of *ʾādām*, "human" and "male," then the text itself has made the elision human = male, erasing woman and designating her as Other.[12]

Trible offers a different kind of formal argument to claim that the phrase "she shall be called woman" (2:23) does not actually constitute the naming of woman, and thus that the man does not exercise the same dominion over the woman that he does over the animals. Her reason is that this verse (2:23), unlike 2:19–20, does not join the verb *qrʾ* (call) with the noun *šēm* (name), into the phrase "to call the name of." Instead, 2:23

merely uses the verb "to call": "She shall be called woman." "Alone," Trible argues, "the verb *call* does not signify naming" (100); she goes on to cite examples from elsewhere in Genesis in which "to name" is also constituted with the phrase "to call the name of." For Trible, "she shall be called" is simply a recognition of sexual difference.

But consider the ways in which ordinary discourse abbreviates syntactic forms in a context where a clear inference can be presumed. For example, although "to give" and "to give blood" are clearly not the same in meaning, "I gave last week" can obviously mean "gave blood" in the context of a discussion in which giving blood has already come up. Now Genesis 2 has set up a sequence in 2:19–22: God forms a creature intended as a companion[13]; God brings the creature to *hāʾādām*; *hāʾādām*, at God's behest, names the creature. The only difference is that with woman alone does God succeed; *hāʾādām*'s role does not change. In fact, Robert Alter implies that the entire sequence is designed to constitute the man's authority to name: "Eve has been promised. She is then withheld for two carefully framed verses while God allows man to perform his unique function as the bestower of names on things" (30). Having set up the sequence in which *hāʾādām* is authorized to name, the text has already generated the context in which "call" may be inferred to mean "call the name of," despite the abbreviated surface form. Repetition of *haššēm* is not needed. The illocutionary act of naming has already been evoked; the surface propositional content of 2:23 simply re-evokes the same illocutionary act. The difference in grammatical construction for the "calling" that occurs in 2:23 might be attributable to the fact that, in contrast to 2:19–20 and to Trible's examples from Genesis 4, 2:23 is direct discourse.[14]

Trible and Bal's final argument about the creation of woman is that even if *hāʾādām* were created first, and as male, creation after and from man would not imply inferiority. Among other arguments,[15] Trible and Bal develop elaborate structural analyses of the full creation story (which in Bal's case begins with Genesis 1[16]) to see 2:23 as a joyful climax signalled by the burst into poetry and direct discourse: "This at last is bone of my bone and flesh of my flesh," which is followed by the consummation "in silence" of man and woman as "one flesh." The creation of woman, they argue, is thus the high point of the entire creation narrative; or, in bumper-sticker language, "Adam was a rough draft."

This argument, although enacted upon a larger structural unit than the sentence, once more stresses the formal properties of the text at the expense of the inferential context in which the structure appears. For what 2:23 actually culminates is the process that begins in 2:18, when God plans to make a helper fit for *hāʾādām*. Any sense of culmination here exists within a context of inferences that have been made about the centrality of *hāʾādām*, who is the subject of this discourse and for whom, after all, this laborious act of creation and re-creation has taken place. The very fact that this moment is represented in the discourse of *hāʾādām* emphasizes that the joy is his; as Hugh White wryly observes, "woman does not respond to this eloquent welcome" (95). Ironically, Bal's own description of this moment unwittingly reproduces precisely the androcentrism of Genesis 2 itself: "God brings the woman "to *hāʾādām*," she says, "who, by the recognition of *the other*, assumes *his own* sexual identity" (emphasis mine). This focus on the male subject is reinforced by the narrator's use, in the very next two verses (2:24 and 2:25) and on three occasions thereafter, of the possessive structure *hāʾādām wěʾištō*—the (hu)man and his woman. It is with this inferential context in mind that John Phillips emphatically considers the claim that woman is the "crown" of creation to be nothing more than "wishful thinking. Given the other features of the story and the purpose of her creation, that notion is utterly impossible. She belongs to the realm of the creatures over which Adam will exercise his lordship" (33).

Even Bal and Trible must admit that sex hierarchy enters the text in 3:16, when God tells the woman that her husband shall rule over her.[17] Confronted with the fact that it is God who pronounces the words that establish male rule, both argue that these words constitute not punishment but consequence; and both consider the man to be the more severely punished of the two. For Bal, whose critical context is a semiotic one, this last section of Genesis 3 generates the emergence of female character, so that only in 3:20 can woman be named. Trible's concern is theological: to avoid the implication that the judgment on the woman constitutes God's justification for patriarchy. She must therefore confront the fact that by the end of Genesis 3, patriarchy has been established. Indeed, by 3:22–24, she says, the name *hāʾādām* has come to signify "the generic man who renders the woman invisible" (137), a sign of the woman's suppression in the new, fallen order of things. But for Trible, this state of affairs is not one in which God participates.[18]

The argument again operates from a formal theory of language rather than a theory of language use. Bal and Trible argue that the absence of an "accusatory formula" ("Because you did this") from God's address to the woman means that the judgment upon her is less severe than upon than man. A theory of inference would argue that the formula "Because you did this" simply carries over from the address to the serpent in 3:14 and is confirmed by the address to the man in 3:17. More central to their arguments is the claim that God's reaction is not a punishment but a consequence for disobedience, an "explicitation of the consequences of the human option" (332) in Bal's terms. At stake is the same kind of speech-act question that "I have an aspirin" evoked: that is, what kind of illocutionary act is God undertaking in 3:16? On what grounds is it possible to determine whether the pronouncement to the woman is what Austin calls an "exercitive"—"a decision that something is to be so"—or simply an "expositive," a "judgment that it *is* so" (155). Is God merely *informing* the woman of her fate, or do his words actually *bring about* the state of affairs announced in 3:16?

Without developing the kind of detailed linguistic analysis that John Searle gives, for example, about promising, let me offer the following less formal description of the stages and conditions that might allow a reader to infer the pronouncement of a sentence or punishment: the speaker issues to the hearer a prohibition concerning a certain act; the speaker has the authority to impose sanctions if the hearer violates the prohibition; the hearer does violate the prohibition; the speaker then utters propositions of the form "Because you did x, then y." All of these conditions obtain, of course, in Genesis 2-3. Indeed, almost all of God's direct discourse in Genesis 2–3 constructs a verbal context for inferring punishment: "Do not eat. . . " "Where are you?" "What have you done?" The conditions of inference are established in which any negative pronouncement, whether in the explicit form "Because you did x, then y" or simply the shorter "Y," will be inferred to constitute a punishment. Moreover, the construction "I will" as a preface to the "consequences" in 3:15 and 3:16, suggests that God is determining and choosing them. In short, the entire narrative, in which God creates the tree, explicitly forbids *hāʾādām* to eat of it, and then calls the man and woman to account for doing so, creates an overdetermined context in which God is *expected* to deliver punishment long before he does so, and the pronouncements of 3:14–19 fulfill this expectation even if their surface form allows other possibilities.

There is, of course, a very important "consequence" at stake. If in fact the state of affairs described in 3:16 is punishment, then God could be charged with ordaining male dominance, all the more as the man is judged not only for eating but for listening to the woman's voice (3:17). [19] This is the point where Bal's and Trible's readings reach their *aporia*—the impasse, the silence, that unravels the argument. For finally neither can explain why male dominance should be the particular consequence of a transgression for which both man and woman are equally, as they argue, responsible. Bal resorts to an uncharacteristically exegetical argument, proposed by Oosten and Moyer, that the cryptic phrase in Genesis 4:7 "and unto you his desire and you shall rule over him" is actually a misplaced portion of Genesis 3:16 which the cultural blindness of patriarchal editors has kept from being reinstated in Genesis 3.[20] Trible attempts the parallel that "the woman is corrupted in becoming a slave, and the man is corrupted in becoming a master" (Trible 128), but surely slave and master, however both odious, are not equivalent roles. Bal's and Trible's readings break down, I suggest, because they press a formal theory of language beyond its own possibilities. A theory of language use that understands the role of inference in the construction of meaning could not yield the reading of Genesis 2–3 as a non-sexist text.

What Bal and Trible have done, however, is what literary critics do virtually as a matter of course: bring to bear upon the reading of a text contexts for interpretation which, like the unspoken rules of language use, are almost never named, especially if they are the accepted tools of what Stanley Fish calls an "interpretive community." Readings like the ones Trible and Bal create are built for the most part on three components, which work together syllogistically:

1. **Observation:** the text states or does x. This proposition identifies a textual feature on the basis of which interpretation will proceed.

2. **Contextualization:** x counts as y [in context c]. This proposition argues that the observed feature has a certain meaning in a particular (social and linguistic) instance.

3. **Implication:** if x counts as y, then z.

In feminist readings of Genesis 2, for example, one might recall the observation that the language of 2:19–20, in which $hā^{ɔ}ādām$ names the animals, differs from the language of 2:23. It is the context we create for reading this observation that will determine whether the same male dominion is established in both passages. Interpretive sequences—or readings—are established when one implication furnishes the premise for further arguments; for example, different arguments about the naming of woman might entail different judgments about whether the subordination of woman is intrinsic to the creation story or occurs only after 3:16.

What I call "contextualization" is the least articulated and least acknowledged component of the interpretive process, and what appear to be disagreements about implications may actually be differences of interpretive context. Literary interpretive practice in particular rarely identifies explicitly the contexts within which observations are transformed to implications in order to yield interpretations of texts. Thus, as it is usually practiced, the formula I have given is carried out simply as "x counts as y"; hence my brackets around the phrase "in context c."[21] Obviously, contexts are particularly powerful when they are assumed but not identified, thereby seeming natural and inevitable rather than constructed and changeable.

Such contextual knowledge, as Wendell Harris puts it, is "of different kinds":

> social custom (including what John Searle calls "institutional facts": the legal system, the monetary system), standard locutions, grammatical principles, cultural attitudes, common experience . . . and the immediate situation in which the language is used. (Harris 123)

For the interpretation of Biblical narrative, of course, one immediately wonders *whose* social custom, grammatical principles, cultural attitudes and common experience one is reading from. To the extent that biblical reading attempts to reconstruct an "intentional" text,[22] a reader will be constituting what she or he imagines to be the probable context—social, cultural, linguistic, etc.—in which the text was *produced*. More than most scholarship biblical interpretation confronts a text whose origins, originating world, and linguistic code will never be fully known; Robert Alter goes so far as to say that "we have lost most of the keys to the conventions out of which [Biblical narrative] was shaped" (47). Meir Sternberg, however, insists that it is utterly necessary to risk engaging in the reconstruction of historical contexts, and particularly in the reconstruction of biblical poetics, as we interpret biblical texts: "From the premise that we are not people of the past, it does not follow that we cannot approximate to this state by imagination and training" (10). In fact, he argues that "once the choice turns out to lie between reconstructing the author's intention and licensing the reader's invention, there is no doubt where most of us stand" (10).

Whether or not "most of us" agree with Sternberg, what he is alluding to is the fact that the environment of the reading subject—social cultural, linguistic, etc.—constitutes yet another, possibly very different context in which the text is *reproduced*. To some extent, in part according to the reader's own self-consciousness, everyone brings cultural and personal contexts to the act of reading—from the ways in which, say, I understand gender relations or the meanings of specific words to my conviction that the Bible can or cannot portray a sexist God. It is not that such assumptions and beliefs do anything so simple as to "bias" the reader; rather, they operate as a kind of grid that obscures certain meanings and brings others to the foreground. Nor is there the possibility of an ideal, objective reading; there are only readings, each of which can be most fully understood by making as visible as possible the acts of contextualization in which the reader seems to have engaged.

In these ways *every* reading creates and is created by its context; no uncontextual reading is possible, and as both Jacques Derrida and Stanley Fish have cleverly demonstrated, a piece of discourse seemingly fixed in meaning can be uprooted by supplying a new interpretive context. As I hope my reading of Bal and Trible has made evident, it would be misnaming to say that speech-act theorists and "political" critics read texts "in context" and that New Critics do not. The differences—and they are crucial ones—lie both in the degree to which context is brought explicitly to bear and in the kind of context the reading creates. As Richard Ohmann argues, "we can conceive Lee Harvey Oswald's act as tensing his forefinger, pulling a trigger, firing a gun, shooting President Kennedy, murdering him or assassinating him."

While each of these statements is technically correct, the implications of Oswald's act are not evident until the context is wide enough. Similarly, the appropriateness of a national holiday honoring the Reverend Martin Luther King, Jr., looks different in the context of a list of those Americans, all U.S. presidents, whose birthdays are already so honored—a kind of formal system—and in the context of the historical struggle of Black Americans for recognition and equality, a pragmatic context which foregrounds the need to redress the legacy of racism that has made a Black presidency historically impossible.

Of all aspects of context, both the most hidden and one of the most consequential for biblical scholarship is the context of understanding brought to the text about the nature of understanding itself. Bal and Trible's understanding of language remained hidden precisely because the formal approach to language that they employ has come to count as *the* "literary" approach both to biblical interpretation and to interpretation in general. When Trible, says that "a literary study of Genesis 2–3 may offer insights that traditional perspectives dream not of" (74), what does she mean by "literary" and what by "traditional"? When she says that "at any rate, such a study fits the text," is she not ignoring the fact that critics also fit texts to their interpretive modes? The problem lies not in the existence of two approaches to language, for surely both decoding and inference are always active in reading; the problem lies in imagining only one approach to be "literary" when in fact it is formalist, as if inference were suspended in the reading of literature.

I have been pressing the role of inference precisely as a corrective to the notion that literary discourse, whether by definition or by default, is discourse privileged beyond the conditions in which communication ordinarily takes place. Obviously the morning news and poetry, to cite extremes, are not the same discursive act, and the formal aspects of language will need far more attention in reading the second than the first. Indeed, while I agree with Pratt that literature is itself a constitutive context, the category "literature" is large and heterogeneous. In seeking a theory of language that accommodates interpretive possibilities, then, I would want to avoid treating not only all discourse, but even all literary discourse as a single mode. If discourses can be located on an axis from those motivated by sheer efficiency, by the desire to communicate information, to those motivated by the desire to please, to play, or to perplex, then literary discourse itself manifests a range, say, from history to parable to lyric to "nonsense" rhyme. Somewhere in the middle of such a spectrum I would locate "ideological literature," the name Meir Sternberg gives to Biblical narrative. Social in its purposes yet complex in form, and regulated, as Sternberg notes, by its need to be both subtle and accessible, Biblical narrative requires, more urgently perhaps than some texts with which literary critics are concerned, attention not only to its formal structures but to the acts of reading that its performance ordinarily entails.[23] While an esoteric reading of Genesis 2-3—a criticism in the wilderness—might excite critics, it also detaches the text from its crucial place in the cultural intertext of human history.

But perhaps texts like Genesis 2-3 continue to rivet us precisely because of the complex and problematic relationships between their formal codes and their structures of inference. Perhaps it is not simply in the interplay, but in the tension between code and speech context— between form and use—that the most exhilarating feminist readings of Genesis 2-3 are to be found. For to the extent that Bal and Trible have identified formal features which other readings have not adequately explained—for example, that the prohibition not to eat is given only to *hā ʾādām*, or that the hierarchical structure *hāʾādām wĕʾištō* belongs to the narrator, not to God or man, who use more reciprocal forms—they create apertures in the reading that is produced by my own theory of inference. Might not the tension between inference and form signify a deep ambivalence on the part of the Jahwist writer or his society about the place of woman? Might such a dis-ease not signify the dissonance within early Judaism between the status of woman in traditional patriarchal society and the theologically egalitarian impulse manifested more openly in the later Genesis 1? Might this not make Genesis 2-3 the document of a patriarchy already beginning to be uncomfortable with itself? If so, I envision a third kind of feminist reading built upon the uneasy relation of context and code, made possible by, but not coextensive with, either Bal and Trible's formalism or the wholly inferential approach which I have opposed to it. It is this third reading, one that negotiates garden and wilderness, for which the feminist critic would indeed be a theoretical pioneer.

NOTES

[1] Contemporary feminist critics would not find Nogarola's argument entirely sympathetic, since it relies on the notion of woman as the weaker sex.

[2] Although I don't know whether he would call himself a feminist, John Phillips performs the most thorough of such readings in *Eve: The History of an Idea*.

[3] Trible's analysis of Genesis 2-3 appears in several essays as well as in the book *God and the Rhetoric of Sexuality* which I cite here. Bal's essay "Sexuality, Sin and Sorrow" is taken from her new book *Femmes imaginaires*, not yet translated into English. My references therefore are to the English text.

[4] Trible's purpose is more openly theological and recuperative, but both writers claim not to be engaged in defending the text. Bal: "my point in this paper is not to establish anachronistically a 'feminist' content of the bible. If my interpretation of Eve's position will show her in a more favorable light than is the case in the common uses of the text, I do not want to suggest that this is a feminist, feminine or female-oriented text" (318); Trible: "I propose not to defend the narrative against [traditional interpretations of male superiority and female inferiority]—

though I am tempted and may sometimes yield—but rather to contemplate it afresh as a work of art" (73–74).

There are numerous differences in substance and rhetoric between Bal's and Trible's positions and major differences in the focus of their attention. Some of these differences will surface in my analysis; others will not. Typically, Bal is more willing than Trible to sustain textual ambiguity. For example, Trible says that the name Eve, which "alone might be a title of honor," confirms woman into "a position of inferiority and subordination" (134); for Bal, while the name "imprisons her in motherhood" (335) it also designates her resemblance as creator to Jahweh, "the consonants H and W being the phonetic actant which opposes the creators to the creatures, signified by D and M" (336).

[5] Trible and Bal do of course rest a few of their arguments on the scenes of disobedience and trial. In brief, both argue that the man and the woman transgress equally, but they also imply that the woman's motives are superior to the man's. After cautioning that "the story does not say that she tempted him; nor does its silence allow for this inference" (113), Trible goes on to make a series of inferences of her own from that very moment of silence (3:6): that the man is weak, "belly-oriented" and acquiescent, while the woman is responding to higher motives such as the physical and aesthetic appeal of the tree and the wisdom it will offer her. In carefully conditional syntax, Trible says: "If the woman is intelligent, sensitive, and ingenious, the man is passive, brutish, and inept" (113).

Similarly, for Bal the woman's "disobedience is the first independent act, which makes her powerful as a character" and through which "speech becomes dialogue" and the relationship between the humans and Jahweh becomes "horizontal" (332). Bal argues also that the two trees of 2:9 are *wisely* confused by the woman in 3:2–3 because she "is open to reality, and ready to assume it" (330). Thus the woman "did not exactly sin; she opted for reality" (332).

For Trible the narrative emphasis on the man in the trial scene creates a textual balance with the emphasis on the woman in the eating scene. Trible also considers the woman's behavior at the trial nobler than the man's because she does not blame Jahweh for creating the serpent as the man blames Jahweh for creating her.

[6] Bal makes this argument not because she believes the text is historically unitary but because she understands coherence as a "reading device" (326 n9).

[7] Trible does not acknowledge that the phrase "she shall be called 'iššâ because she was taken from 'iš" would be meaningless were there no 'iš prior to the creation of 'iššâ from which she could be "taken." Bal does try to resolve this problem, and offers "two ways out": either "the man retrospectively assumes that he always had this sexual identity" or—the version she prefers—"taken from" actually means "differentiated from" (324).

[8] Bal argues that "the eventual authors of the younger, first version, did not present a theological counterstatement to the second, older one. They were accurate readers and wrote a piece that completed retrospectively the imaginary representation of this particular conception of creation through differentiation" (326 n9). This allows her to accept the documentary theory and yet use the plural pronouns of Genesis 1:27 (as well as 5:2) as the context for reading hā'ādām as sexless and man and woman as equal.

Bal's reading is the only one to explain satisfactorily, I think, the "problem" that the injunction not to eat the fruit is given only to hā'ādām. If hā'ādām has yet no gender, the prohibition is effectively being given to both future characters.

[9] Significantly, such assumptions are usually identified only in cases of perceived *mis*understanding, as in "Oh, I thought you meant x." But even here, it is normally the misunderstanding rather than the language rule that will be discussed.

[10] The effort to articulate these rules and conventions was begun mainly by H. P. Grice, who posited what he called maxims of conversational implicature. Many philosophers of language are now at work on developing a more precise theory of inference. As far as I know, the most up-to-date bibliography of philosophical (though not literary) research on inference can be found in Sperber and Wilson, pp. 265–74.

[11] Trible's qualification—"frequently, though not exclusively"—is imprecise. As she will ex-

plain later, *hāʾādām* systematically refers to the man until 3:22–24. Trible also claims that "the retention of the word *hāʾādām* allows for both continuity and discontinuity between the first creature and the male creature just as the rib allows for both continuity and discontinuity between the first creature and the female creature" (98). But the rib is hardly equivalent to *hāʾādām*, nor does the text take up in any way the word or idea of *ṣēlāʿ*, rib, in designating the woman.

¹²I refer here to Simone de Beauvoir's argument in *The Second Sex* that man is both the positive and the neutral pole in the binary set male/female; that is, man is both the signifier for male and the signifier for human; woman is the signifier only for female, never for human.

¹³I give Trible and Bal the benefit of the doubt here in translating *ʿēzer* as "companion" rather than as "help" or "support." One of the characteristics of Trible's discourse (and by adoption of Bal's) is the rendering of the text into an English that is most favorable to their interpretation. Hence *hāʾādām* is translated as "earth creature," as if *ʾādām* were actually a derivative of *ʾādāmâ* rather than sharing the same root. Similarly, *hāʾādām* is designated by the pronoun "it" rather than "he," a freedom, of course, that the Hebrew technically permits. But the effect of such choices on an English-language reader unfamiliar with the Hebrew is to validate what are in fact interpretive choices, not necessities of the Hebrew text.

¹⁴I am grateful to Joan Radner for pointing this out to me.

¹⁵Bal also disagrees on semantic grounds: "The verb used for Jahweh's forming of the earth creature was the specific verb for pottery; the verb used in 2:22 refers specifically to architecture and the construction of buildings. The action is both more difficult, more sophisticated, and requires more differentiated material. The difference would indicate a higher level of creation" (323). But the semantic argument also yields different conclusions: is it necessarily more difficult to create a person from a rib than to create a person simply by breathing on dust? Might it not be a greater miracle to create from *less* differentiated materials? The interpretive impasse I reach when I try to weigh my interpretations against Bal's may suggest that formal analysis alone cannot provide the bases upon which a reading can stand. We are thrown back once again to questions of context.

¹⁶Bal sees both creation stories as leading to "the climax of the creation of the world" (323). One could easily argue that the careful progression of creation in Genesis 1 is already disrupted in Genesis 2 by the creation of *hāʾādām before* the animals.

¹⁷Curiously, for Bal male dominance is merely an "afterthought" attached to the main consequence which is pain in childbirth.

¹⁸Trible's claim here is problematic. She argues that God continues to see man and woman as equal and to offer them equal care, as when he clothes them both in 3:21. But God (in 3:22) as well as the narrator uses the word *hāʾādām* in precisely the woman-erasing mode Trible has seen as a sign of male dominance.

¹⁹The ideological context of Trible's analysis, though she does not say it as openly in this essay as she does in "Genesis 2–3 Revisited," is salvation history, and with it the belief that patriarchy is not God-given and inevitable, but the unhappy consequence of the Fall and hence a state that Christian redemption can reverse.

²⁰This is Bal's rendering of 4:7; the Anchor version is less blatantly parallel to 3:16:

> Surely, if you act right, it should mean exaltation. But if you do not, sin is the demon at the door, whose urge is toward you; yet you can be his master.

As a lay person in relation to exegetical matters, I find Oosten and Moyer's hypothesis fascinating.

²¹Actually the formula for "contextualization" embeds two separate propositions: that context *c* is indeed the appropriate context in which the observation is to be understood; and that in context *c*, *x* carries the meaning *y*.

²²I mean "intentional" here not in the complex ways evoked by speech act theory but simply in Meir Sternberg's sense of historical intention as embodied or objectified in the text. "'Inten-

tion,'" says Sternberg, "no longer figures as a psychological state consciously or unconsciously translated into words. Rather, it is a shorthand for the structure of meaning and effect supported by the conventions that the text appeals to or devises: for the sense that the language makes in terms of the communicative context as a whole" (9).

[23] In fact, I wonder what kinds of interpretive practices might emerge from a literary theory that takes biblical narrative as its starting point. I would agree with my colleague Joseph Sitterson that the liaison of literary theory and biblical criticism has been too unidirectional, from literary theory to biblical hermeneutics, and that biblical hermeneutics could provide to literary theory a valuable "chastening perspective" about "relations between readers and texts" (p. 1).

WORKS CONSULTED

Alter, Robert
    1981   *The Art of Biblical Narrative*. New York: Basic Books.

Austin, J. L.
    1975   *How to Do Things With Words*. (2nd ed.) Ed. by J. O. Urmson and Marina Sbisà. Cambridge: Harvard University Press.

Bal, Mieke
    1986   "Sexuality, Sin and Sorrow: The Emergence of Female Character [A Reading of Genesis 2–3]." Pp. 317–338 in *The Female Body in Western Culture*. Ed. Susan Rubin Suleiman. Cambridge: Harvard University Press.

Fish, Stanley
    1980   *Is There a Text in This Class? The Authority of Interpretive Communities*. Cambridge: Harvard University Press.

Grice, H. P.
    1975   "Logic and Conversation." In *Syntax and Semantics. Vol. 3: Speech Acts*. Ed. Peter Cole and Jerry L. Morgan. New York: Academic Press.

Harris, Wendell V.
    1986   "Toward an Ecological Criticism: Contextual versus Unconditioned Literary Theory." *College English* 48 (2): 116–31.

Hartman, Geoffrey
    1980   *Criticism in the Wilderness: The Study of Literature Today*. New Haven: Yale University Press.

Nogarola, Isotta
    1983   "Of the Equal or Unequal Sin of Adam and Eve" (1453). In *Her Immaculate Hand: Selected Works by and About the Women Humanists of Quattrocento Italy*. Binghampton, N.Y.: Medieval and Renaissance Texts and Studies, No. 20.

Ohmann, Richard
    1973   "Literature as Act." Pp. 81–107 in *Approaches to Poetics: Se-*

lected Papers from the English Institute. Ed. Seymour Chatman. New York: Columbia University Press.

Oosten, Jarich and David Moyer
    1982   "De mythische omkering; een analyse van de sociale code van de scheppingsmythen van Genesis 2.4b–11." *Anthropologische verkenningen* 1 (1): 75–91.

Phillips, John A.
    1984   *Eve: The History of an Idea*. New York: Harper & Row.

Pratt, Mary Louise
    1977   *Toward a Speech Act Theory of Literary Discourse*. Bloomington: Indiana University Press.

Rickheit, Gert, Wolfgang Schnotz, and Hans Strohner
    1985   "The Concept of Inference in Discourse Comprehension." Pp. 3–49 in *Inferences in Text Processing*. Amsterdam: North Holland.

Schmidt, S. J.
    1975   "Reception and interpretation of written texts as problems of a rational theory of literary communication." Pp. 399–408 in *Style and Text: Studies Presented to Nils Erik Enkvist*. Stockholm.

Searle, John R.
    1969   *Speech Acts: An Essay in the Philosophy of Language*. London: Cambridge University Press.

Showalter, Elaine
    1982   "Feminist Criticism in the Wilderness." Pp. 9–36 in *Writing and Sexual Difference*. Ed. Elizabeth Abel. Chicago: University of Chicago Press.

Sitterson, Joseph
    1986   "The Will to Power in Biblical Interpretation." Paper delivered at the Modern Language Association Convention.

Sperber, Dan and Deirdre Wilson
    1986   *Relevance: Communication and Cognition*. Cambridge: Harvard University Press.

Sternberg, Meir
    1985   *The Poetics of Biblical Narrative: Ideological Literature and the Drama of Reading*. Bloomington: Indiana University Press, 1986.

Trible, Phyllis
    1975   "Genesis 2–3 Revisited." In *Womanspirit Rising: A Feminist Reader on Religion*. Ed. Carol Christ and Judith Plaskow. New York: Harper and Row.

Trible, Phyllis
    1978   *God and the Rhetoric of Sexuality*. Philadelphia: Fortress Press.

Westermann, Claus
    1984   *Genesis 1–11: A Commentary.* Trans. John J. Scullion, S. J. Minneapolis: Augsburg.

White, Hugh
    1980   "Direct and Third Person Discourse in the Narrative of the 'Fall.'" *Semeia* 18: 91–106.

SPEECH ACT THEORY AND BIBLICAL EXEGESIS

Daniel Patte
Vanderbilt University

ABSTRACT

This essay explores the interface of speech act theory and biblical exegesis, and ends up calling for the development of a "speech act exegesis." The conclusion that such a type of exegesis is needed, and promises to be quite fruitful, is reached by addressing a series of questions.

1) In which ways does the conceptual framework of speech act theory challenge the hermeneutical paradigm of other types of exegesis?

2) How is the phenomenon of religion perceived from the perspective of speech act theory?

3) How is religious discourse to be perceived from the perspective of speech act theory?

4) What neglected dimensions of the meaning of religious texts could speech act exegesis help us elucidate?

The concluding part of the essay formulates some suggestions outlining steps which need to be taken to develop such a "speech act exegesis."

When a Title Conveys What is Intended by an Essay.

"*Speech act theory and biblical exegesis.*" The title of the essay expresses that I propose to explore the interface between these two fields of inquiry. This is the "propositional content" (Searle, 1969, and 1979) of the title. As we shall see, exegetes have much to learn from speech act theory. But at first this is not self-evident. Indeed, what can exegetes expect to learn from such a "philosophy of language" (see the subtitle of *Speech Acts,* Searle 1969)? Actually, my title conveys it, although in a subtle way!

Reading and rereading this title with our usual exegetical tools, we as exegetes would normally be left perplexed. An exegetical *analysis* of the title does not reveal anything about "what exegetes can learn from speech act theory!" And yet the title expresses it!

In order to perceive it one needs to abandon our traditional exegetical perspectives and to adopt another perspective. Indeed, when one reads the above title from the perspective of speech act theory, one can recognize the "illocutionary force" (Searle 1969 54–71; Searle 1979 1–29) and the "intentionality" (Searle 1983) of this title as a "speech act." Then, what is not in this title, and yet is expressed by it, appears.

An explanation of these introductory comments about my title will simultaneously clarify the aim of this essay (what I *intend* to argue) and begin to show what exegetes can learn from speech act theory.

In order to perceive the "intentionality" which is expressed by the title of my essay, one needs to note the order of its terms—an order which is far from innocent. Indeed, one can envision two kinds of interrelations between speech act theory and biblical exegesis.

1) One might want to give *priority to biblical exegesis* by seeking to appropriate from speech act theory certain tools (categories, taxonomies, methodological tools) which could be used to carry out the exegetical task. In Searle's terms, "the direction of the fit" (an important concept used for establishing a taxonomy of illocutionary acts, Searle 1979 3–4) is "from speech act theory to exegesis;" *speech act theory is made to fit the exegetical task* as previously defined. This "direction of the fit" is fruitful in the sense that exegesis gains new tools which enhance the exegetes' ability to carry out a task previously defined. This involves "plundering" speech act theory for whatever might be usable in biblical exegesis—for instance, the taxonomies of speech acts—, and discarding what does not "fit" the exegetical task as defined. More specifically, what is discarded is the "conceptual framework" of speech act theory, so as to preserve the "conceptual framework" which determines the nature and goals of the exegetical task.

2) On the other hand, one might want to give *priority to speech act theory,* as I did in the title of this essay. "The direction of the fit" that I propose is from biblical exegesis to speech act theory: I "intend" to investigate what happens when *the exegetical task is made to fit speech act theory.* From this perspective, the first move is not to seek to appropriate from speech act theory ready-made categories or tools, but rather to envision the implications of speech act theory for our understanding of the exegetical task. This approach involves taking the risk of rethinking the nature and goals of exegesis in terms of the conceptual framework of speech act theory.

I chose this second approach despite its risks because it proved to be the most fruitful in a similar case: when structural semiotics was brought to bear on biblical exegesis. Our previous experience with "structural

Applications of Speech Act Theory

semiotics and exegesis" provides us with a model for the way to proceed when attempting to appropriate speech act theory as exegetes. Learning from this experience will allow us to avoid the many unnecessary "detours" we took as we strove to discover the implications of semiotics for exegesis. It is because of this experience that when considering the interface between speech act theory and exegesis we give priority to the former. As long as we simply sought to appropriate from structural semiotics (Greimas's semiotics) analytical techniques so as to pursue our traditional exegetical goals, the results were quite disappointing. But when we took the risk of rethinking the exegetical task in terms of the conceptual framework offered by structural semiotics—and thus developing a "structural exegesis"—a very fruitful study of biblical texts could be envisioned.

In retrospect, the steps involved in the development of a "structural exegesis" can be listed in a coherent manner. 1) The first step involved, of course, becoming familiar with structural semiotic theory, so as to apprehend its conceptual framework and more specifically the way in which "meaning in/of text" is to be interpreted (its hermeneutical paradigm). (See Patte 1976, ch. 1.) 2) Since our goal was the exegesis of "religious" texts, the second step involved raising the question: How is the phenomenon of "religion" to be perceived from a semiotic perspective? 3) This second step was quickly followed by a third one: How is a "religious" discourse to be perceived from that perspective? (See Patte 1982.) 4) The fourth step raised the question: What neglected dimensions of the meaning of religious texts could structural semiotics help us elucidate? (See Patte 1978.) 5) Once this was determined, the fifth step involved the development of an exegetical method based on structural semiotic theory—a method which then was, and still is, progressively refined as it is used.

The development of a "speech act exegesis" should follow the same steps. Obviously, in the limits of this essay, we cannot hope to develop such an exegetical method (the fifth step). We cannot even hope to cover fully the other steps which would demand to be totally immersed in speech act theory—and I do not pretend to be. All we can do is to explore in a preliminary way the interface of speech act theory and exegesis so as to ascertain whether or not it is worth pursuing the development of a speech act exegesis. Thus this essay merely attempts to envision the contributions that a speech act exegesis could make to the interpretation of biblical texts. The subtitle for this essay could have been: "Prolegomena to the development of a speech act exegesis."

I have first to confess that, when I began this investigation, I was quite sceptical. I was not expecting that such a philosophy of language would have much, if anything, to contribute to exegesis. But, to my surprise, it does! A speech act exegesis promises to help us take into account dimensions of the meaning of biblical texts which we have neglected and occulted for too long a time. Thus, this essay ends up advocating a long-term and collaborative research project aimed at developing a "speech act exegesis."

As is clear from the preceding comments, I had first to overcome my own scepticism which, I anticipate, is also shared by other exegetes. A first reason for this scepticism could be that speech act theory does not offer any clear method which could be directly applied to the study of texts (most of the examples used by Austin and Searle are short sentences rather than more complex discourses). But, as is clear, I do not believe that the main contribution of speech act theory to exegesis would be such ready-made methods. For me, this scepticism arose from the fact that the premises of speech act theory contradict those of structural semiotics on important points. Adopting a speech act perspective demanded from me to risk perceiving the nature and goals of exegesis in a way quite different from the view of the nature and goal of exegesis that I gained from structural semiotics. Generalizing this point, I can say that speech act theory challenges in a similar way any other exegetical methodology. In order to overcome this initial scepticism, we need to take the risk of perceiving the nature and the goals of exegesis from a new perspective. This risk can be accepted when we remember that any exegetical methodology is based upon preunderstandings which have the twofold effect of allowing us to perceive clearly certain dimensions of the meaning of texts and, simultaneously, of blinding us to other dimensions of their meaning. When this is recognized, one does not need to feel threatened by new methodologies. They do not negate the value of the results of our current methodologies. A new exegetical methodology such as a "speech act exegesis" (which remains to be envisioned) will certainly elucidate dimensions of the meaning of texts that we cannot presently perceive, or that we only perceive dimly. Thus, we can be confident that such a new methodology will not deprive us of the "gains" we see in our own methodology, but rather enrich us by allowing us to gain new insights into the biblical texts—new insights the need of which is already expressed in aspects of the quest for literary methodologies.

In what follows, I will therefore sketch some of the points which convinced me that the development of "speech act exegesis" would be fruitful. This is to say that I will limit myself to a series of programmatic statements suggesting the way in which we need to proceed to develop such an exegetical method.

1. Texts as Speech Acts. The Challenge of a New Hermeneutical Paradigm.

As is well known, Austin's essential lesson is that a linguistic sequence, far from simply describing actions, is itself an action (Austin

1962). This view, which at first excluded purely descriptive or constative sentences, was soon extended to apply to all sentences, as is the case in J. R. Searle's work (Searle 1969 and 1979). Although in the process of developing speech act theory Austin and Searle usually limit their examples to sentences, the length of "linguistic sequences" is not at issue. In other words, their theory applies to discourses of any length, and thus to any text. Texts are to be viewed as speech acts.

This basic lesson of speech act theory can be readily accepted. Intuitively, it makes sense: one speaks to achieve some kind of effect upon hearers, and thus one acts upon them. More specifically, it is clear that the meaning of a statement will be different if it is perceived, e.g., as a promise, a prediction, or a report; as a request, an order, an asking, or a plea; as a congratulation, a felicitation, or a welcome. Furthermore, rhetoric views discourses as a means to affect audiences; literary theories take more and more into account the role of the reader, and thus the ways in which readers are affected by a discourse or text; and structural semiotics speaks of meaning as a "meaning effect" and consequently takes into account the process of enunciation (or discursivization). The speech act theory seems to express something which is quite commonly recognized, although formulated in different ways, and thus one could conclude that there is nothing really new in speech act theory. But this is missing the point. In order to appreciate the challenge that speech act theory constitutes, we need to elucidate its conceptual framework by comparing it to the conceptual frameworks of other views of discourses and texts.

First, we can note that the view of speech and discourse as acts is based on the same fundamental insight which gave rise to the development of structuralism and semiotics, namely, that the linguistic phenomenon can be homologated to other dimensions of human experience. Language and its use is only one way among many through which human beings produce meaning, communicate, and exist in a meaningful universe. But the homologation of the linguistic and of the non-linguistic domains was done in opposite ways by speech act theory and by structural semiotics. In effect, Austin's insight was that what is known about a non-linguistic domain of human experience, namely "actions," can be used to understand speech; speech is an act. To paraphrase Searle, the fit is "language to world": *language is made to fit the world of concrete actions* as paradigm of any process through which human beings affect their world. For instance, consider how Searle studies "Intentionality" in the book with this title (Searle 1983). The intentionality of speech acts (chapter 6) is understood on the basis of study of intentionalities of perception (chapter 2) and of action (chapter 3) and of their causation (chapter 4) and background (chapter 5). By contrast, Lévi-Strauss, Barthes, and Greimas developed structuralist and semiotic theories by applying what is known about language (e.g., Jakobson's phonology,

Hjelmslev's linguistic theory) to non-linguistic domains of human experience (e.g., kinship systems, ritual, fashion, painting, etc.), and on this basis developed theory concerning discourses. The fit is world to language: *the world is made to fit language* as paradigm of any meaningful phenomenon.

If these domains are indeed homologable, both moves are legitimate. The non-linguistic domain should help understand the linguistic domain, and vice-versa. But as speech act theory shows, the *direction of the fit* is not inconsequential! A fundamental difference between structural semiotics and speech act theory appears when one first notes another point of agreement, namely, that the production of meaning is *rule governed:* in speech act theory it is the existence of such rules which allows Austin and Searle to classify illocutionary forces (see e.g., Searle 1969 33–42); in structural semiotics structures are rules governing the production of meaning (see Greimas and Courtes 1983 313–318). Yet these "rules" are quite different. For structural semiotics, these rules are structures which are *manifested by the linguistic utterances*—and are thus inscribed in the discourses. For speech act theory, the rules governing illocutionary forces are *not inscribed in the linguistic utterances*. Thus Bierwisch complains that a basic weakness of speech act theory (what he calls its "original sin") is that it does not account for the rules (structures) manifested in the text (Bierwisch 1980). Yet, instead of complaining about this difference and attempting to overcome it in a theory which would account for both types of rules, as Bierwisch proposes, we first need to acknowledge this basic difference resulting from the difference of the "direction of the fit." Since for speech act theory the fit is "language to world," the rules governing concrete actions in the world are the focus of attention, and these rules are not inscribed in the text, even though the text might provide markers pointing to them. These rules are extra-textual. Thus studying a text as a speech act involves taking into account *something which is not in the text,* and yet is part of the communication of meaning by that text. This approach goes against the basic principles of accountability of structural exegesis (as well as of other exegetical methods, including rhetorical criticism) which demand that what is stated about the meaning of the text be grounded on what is *in the text*. This observation already suggests that the basic approach demanded by structural exegesis (and other exegetical methods), namely, the *analysis* of features of a text as the basis for interpretation, is not appropriate to account for the intentionality of the text. An approach other than "analysis" is necessary.

In order to begin conceptualizing this "other approach" which seems to be demanded by speech act theory, we need to take note that this theory appears to be closely related to the methodologies which, in the interpretation, take into account an "extra-text." It is most directly related to such approaches which also emphasize that the production of meaning is rule governed. I want to refer to "reader criticism" derived from the work of Iser (Iser 1974 and 1978). Yet, right away, an essential difference appears. While both theories are pragmatic theories (Parret, 1983: 94–98; despite Abrams's taxonomy which would, I guess, classify speech act theory as "expressive;" Abrams 1953), the focus of attention is on different extra-textual domains: the production of meaning by the author, for speech act theory, the production of meaning by the reader, for reader criticism. From the perspective of New Criticism, these two approaches seem to fall once again into the traps of "the intentional fallacy" and of "the affective fallacy," respectively (see Wimsatt and Beardsley 1954). Since the focus is on extra-textual rules, the text itself, as an object of critical judgment, tends to disappear. But rather than construing this comment as a negative assessment, let us view it as expressing that speech act theory and reader criticism are a necessary complement to those approaches which are exclusively text centered. And obviously, speech act theory with its emphasis on the "intentionality" of the author complements reader criticism with its emphasis on the reader or interpretive communities (Fish 1980).

The similarities between reader criticism and speech act theory provide us with a way to conceptualize how we can speak of the way in which the "intentionality" of an utterance is expressed by this utterance without being in it. Speech act theory underscores that the propositional content should not be viewed as the total meaning of an utterance; one also needs to account for its illocutionary point and its illocutionary force (Searle, 1979 2–3). For instance, the propositional content "I'll be there before you" can be uttered as a promise, a prediction, a warning, or a remark, that is, as different speech acts with different illocutionary forces (Bierwisch, 1980 1). The intentionality (illocutionary force) which is part of the meaning of this utterance is not marked in the text (propositional content) itself. It takes the form of an "absence," or, in Iser's terminology, we could say that it is a "gap," indeed a gap that the reader has to fill in so as to make sense of the text.

It follows that the development of a "speech act exegesis" should include a comparative examination of the methodological strategies involved in reader criticism with the methodological strategies described or implied in speech act theory. Theoretically speaking, the methodology of reader criticism should provide us with strategies which could apply to the task of apprehending the "gaps" which express in the form of absence the intentionality of a text. But conversely, speech act theory should help clarify and refine the methodology of reader criticism. To begin with, speech act theory should challenge reader criticism to acknowledge and take stock of the fact that its approach cannot be primarily an "analysis." More specifically, the development of speech act exegesis could help reader criticism take seriously into account what is involved in reading a "religious text."

2. How is the Phenomenon of Religion to be Perceived from the Perspective of Speech Act Theory?

I am not prepared to address this question. I simply want to make explicit the importance of this question in the process of developing a "speech act exegesis" by marking in this essay the place which should be occupied by a close examination of this issue. In a significant way the essay by Ronald Grimes in this volume of *Semeia* begins to address this issue by asking the question: How can speech act theory be applied to the study of religious acts? It proceeds by taking note of the taxonomies of speech acts proposed by Austin, Searle, and their followers (Searle, 1980) and applying them to the study of religious phenomena. But note that in this essay the author soon discovered that he could not simply adopt the taxonomies proposed by Austin and Searle. In order to account for rituals one needs to modify these taxonomies at least by expanding them. This is to say that a view of "religion" from the perspective of speech act theory need not only take into account the categories set in speech act theory to account for "religious speech acts" and "religious illocutionary forces" (for instance, as part of the "sincerity conditions," Searle 1979 4–5). It also needs to consider the entire phenomenon of religion (as understood in "religious studies") from the point of view of the conceptual framework of speech act theory. This would involve rethinking the results of traditional studies of religious acts in categories which would allow us to perceive their relationship with speech acts; this would also involve taking more seriously into account that "religious utterances" are in their own right religious acts. Furthermore, one would need to take into account the "intentionality" of religious acts, a dimension of the phenomenon of religion which might have been conceptualized in other ways by our traditional theories concerning the phenomenon of religion. But once again I am not immersed enough in speech act theory even to begin to do so at this time.

3. How is Religion Discourse to be Perceived from the Perspective of Speech Act Theory?

I can be more specific, but no less programmatic, in addressing this new question. We have noted that the essential lesson of speech act theory is that any utterance—and thus any discourse or text—should be viewed as a speech act. For the development of a "speech act exegesis," this means that *a biblical, that is religious, text should be viewed as a religious act.*

By itself this observation opens a vast and mostly unexplored territory for biblical studies or, more generally, for the study of religious texts. In brief, the study of biblical texts conducted by members of the Society of Biblical Literature needs to be related to, and enriched by, the work of our colleagues of the American Academy of Religion who study religious acts. One might object that there is nothing new in this proposal. Have we not taken into account, for instance in form critical studies, aspects of research on religion, on rituals, on myth, so as to understand, for instance, the *Sitz im Leben* of a biblical form? But it must be acknowledged that, in most instances, we viewed the biblical texts as reflecting, through their forms or through some other features, religious acts. In other words, we viewed these religious texts merely as expressions of religious acts, as linguistic sequences were viewed, before Austin, as expressing actions. By contrast, speech act theory calls us to view religious discourses as religious acts in their own right. While in isolated instances the fact that the religious discourses are religious acts has been taken into account, this has not been done in any systematic way.

What can be envisioned, thanks to the essential lesson of speech act theory, and indeed what is called for by it, is a cooperative effort between scholars who study rituals and other religious acts *per se*—whatever might be their methodology—so as to understand how and in which way religious discourses such as those of the biblical texts function as religious acts.

What does this mean? What will we learn about biblical texts in the process? Quite frankly, I do not know. As I noted above, all that I can do is to make a series of programmatic statements! But reflecting on how speech act theory could help us in our task in biblical studies convinced me that considering biblical texts as religious acts, and this on the basis of the study of ritual acts, is a very fruitful field of investigation. I cannot say much more on this point, because I have everything to learn in this field that I had not envisioned as part of my research in New Testament. I am sure others have already worked in this area. I want to refer, for instance, to William Beardslee's proposal in *Literary Criticism of the New Testament* (1970: 27ff.) which, unfortunately, has not had the impact that it should have had. In brief, Beardslee called for an interpretation of the beatitudes as religious acts of "blessing," emphasizing what Searle would term the illocutionary and perlocutionary forces of such utterances; for the hearers they establish a new reality. And, of course, one could make the same comment regarding utterances such as the "woes," or curses in Matthew 23.

I would dare to suggest that such proposals were not received as they deserved to be because of the lack of a conceptual framework which would allow us to generalize them. Speech act theory could provide this framework. When the results of the studies of such ritual acts as blessings and curses conducted by our colleagues of the AAR will have been related to the categories of speech act theory, that is, when these results will have been reinterpreted so as to permit speaking simultaneously of concrete religious acts and of religious discourses as religious speech acts, it will become possible to carry on the task suggested by Beardslee's proposal about the beatitudes. This will involve viewing as religious speech acts each biblical text as a whole, as well as each of the passages of these texts, including, for instance, such unlikely passages as the words through which Matthew introduces the Sermon on the Mount, even though they might not directly express in a verbal form any specific religious act (following Searle's warning that illocutionary acts should not be confused with, and thus limited to, the presence of illocutionary verbs as Austin tended to do; Searle 1979: 10–11).

4. What Neglected Dimensions of the Meaning of Religious Texts Could Speech Act Exegesis Help us Elucidate?

The answer to this question depends upon the answers we shall ultimately give to the preceding two questions. Since we had to limit ourselves to general suggestions concerning these questions, we are in a weak position to point out what could be the specific goal of a "speech act exegesis." Yet we can make several suggestions by coming back to our earlier observation that the approach represented by the works of Austin, Searle, and other practitioners of speech act theory involves a shift of conceptual framework.

One can already recognize this shift of conceptual framework in the fact that linguistic sequences were viewed as expressing actions, but that now they are viewed in and of themselves as actions. Such a shift of conceptual framework affects all the issues raised by speech act theory. For instance, Searle opens his discussion of the intentionality of perception by noting: "Traditionally the 'problem of perception' has been the problem of how our internal perceptual experiences are related to the external world" (Searle 1983: 37); then he challenges the underlying assumptions of this traditional view by emphasizing how the *external* world is related to our perceptual experiences. It is this shift of conceptual framework which allowed Austin and Searle to show dimensions of the linguistic phenomenon which were hidden from other perspectives.

Similarly, adopting the speech act theorists' approach and conceptual framework will demand from us to look at religious phenomena and discourses from a different perspective, a perspective which will reveal dimensions of religious phenomena and discourses hidden from us as long as we continue to look at them from our usual perspectives. Yet, adopting such a different conceptual framework is not easy. It necessarily involves transgressing taboos!

What are the fundamental characteristics of the conceptual framework espoused by speech act theory? Searle points them out in his book on *Intentionality* which "is to provide a foundation for (his) two earlier books, *Speech Acts* and *Expression and Meaning*" (1983: vii). In these two books Searle had constantly emphasized that the speakers have specific intentions, and moreover that they intend that these intentions be recognized. In *Intentionality*, Searle makes explicit the conceptual framework which he presupposed. It demands that the entire investigation be based upon the "fundamental capacities of the mind (or brain) to relate the organism to the world by way of such mental states as belief and desire, and especially through action and perception" (Searle 1983: vii).

The mention of "mind," "brain," and "mental states" makes us cringe. At the very least we are not accustomed to using such categories with regard to the practitioners of the religion we study or with regard to the authors of the biblical texts we consider, let alone to making these categories the central concern of our investigations. Actually, as was pointed out by Herman Parret in his book *Semiotics and Pragmatics: An Evaluative Comparison of Conceptual Frameworks* (Parret 1983; a major work which has the merit of studying in great detail the conceptual framework of speech act theory as a branch of pragmatics), such an emphasis on intentionality expresses that the dominant category is "subjectivity" (Parret 1983: 106–115). In brief, using a speech act theory approach means that when studying religious acts and religious discourses, the primary concern should be to account for the subjectivity of the religious practitioners or of the authors of a religious text.

As is clear, adopting such an approach demands that we transgress a taboo in religious studies which, along with the rest of the social sciences, taught us to distrust every variant of subjectivism along with historicism and psychologism. Of course, we do not want to deny the existence of "subjectivity," but we have been so preoccupied to avoid subjectivity in our own research—otherwise our work cannot claim to be "scholarly"—, that we have bracketed subjectivity out of the texts or phenomena we study. Precisely, we study "phenomena," religious phenomena, that is "objects" that we envision more or less spontaneously as a result of what Husserl would call a "phenomenological reduction." For us, the subjectivity related to the performance of a religious act or to the production of a religious text under study is a residue, a remnant, which has no true bearing upon the significance of the religious phenomenon or text we are studying. Yet, here we are! Speech act theory invites us, indeed, challenges us, to make this subjectivity the primary concern of our study. Here is a neglected dimension of the meaning of religious acts and of biblical texts that speech act theory promises to help us elucidate.

We cannot but resist this shift of conceptual framework. We do so even when we are convinced that speech act theory has something to teach us and when we try to apply it to our field. Thus, for instance, at the end of his excellent essay on "Infelicitous Performances, or How Rituals Fail," Ronald Grimes felt compelled to note: "I believe it is a mistake always to blame persons rather than rituals—a tactic that prevents ritual criticism." This incidental remark seems to me to be in contradiction to the use of the approach of speech act taxonomies presented in the essay. It does not invalidate the essay, but shows that Grimes believes that one can use speech act theory for the purpose of establishing a "ritual criticism" which will be "scholarly" because it will be exclusively based on the study of what is "objective," the ritual, rather than on the subjectivity of the practitioners, an inconsequential and insignificant residue as far as ritual criticism is concerned. What is surprising is that Grimes underscores this at the end of an essay which uses a taxonomy established on the basis of the intentionality of the speakers! (Yet, to be fair, I need to note that, since he focuses his study on Austin's notion of "infelicity," Grimes primarily uses Austin's taxonomy which does not make explicit the role of intentionality and of subjectivity as much as Searle's work does).

These comments are not intended as an attack against Grimes's essay, from which I learned much and which is an excellent piece. They are exclusively made in order to call attention to the radical shift that the use of speech act theory demands from us, a shift that we must accept if we truly want to harvest all the benefits that a view of religious acts and religious texts from the perspective of speech act theory might, and I am sure will, offer us. But for this we have to be patient and take the time to take upon ourselves the conceptual framework of speech act theory before looking at religious acts and religious texts.

What is involved in adopting the speech act theory perspective? Of course, it does not mean that we should become subjectivist. In the same way that we have learned to be objective without falling into the trap of objectivism, we have to learn to account for the subjective dimensions of religious acts and texts without falling into the trap of subjectivism— either subjectivism on our part as scholars, or subjectivism with regard to the practitioners of religion. In this latter case subjectivism would involve "blaming" or "attributing to" a *mysterious* state of mind of the practitioners the significance of the religious acts or texts; and, by definition, a "mysterious" state of mind cannot be studied. In fact, speech act theorists, and especially Searle, strive to explain what subjectivity is in such a way that it will no longer be possible to view it as a mysterious reality.

For them it is *a process which can be studied because it is rule governed* (Searle's major contribution, beyond Austin's work, in *Speech Acts* and his subsequent books). In other words, adopting the perspective of speech act theory in our own study means that we need to learn to account for the role of subjectivity in religious acts and texts, a role which is far from insignificant.

Obviously, in the rest of this paper I cannot express all that is involved in this shift. A few pointers, programmatic statements, will have to suffice.

First, I would like to underscore that the emphasis on subjectivity does not mean that we need to abandon a critical stance. Speech act studies of religious acts and texts will be ritual criticism and biblical criticism. But the definition of criticism will be altered. According to our various methods, a critical study is before all the *analysis* of an object (a ritual, a biblical text). An analysis is sound and solid if, and only if, all the elements of its conclusions can be shown to be present in the phenomenon (a text, a corpus, a ritual, all a series of religious manifestations) which globally is perceived as an object to be analyzed. Thus, for instance, in Matthew 5:19, the condemnation of those who relax one of the least of the commandments and teach this to others is at times interpreted as an attack against Paul. Yet, the exegete cannot simply make such a statement; he or she needs to show that this conclusion is grounded on features of the object under investigation, in this case both the text of Matthew and Paul's letters. The validity of this claim is assessed in terms of the validity of the analysis, that is, whether or not the analysis takes correctly into account the various features of these texts.

Thus, for us, analysis is the only legitimate procedure for grounding a critical study. Yet, as the linguist Louis Hjelmslev first pointed out (Hjelmslev, 1953), "analysis" is only one of the two procedures which can be used, and are indeed used, in critical studies. Besides *analysis*—which, following Hjelmslev, Greimas defines as establishing "relations among the parts of an object, on the one hand, and, on the other hand, between the parts and the whole which it constitutes" (Greimas and Courtes, 1982:13)—there is another procedure that Hjelmslev called *catalysis*. It involves accounting for *elliptical* elements and making them explicit. As Greimas expresses it, catalysis "is carried out with the help of manifested contextual elements, and thanks to the relations of presuppositions which they have with implicit elements." (Greimas and Courtés 1982: 26).

As is clear, catalysis is actually quite frequently used as we interpret elliptic statements by spontaneously supplying the words which have been omitted; or, in the case of ellipses in narrative, by spontaneously presupposing that a series of events which are demanded by the one which is described have indeed taken place. And, of course, we could multiply the examples. But note the process: we perform such a catalysis by *applying a general principle or rule*. We supply a missing verb in an elliptical sentence because grammar demands that a sentence include a verb; and we do so by *inferring* from the context (that is, from what is present in the text) which specific verb should be presupposed. In the same way, in the example of an elliptical narrative we make use of our knowledge of the rules governing the unfolding of narrative plots.

Similarly, as speech act theory points out, a linguistic statement does not make sense as long as one does not take into account the intentionality of the speaker. By not doing so, we might mistake, for instance, a sincere promise and an insincere promise (Searle 1969:57–62). Yet the intentionality of the speaker, the subjectivity and the illocutionary force, are by nature largely elliptical. Therefore they need to be *inferred* on the basis of what is manifested in the statement, of its context, and this in terms of the rules which govern intentionality.

Of course, this is what we do spontaneously when we listen to a speaker. Subconsciously making use of such rules, we infer what is the intentionality of the speaker; otherwise, the speech act would fail. In the case of "live speeches," this is a fairly reliable process which allows for communication to take place, even though it is somewhat haphazard, frequently involving trials and errors, guesses which are subsequently corrected, etc. In the case of texts, and especially texts from a removed historical period and from a foreign culture, the chance of error greatly multiplies. Yet, as long as we refuse to make the study of the subjectivity and the intentionality of the author a legitimate part of our critical investigation, we simply pretend that we can spontaneously apprehend them correctly! Actually, we occult this important dimension of meaning. A critical study of the intentionality of a text will allow us to recover it. For this purpose, unlike the spontaneous filling in of the ellipsis of live communication, we need to make a self-conscious use of the rules which govern intentionality.

As we learn to consider religious acts and religious discourses from the perspective of the conceptual framework of speech act theory, we will progressively discover the specific place and role of "intentionality" in religion and religiuns discourses. I suspect that we shall discover that what speech act theory terms "illocutionary point," "illocutionary force," "perlocutionary force," etc., corresponds to aspects of religious experience which believers designate in their own ways. Conversely, our examination of religious acts and religious discourses will certainly lead us to recognize illocutionary acts which are not yet included in Austin's and Searle's taxonomies (as Grimes has begun doing). We will then be in a position to define more specific goals for a "speech act exegesis." Yet it will remain that such an exegesis will be focussed upon the intentionality of the biblical texts, and thus will need to use as its basic procedure "catalysis" rather than "analysis."

5. Development of a Method of Speech Act Exegesis.

At this point of our reflections, the steps that one needs to take in order to develop a method of "speech act exegesis" appear clearly. In conclusion of this programmatic essay it is enough to list them.

(a) First, we need to learn the rules which govern "intentionality." Here Searle's book on *Intentionality* is an essential starting point. Categories such as "conditions of satisfaction of the intentional component" and "nature of the self-reference of the intentional component" appear to be excellent heuristic categories. In addition, Parret's points regarding other characteristics of intentionality (Parret 1983 106–126) should be accounted for. Especially, we need to keep in mind that the rationality involved in intentionality is neither "causal thought" nor "paradigmatically determined" but rather an "inferential reasoning." This point is particularly important for practitioners of structuralism and semiotics; it clearly means that the rationality involved in intentionality is neither like the logic of narrative syntax nor like the logic of semantic systems—the two kinds of "logic" which are the focus of structural exegesis. Yet it is no less important for practitioners of other exegetical methods, since by learning how to recognize the role of "inferential reasoning" in the production of a meaningful discourse one is led to view in a different way textual phenomena such as "reference," "predication," "proper names" (Searle 1969), "grammatical syntax," "indirect speech," "fictional discourse," "metaphor" (Searle 1979), as well as "modality" (wanting, being able, knowing), "deixis" (of time, space, or actor; such as "now," "here," and "I, you, she"), and "character" (or actor, Parret 1983: 118–126). In other words, by learning to recognize the role of "inferential reasoning" in the production of meaning we also learn *how to recognize its traces* (in the form of "gaps," or "absence") *in the textual manifestation*. For instance, Searle shows how his taxonomy of illocutionary acts corresponds to certain syntactic features in English syntax (Searle 1979: 12–27). This understanding of the rules which govern "inferential reasoning" in speech acts and of the traces that this reasoning leaves in a text will provide a basis for the *"catalysis"* which needs to characterize "speech act exegesis" as method of interpretation.

(b) In a second step, still quite theoretical, we need to take a creative leap by placing these rules in the religious context. As we envision to what dimensions of religion and religious experiences these rules correspond (see above), we can then select specific goals for a "speech act exegesis." This selection of goals will then allow us to identify the specific rules which will need to be used in our critical study of the intentionality of religious texts. These specific rules will define the kind of "gaps" which will become the focus of the "catalysis." As we consider certain kinds of fit between the religious texts and the world, we will need to become aware of the textual features which, according to these rules, mark the "absence" and point toward it.

(c) It is only at this point that the development of specific exegetical methods which will be able to account critically for the religious intentionality of the biblical texts will become possible. The big temptation will be to attempt to relate these new exegetical methods to existing methods too early. Are not concepts such as "fit to the world" closely associated with procedures of historical criticism? Are not concepts such as "speech acts" closely associated with the process of enunciation governed by the discursive structures described by structural semiotics? The methods of a "speech act exegesis" must first be developed in the conceptual framework of speech act theory. The only possible exception might be, as we suggested above, reader criticism, since its methods involve the study of "gaps." Yet, since reader criticism has other goals, and apparently a different conceptual framework, its methodological insights can only be appropriated after the necessary transpositions. One will be able to benefit more directly from the works in literary criticism which already strive to account for speech act theory. I want to refer to the excellent books by Susan Sniader Lanser, *The Narrative Act: Point of View in Prose Fiction*, and Mary Louise Pratt, *Toward a Speech Act Theory of Literary Discourse*. Yet, once again, since the concern of "speech act exegesis" will be "religious intentionality," Lanser's and Pratt's proposals will need to be appropriated after the necessary transpositions.

These last comments bring to the fore one of the fundamental presuppositions of this entire essay: *religious discourses are peculiar speech acts* which cannot be assimilated to other kinds of speech acts. I believe this presupposition to be demanded by speech act theory. Insofar as one acknowledges the specificity of religious acts, one has to acknowledge the specificity of religious speech acts! Actually, it might be that what makes a discourse a religious discourse is its characteristic illocutionary points and forces and its characteristic intentionality. In other words, I suspect that speech act theory might provide us with the solution to the vexing problem that can be formulated by the question: What are the formal distinctive characteristics of religious discourses and texts? As long as one looks for an answer to this question through the "analysis" of such discourses as objects, one cannot really distinguish religious discourses from other discourses. Their propositional contents and structures are often the same as that of other discourses! I suspect that what makes a discourse or text "religious" is its peculiar intentionality and its illocutionary points and forces (and possibly also its peculiar perlocutionary forces).

Since speech act theory does not present a systematic study of this specific kind of speech acts, much work needs to be done for developing a method of "speech act exegesis." Indeed, most everything. My hope is that this essay will have succeeded in communicating my convictions concerning the promises of such a venture to the point that some will want to participate in such a long-term research project. If "speech act exegesis" keeps all its promises, a most important dimension of the meaning of religious experience and of religious texts will be, at last, incorporated into the critical study of religion and of religious texts instead of being dismissed as inconsequential and insignificant residue. And this long-neglected dimension of meaning might be nothing less than the very religious character of religious texts!

WORKS CONSULTED

Abrams, M. H.
    1953   *The Mirror and the Lamp. Romantic Theory and the Critical Tradition.* New York: Oxford University Press.

Austin, J. L.
    1962   *How to Do Things With Words.* Oxford: Oxford University Press.

Beardslee, W.
    1970   *Literary Criticism of the New Testament.* Philadelphia: Fortress Press.

Bierwisch, M.
    1980   "Semantic Structure and Illocutionary Force." Pp. 1–35 in *Speech Act Theory and Pragmatics* Eds. J. R. Searle, F. Kiefer, and M. Bierwisch. Dordrecht, Holland: D. Reidel Publishing Company.

Fish, S.
    1980   *Is There a Text in this Class? The Authority of Interpretive Communities.* Cambridge, Mass.: Harvard University Press.

Greimas, A. J., and Courtés, J.
    1982   *Semiotics and Language. An Analytical Dictionary.* Trans. L. Crist, D. Patte, et al. Bloomington: Indiana University Press.

Hjelmslev, L.
    1953   *Prolegomena to a Theory of Language.* Bloomington: Indiana University Press.

Iser, W.
    1974   *The Implied Reader. Patterns of Communication in Prose Fiction from Bunyan to Beckett.* Baltimore: Johns Hopkins University Press.

1978 *The Act of Reading. A Theory of Aesthetic Response.* Baltimore: Johns Hopkins University Press.

Parret, H.
1983 *Semiotics and Pragmatics. An Evaluative Comparison of Conceptual Frameworks.* Amsterdam, Philadelphia: John Benjamins Publishing Company.

Patte, D.
1976 *What is Structural Exegesis?* Philadelphia: Fortress Press.
1982 "The Interface of Semiotics and Faith: Greimas's Semiotics Revisited in Light of the Phenomenon of Religion," *Recherches Semiotiques/Semiotic Inquiry* 2 no. 2 (1982).

Patte, D. and Patte, A.
1978 *Structural Exegesis: From Theory to Practice.* Philadelphia: Fortress Press.

Pratt, Mary Louise
1977 *Toward A Speech Act Theory of Literary Discourse.* Bloomington: Indiana University Press.

Searle, J. R.
1969 *Speech Acts. An Essay in the Philosophy of Language,* Cambridge: Cambridge University Press.
1979 *Expression and Meaning. Studies in the Theory of Speech Acts.* Cambridge: Cambridge University Press.
1983 *Intentionality.* Cambridge: Cambridge University Press.

Searle, J. R., F. Kiefer, and M. Bierwisch, eds.
1980 *Speech Act Theory and Pragmatics.* Dordrecht, Holland: D. Riedel Publishing Company.

Wimsatt W. K. and Beardsley, M. C.
1954 *The Verbal Icon. Studies in the Meaning of Poetry.* Lexington, Ky: University of Kentucky Press.

INFELICITOUS PERFORMANCES AND RITUAL CRITICISM

Ronald L. Grimes
Wilfrid Laurier University

ABSTRACT

Based on the premise that rituals can fail to do what participants intend them to do, this article uses speech act theory as a basis from which to begin the task of ritual criticism. Although J.L. Austin intended his theory to apply to speech, his examples and asides indicate that he knew it had applicability to ritual. A full ritual criticism would have to account for more than speech; it would have to include non-verbal gestures and more. But Austin's outline of the ways "infelicitous" speech acts occur, can be extended to take account of other sorts of ritual failure. Here I add some additional categories and supporting examples from biblical literature to show the necessity for, and complexities of, making judgments about ritual. The result is not a complete typlogy, only a suggestive beginning. I conclude by identifying a number of problems with ritual criticism that await reflection, if not resolution.

No enchantment against Jacob,
No divination against Israel (Numbers 23:23)

> The magicians tried by their secret
> arts to bring forth gnats, but they
> could not (Exodus 8:18)

But for Cain and his offering
he [God] had no regard (Genesis 4:5)

> Now he [Jacob] has taken away my
> blessing (Genesis 27:36)

And [Nadab & Abihu] offered unholy fire before the
Lord, such as he had not commanded them. And fire

came forth from the presence of the Lord and devoured
them (Leviticus 10:2)

I hate, I despise your feasts,
and I take no delight in your
solemn assemblies (Amos 6:21)

Do not lay your hand on the lad [Isaac]
or do anything to him (Genesis 22:12)

Rituals do not always go smoothly; often they seem to be more trouble than they are worth. Amos' God has little use for solemn assemblies. Nadab and Abihu are killed for performing an unauthorized rite. Esau loses the benefits of the blessing rite to his brother Jacob. Cain's offering is disregarded for some unspecified reason. The Egyptian magicians' magic cannot match that of Moses and Aaron. Balak cannot get Balaam's oracle to tell him what he wants to hear. And if Abraham's ritual sacrifice of his son had been successful, it would have failed.

Curiously, little has been done in a theoretical way to take account of ritually related trouble, but speech act theory has some promising features that might enable us to begin rectifying this gap in the phenomenology of religion. Speech act theory, which developed out of philosophical linguistic analysis, is usually applied only to verbal phenomena. I propose to extend its application to ritual, a performative phenomenon.

Specifically, I will demonstrate the applicability of J.L. Austin's typology of "infelicitous" [his term] performances to both biblical and non-biblical examples of troublesome ritual. The reasons for putting speech act theory to this use are simple: (1) some of the examples used by Austin are ritualistic and (2) ritual contexts, more than any other, make use of what he calls performative utterance, that is, speech insofar as it accomplishes tasks rather than merely describing them. Speech act theory has proven generally useful in understanding the relations between "things said" and "things done" (to paraphrase Jane Harrison), but I want to explore one specific dimension of the theory. My hypothesis is that Austin's typology is applicable not only to things said in ritual contexts but also to things done in them, especially if the things done seem to go awry. There is no necessary reason why one has to apply speech act theory to failed rites as opposed to successful ones, but applying it to "happy" (his term) instances has been done; applying it to unhappy ones has not.

In my view ritual is not a single kind of action. Rather it is a convergence of several kinds we normally think of as distinct. It is an "impure" genre. Like opera, which includes other genres, for example, singing, drama, and sometimes even dancing, a ritual may include all these and more. Accordingly, applying speech act theory to ritual is unlikely to explain every sort of action that can transpire in a rite. Initially, one might expect it to be of use only in understanding the verbal aspects of it, particularly those facets of ritual language that do rather than merely refer.

All speech acts are not ritual acts, and not all ritual acts include speech acts. Therefore we would suppose speech act theory would be of little use in rites characterized mainly by, say, silence or movement. Ritual is a more complex cultural form than speech, because it can include all the variants of speech, but speech cannot include all the varieties of ritual.

Just as what we label with the single term "ritual" is a multifold phenomenon requiring multiple methods to understand it, so there are numerous ways a rite can succeed or fail. A fertility rite may not make crops grow; nevertheless, it can fail empirically while it succeeds socially. Worship can lapse into civil ceremony and thus serve a vested political interest thereby failing ethically. Meanwhile, it can succeed in providing symbols that nourish or comfort individuals. A wedding may legally bind a couple but fail to generate a festive air. And so on. In short, different kinds of ritual fail in different ways. And a rite need not fail on every level or from every point of view for it to be worth our while to consider the question of ritual infelicity.

Since rites are often multi-phased as well as multi-leveled, and since symbols have a "fan" of overlapping meanings as well as several kinds of meaning, one can seldom demonstrate that a rite has failed in all phases and on all levels. Of the many varieties of human behavior ritual is probably the most difficult to evaluate. And when we do evaluate it, justifying our assessments is notoriously difficult. Consequently, quarrels over ritual are often settled by violence or counter-ritualization—not by discussion, argument, or vote-taking. Furthermore, criteria for considering a ritual as successful or failed may be inescapably religio- or ethnocentric. I am still uncertain about this issue.

Despite these difficulties and caveats, people still engage in ritual criticism. As religious traditions and cultures clash and converge and individuals engage in overt and covert syncretism, criticism becomes increasingly necessary—if not for participants themselves, then for us who study ritual behavior.

Religious studies generally, and ritual studies in particular, typically ignore rites that do not do what they are purported to do. Although participants probably experience the failure of ritual as often as they do the success of it, people who study rites pay little attention to the dynamics of ritual infelicity. Questions such as the following remain not only unanswered but scarcely even considered: Does it make sense to consider rituals "happy," "true," or "successful," hence, "unhappy," "false," or "failed?" By what criteria do participants judge rites? Why is there such resistance to ritual criticism? Are there any cross-culturally valid ways to assess a rite? Are there specifically ritualistic, as opposed to moral, criteria? What do we mean when we say a ritual "works"? Is "working" a criterion equally applicable to every kind of ritual?

Understandably, anthropologists usually avoid making explicit, written judgments about the failure or success of the rites they observe and record. Liturgists are more likely to do so because of the normative, religious nature of their work. Even so, liturgists do not pose their criticisms so as to make them open to cross-cultural assessment, nor are they always explicit about their grounds for engaging in ritual criticism in the first place. An interesting question—one I will be unable to pursue in this essay—is: What are the motives and mechanisms of the widespread evasion of the fact of ritual infelicity?

To open the discussion of some of these questions I will first summarize some of the research of speech-act theorist J. L. Austin and then inquire how his theories have been used to understand ritual. Finally, I will critically reformulate and illustrate the categories in order to make them more useful in ritual studies.

RITUAL INFELICITY IN SPEECH-ACT THEORY

Austin's *How to do Things with Words* (1965) was originally delivered as the William James Lectures at Harvard in 1955. In it Austin introduces the idea of "performative utterance," which has become the foundation of modern speech act theory, whose leading contemporary proponent is John Searle. His *Speech Acts* (1969) and *Expression and Meaning* (1979) elaborate and refine Austin's original research.

Austin's stated intention is to describe the way words do things, as opposed merely to describing or expressing them. He employs a set of classifications that (1) enable us to distinguish words that say something ("constatives") from those that do something ("performatives"), and (2) help us judge when performatives are "happy," on the one hand, or "infelicitous," on the other. Here I am concerned with types of "infelicitous performance" and the light they shed on ritual failure.

I do not believe that I am stretching Austin's terminology. He recognizes that it has implications for ritual (see, e.g., 17, 20, 24, 36, 76, 84-5), but does not develop them. In the most explicit passage he says, ". . . Infelicity is an ill to which *all* acts are heir which have the general character of ritual or ceremonial, all *conventional* acts . . ." (18-19).

Which infelicities are likely to occur in which types of ritual Austin never says. Nor does he claim to consider any kind of act other than that of uttering words. So we are left to infer and imagine how to proceed from the kind he treats. He proposes two large categories of infelicity:

"misfires" and "abuses." When a ritual misfires, its formula is not effective; the act is "purported but void." An example of a misfire would be a wedding performed by someone unauthorized to do it, say, the choirmaster rather than the priest. When a rite is abused, it is "professed but hollow." An abuse would be saying "I do" while secretly resolving not to do.

It is clear from Austin's analysis that recognizing ritual misfires requires attention to the total situation of the speech act not just to the words alone. Assessment requires a consideration of the tradition and social context. Recognizing ritual abuses requires that attention be paid to the psychology of the ritualist, especially insofar as one can infer such psychology from tones of voice, grammatical moods, and gestures.

Some performatives are easy to recognize, because they include explicit grammatical cues such as the first-person singular or certain adverbs: "*I* bid you welcome" or "I *hereby* name you the Queen Mary." But the line between explicit and implicit performatives is not always so clear. "I am sorry" can be the description of a feeling or the enactment of an apology, and pipe smoking can be either an habitual activity or a sacred gesture.

In John Searle's refinement of Austin's research a great deal of effort is spent reformulating the taxonomy of illocutionary acts (see Searle 1979: chap. 1) and almost none on the infelicities. Searle (1969: chap. 5) argues that predication ("saying") is also an act, thus softening Austin's contrast between constatives and performatives. In addition, Searle (136 ff) identifies the "speech act fallacy" that results from trying to overextend speech-act theory. But "defective" (see 54) performatives receive little attention from him. So the main contribution of speech act theory to a theory of ritual failure still consists of Austin's taxonomy, which he himself took to be provisional and incomplete.

SPEECH ACT THEORY IN THE STUDY OF RITUAL

Speech act theory has not been used often in religious studies generally nor in the study of ritual specifically. But it may be useful to summarize what has been done so far.

Although not explicitly based on Austin's theories, anthropologist S. J. Tambiah's article, "The Magical Power of Words" (1968), is sometimes referred to in subsequent discussions. Tambiah argues that ritual is not action (as opposed to language) but rather a way of connecting action and language. He notes the wide, cross-cultural occurrence of three ways of accounting for the power of language: that it is from the gods, that is from human beings, and that it is indigenous to words themselves. In an extended re-analysis of the data on Trobriand magic (first presented by Malinowski) he goes to great lengths to demonstrate that magical utterances are not mumbo-jumbo or mere emotional release. Instead he tries to show that it is a metaphoric means of constructing blueprints or self-fulfilling prophecies. His summary of the argument is worth quoting:

> Thus it is possible to argue that all ritual, whatever the idiom, is addressed to the human participants and uses a technique which attempts to re-structure and integrate the minds and emotions of the actors. The technique combines verbal and non-verbal behaviour and exploits their special properties. Language is an artificial construct and its strength is that its form owes nothing to external reality: it thus enjoys the power to invoke images and comparisons, refer to time past and future and relate events which cannot be represented in action. Non-verbal action on the other hand excels in what words cannot easily do—it can codify, and analogically by imitating real events, reproduce technical acts and express multiple implications simultaneously. Words excel in expressive enlargement, physical actions in realistic presentation.
>
> It is a truer tribute to the savage mind to say that, rather than being confused by verbal fallacies or acting in defiance of known physical laws, it ingeniously conjoins the expressive and metaphorical properties of language with the operational and empirical properties of technical activity. It is this which gives magical operations a realistic colouring and allows them to achieve their expressiveness through verbal substitution and transfer combined with an instrumental technique that imitates practical action (202).

Because Tambiah concentrates on showing how ritual language works, he does not entertain questions about its failure. On the contrary, he thinks Malinowski misinterpreted his own data insofar as he regarded Trobriand magic as "prosaic pedantry" (Tambiah 1968: 192). The failure, he shows, was the anthropologist's not the magicians'.

Ruth Finnegan's, "How to do Things with Words: Performative Utterances Among the Limba of Sierra Leone" (1969), appeared a year later than Tambiah's and in the same anthropological journal. Her claim, which she amply supports with both linguistic and behavioral data, is that for the Limba performative utterances have broader currency than they do in English. She shows that accepting gifts, announcing, pleading, greeting, and saying good bye are highly valued; they are not just polite expressions but substantive social acts. Among the Limba failure to perform them at the proper time or in the correct way has serious social consequences. But beyond this gross point of omission, Finnegan does not analyze the dynamics of such failure.

Benjamin Ray in "'Performative Utterances' in African Rituals" (1973), shows that ritual language in Dinka and Dogon ceremonies do not merely symbolize and express meanings. Rather, they accomplish ends by virtue of "the *authority* involved *in the act of uttering the words*" (28). Ray accepts Finnegan's data as supportive of his own findings, but he is sharply critical of Tambiah. He charges Tambiah with implying that the efficacy of magical words lies only in the overt actions accompanying them (25). This interpretation violates ritualists' own beliefs that their words direclty affect the objects toward which they are directed (see 28). Ray contends that ritual language is not metaphoric or symbolic at all, but rather performative in Austin's sense of the word.

What Ray actually succeeds in demonstrating is only that the expressive/instrumental dichotomy, as applied to the Dinka and Dogon understanding of ritual, violates the practitioners' own views of it. In short, he shows that speech act theory is homologous with Dinka and Dogon views on the matter—a thesis resembling Finnegan's regarding Limba usage. Ray does not really demonstrate *that* or *how* their utterances achieve their effect. If he had, he might have been forced to deal with some instances of their ineffectiveness—with infelicitous as well as happy instances.

Another effort in religious studies to use speech act theory is Hugh White's "A Theory of the Surface Structure of Biblical Narrative" (1979). White contends that the Bible's heavy use of direct, first-person discourse (of the divine voice) makes it "performative" rather than "classical." The classical mode, as he defines it, encloses discourse in a third-person narrative framework. Like Ray and Finnegan, White basically wants to show how a particular tradition of usage illustrates Austin's description. But once again it is beyond the scope of his treatment to consider infelicitous instances. All of the examples are "happy."

As far as I can tell, the only extended treatment of the failure of ritual language in terms of Austin's theory is Fenn's book-length examination of conflicts between the requirements of court-room utterances and those of the liturgy. In *Liturgies and Trials* (1982) he examines three cases: "In the Matter of Maria Cueto," "In the Matter of Karen Ann Quinlan," and Daniel Berrigan's *The Trial of the Catonsville Nine* (1970). In each court case he shows how religious utterances are reduced in court to mere opinions. The liturgy, he argues, is the only context which comes near to being "the closed linguistic garden of paradise" (xv). The arena within which religious utterances have actual performative force, he shows, has become quite small. What is a felicitous utterance in the one social context is infelicitous in another. Fenn demonstrates how context-dependent the failure of ritual language is.

Prophetic and kerygmatic speech, one might suppose, are two of the most performatively oriented types of Biblical language. Both Fenn and White seem to imply as much. What Fenn (173) claims, however, is that the church, by attempting to establish permanently, the meanings of these kinds of religious speech, unwittingly secularized them, making them precarious and transient. By "secularizing," he means, "the identifying of ambiguous and open-ended terms with referents and meanings that are so specific as to become outmoded and irrelevant in other contexts and at later times and occasions" (172). Furthermore, prophetic and kerygmatic speech-acts are disallowed in the courtroom; only a specialized form of testimony is permitted even from religious authorities who, in other contexts, have the authority to utter things performatively. By controlling the ritual proceedings, the courts further contribute to the secularization of speech initiated by religious groups. The outcome is often ritual conflict and failure. And "when ritual fails, individuals and groups break the usual role for testimony and speak for themselves outside the context of their institutional roles" (141). Loss of legitimacy and loss of illocutionary force accompany one another. In such a crisis symbols no longer evoke what they represent. What was once a performative utterance now only expresses a pious wish. A good example of this kind of failure—though not one offered by Fenn—is Charles Winquist's (1983: 296) assumption that theology is a speech act. If he intends this as a description of theological practice, I seriously doubt his claim. Theology, unlike prophetic and kerygmatic speech, has seldom been performative. If he intends it merely as an expression of hope, I, of course, could agree.

Curiously, Fenn's pioneering treatment makes no use of Austin's typology of infelicities even though he makes good use of Austin's conception of illocutionary force and acknowledges (124 ff.) heavy dependence on speech act theory. Why do Fenn, White, Ray, Finnegan, and even Searle not make use of the typology of infelicities? Are there unconscious apologetic motives? Clearly not in the case of Fenn; probably not in the case of Searle. Why do these scholars depict religious speech only when it is happy? Do they think Austin's typology is either wrong or too restricted for use in religious contexts? Not one of them criticizes Austin's discussion of ritual failure. However, I will give them the benefit of the doubt and assume that they examine Austin's positive thesis as a prelude to considering his negative one at a later time. Let us assume that they have presented a convincing case that Biblical, Dinka, Dogon, and Limba speech make considerable use of illocutionary constructions. The next step, I propose, is inquiring into the dynamics of the loss of illocutionary force.

TYPES OF INFELICITOUS PERFORMANCE

Not all of Austin's examples depend solely on language related features. His taxonomy turns out to be much broader than his declared intentions of developing a theory of utterance; it includes instances in which failure stems from some problem with attitude or action. In fact, examined carefully, only "breaches" *necessarily* involve words. In all the other categories failure could occur without the involvement of language at all, even though Austin often gives examples that are language oriented. His categories are more general than one might initially suppose. Furthermore, we might surmise from the amount of space he devotes to infelicities, that he expected them to occur as frequently as he did happy performatives.

Austin identifies two major types: (1) "misfires" and (2) "abuses." I will describe the various subtypes and provide actual ritual examples to illustrate their usefulness beyond the arena of language.

(1.11) "Non-plays" are procedures that do not exist, therefore the actions are disallowed. Strictly speaking, there would be not examples for this category (which may be one reason Austin never found a term for it that satisfied him). However, his intention seems to be that of defining a category of rites that someone, say, a ritual authority, believes to be non-existent or illegitimate. I use the term to include invented or recently borrowed rites that are disconnected from the structures that might legitimate them. Austin says that non-plays lack "an accepted conventional procedure" (14). Such a procedure does not fall within the boundaries of legitimacy or the domain of efficacy. For instance, when William O. Roberts, Jr., (1982: 11) designed initiation rites for the youth of First Church of Christ in Middletown, Connecticut, a denominational executive responded, "In Christianity we confirm faith. We do not initiate people." In his view Christian initiation is a non-play.

(1.12) If a rite fails by "misapplication," it is a legitimate rite but the persons and circumstances involved in it are inappropriate. An example is the funeral in 1954 of a ten-year old Javanese boy named Paidjan. Clifford Geertz's (1973: 153 ff.) sensitive description and probing analysis show how the *slametan* (a communal feast) of the funeral became arrested because of social and political circumstances—because of what he deems "an incongruity due to the persistance in an urban environment of a religious symbol system adjusted to peasant social structure" (169). One might wish to add to this category procedures that fail because they are ill-timed, such as harvest celebrations (e.g., Thanksgiving) that occur two months later than the actual harvest, or weddings that are undergone too soon or late.

(1.21) "Flaws" are ritual procedures that employ incorrect, vague, or inexplicit formulas, including, I would add, non-verbal or gestural formulas. Indigenous attempts to account for the failure of magical rites often appeal to some such notion. If a ritual is considered merely flawed, participants may easily be convinced to repeat it. Obviously, ritualists themselves are not eager to keep records of their mistakes, so, even though flawed enactments may be rife, recorded examples are rare. An interesting one is reported by Morris E. Opler (1969: 92-93). Look-

Around-Water, a Mescalero Apache, believed that a protective rite failed, allowing him to be struck by two bullets, because he had been singing a deer song instead of the one that properly belonged to him. As soon as he changed his song he was healed.

(1.22) "Hitches" are misexecutions in which the procedures are incomplete. One of Austin's (37) fictional examples is the official who declared, "I hereby open this library," only to discover that the key had broken off in the lock. A more poignant instance is the case of Lulu (Leacock 1975: 200ff), a forty-year old Afro-Brazilian woman, who for twenty years was unable to have a trance experience even though she repeatedly showed the usual signs of incipient possession.

(2.1) "Insincerities" are a type of "abuse"—an act "professed by hollow." Ritual insincerity amounts to saying—I would add, doing—things without the requisite feelings, thoughts, or intentions. Levi-Strauss (1967: 169ff), re-tells the story (first told by Franz Boas) of Quesalid, a Canadian Kwakiutal who did not believe in shamanism but so learned it in order to expose it. Later, he continued to practice this "false supernatural" without believing in it, because people believed in him, and because he knew of techniques even more false than his own.

(2.2) "Breaches" are failures to follow through; they are abrogations of ceremonially made promises. Since "breaches" includes breaking promises and failure to abide by contracts, it is one of the more familiar types of infelicity. Sometimes rites fail to bind. One can avoid the conclusion that the fault is the rite's by claiming that persons, not ceremonies, fail—that rites are "victims," not agents. A widely publicized breach was former U.S. President Nixon's violation of his oath of office by his involvement in Watergate. No longer "protecting and defending," he was guilty of undermining and attacking—at least this seemed to be the public verdict.

Here Austin's typology ends, yet there remain other examples that could not be handled by his scheme, so further additions to the typology are necessary:

(2.3) "Glosses" are procedures that hide or ignore contradictions or major problems. Glossing over conflict is a function that rites proverbially (in anthropological theory) do well. In fact, some scholars would argue that this is its primary function. However, rituals may also fail because a gloss is too thin and people see through it, or because it is too thick and only recognizable by its repercussions in the psyche or social structure. I recently attended a wedding in which the bride was pregnant, followed a few months later by a child-blessing in which this same new wife participated with a black eye from her husband. Both ceremonies were "applied" in the same manner (and about as successfully) as her eye make-up. They "glossed" rather than "bridged" the chasms. It is not uncommon for participants to believe that one's wedding day should be perfect—ideal and unmarred by any recognition of difficulties.

(2.4) In a "flop" all the procedures may be done correctly but the rite fails to resonate. It does not generate the proper tone, ethos, or atmosphere. In some rites mood is less important than precise execution of procedures; this might be true of a healing rite or baptism. But in a fiesta or birthday party, having a good time and being festive is a primary aim. At a retirement ceremony for a colleague, things went without hitch or flaw (in Austin's sense of these terms), but the praise was so exaggerated and the jokes so strained that the farewell went flat; it flopped.

(3) Austin thinks of illocutionary acts almost solely in the context of interpersonal relations and legal procedures. Consequently, he omits consideration of the performative utterances that would be most obvious to scholars in religious studies and anthropology, namely, magic. Hence, I propose the major category, "ineffectuality."

Ineffectualities are procedures that fail to bring about intended observable changes. Ineffectualities are more serious than flaws, because the latter are partial. In the case of the former a rite may be properly performed, but it does not produce the goods. For instance, Maria Sabina (Halifax 1979: 213), a Mazatec shaman, was unable to heal seventeen-year old Pefecto Jose Garcia and concluded her chant,

> Dangerous things are being done, tragedies are being worked out. We are left only perplexed, we mamas. Who can stand all these things? It's the same; it's the same here. Really this thing is big.

The chant may have prepared those present for grief and loss; it was not a "flop." But it was, in her view, ineffectual inasmuch as the boy died.

(4) Ritual "violation," as I use the term, reflects a moral judgment. Violations may be effective, but they are demeaning. From some point of view they are judged to be deficient. Rites such as initiations that deliberately maim or inadvertently degrade are difficult analytically as well as morally. Clitoridectomies are a case in point. Recently, some anthropologists, particularly women, have attacked them regardless of their indigenous support. Judging actions to be moral violations may be culturally relative, but this does not relieve us of moral responsibility. An example about which there seems to be obvious warrant for debate (at the very least) is the Aztec ceremony (see Vaillant 1962: 205) in honor of Huehueteotl, the fire god. In it priests danced with prisoners bound to their backs and then, one by one, dumped them into the flames. Before death could relieve the pain, the priests dragged the captives out with hooks and cut out their still beating hearts. Burnings at the stake, head

hunting, and human sacrifices challenge the easy cultural relativism of broad-minded academics.

(5) Ritual "contagion" occurs when a rite spills over its own boundaries. It may be effective, but it is uncontained. In *Violence and the Sacred* René Girard (1977: 31ff) has offered the most provocative analysis of this sort of infelicity. However, he typically emphasizes the way rituals contain the social contagion of violence, rather than the way in which rituals themselves can contaminate. Maya Deren (1970: 254ff; 322, n. 8), a film maker, tells how the Voodoo rite she went to Haiti to study, broke its bounds. It is rare for a non-Haitian to be possessed, but Deren was, producing considerable complications for her recording project. From one point of view this occurrence shows the power of the rite. From another it is a problem, if not evidence of some sort of failure.

"Rituals of conflict" (Norbeck 1967: 226) often spread as if they were a contagious disease. From the point of view of rebels and proponents of social change, this is as it should be. From the point of view of the established elite, contamination is tantamount to failure.

(6) In instances of ritual "opacity" a ceremony or some element in it is experienced as meaningless; the act is unrecognizable or uninterpretable. Either it fails to communicate or it communicates such conflicting messages that someone—either participant or observer—fails to grasp its sense. There are short-lived varieties of opacity, but there are long-range ones too. Most rites probably contain some opaque symbols, and most religions some opaque rites, but the situation becomes problematic if opacity is widespread. Opacity may incite one to curiosity, but when rife or sustained, it can damage a rite. Perhaps the most common example of opacity is the use of a sacred language (Latin, Hebrew, or Sanscrit, for instance) to such a degree that it ceases to create mystery and begins to obfuscate. How much opacity participants can tolerate seems to differ widely from culture to culture.

When tourists witness the Pueblo corn dance at Santo Domingo Pueblo, New Mexico, it is opaque to most of them; hence their concentration on the rhythm of the drums, the weather, or the color of costumes. The opacity may protect the rite from meddling, but it sometimes results in the spectators' inadvertently interrupting a sacred performance by an inappropriate response. In this case opacity is the result of being a outsider.

In the following case, recounted by Apuleius (1962: 248-249) ritual opacity is deliberate, the result of priestly mystification:

> Thereupon the old man took me by the hand and led me towards the spacious temple. . . . He produced from the secret recesses of the shrine certain books written in unknown characters. The meaning of these characters was concealed, at times by the con-

centrated expression of hieroglypically painted animals, at times by wreathed and twisted letters with tails that twirled like wheels . . . so that it was altogether impossible for any peeping profane to comprehend.

(7) Ritual "defeat" is more common than might be supposed, because ritual competition and conquest are widespread. In a ritual defeat one ritual performance is accepted as invalidating another. The eighteenth chapter of I Kings, for instance, tells of a contest between Elijah and Baal's prophets. The story is told from the point of view of the victors, so they are the ones who conclude that the opposing rite (and its attendant deity) are failures. Often a ritual defeat is followed by ritual "theft," that is, the plundering of a conquered ritual system for its symbolic wealth. That ritualists explicitly compete in magical battles is obvious enough. What scholars sometimes fail to notice is how rites may be thrown implicitly into competitive, "market" situations. Fenn's (1982) analysis seems to imply that liturgy is sometimes defeated by courtroom ceremony. On occasion rites from the same system inadvertently become competitors, e.g., a Sunday worship service and its televised counterpart.

(8) In cases of ritual "omission" the rite does not fail; rather one fails to perform it. Ruth Finnegan (1969:545) says that if a Limba husband can complain against his wife, "You haven't greeted me," it is a serious breach of decorum. Like "flaws," omissions are a favorite way for participants to account for trouble. If one fails to make prayerful requests, offer the expected sacrifice, or give due thanks, then it is easy to claim that such omissions account for subsequent suffering or disaster. Omissions are the opposite of "non-plays." In the former there is no accepted procedure; in the latter there is a procedure but it is left undone.

(9) Outsiders are more likely than insiders to commit "misframes." When we misframe a rite, we misconstrue its genre. The result is akin to missing the point of a joke or taking irony literally. Perhaps we understand it on some level—it is not "opaque" to us—but on some other we miss the point. If one does not understand the shit devil rites described by Jeanne Cannizzo (1983: 124-141), one might assume that boys who stumble, defecate, and wear ragged clothes were mentally ill instead of engaging in ritual caricature. It is not always easy to tell whether we are witnessing drama, symptoms, or ritual. It is a common error to misconstrue magic as drama or vice-versa. Since frames can shift or multiply in the course of a single cultural performance (e.g., a dramatic pageant within, or subsequent to, a civil ceremony), even participants can misframe the activities in which they participate. Sometimes this is an advantage, allowing ritualists to believe they share a common definition of the situation. In other instances, however, the misframing is disastrous

or funny. Erving Goffman's *Frame Analysis* (1974: 324) is replete with examples such as the story of a thousand enraged Mexican farmers who drive their priest out of town because he will not celebrate Mass at a tree that, after lying five years dead on its side, is found upright after a thunderstorm. They frame the event as "miracle"; he does not.

To summarize, the complete typology, consisting of Austin's as well as my own descriptions (in quotation marks) is as follows:

1. Misfire (act purported but void)
    1.1 Misinvocation (act disallowed)
        1.11 Non-play (lack of accepted conventional procedure)
        1.12 Misapplication (inappropriate persons or circumstances)
    1.2 Misexecutions (act vitiated)
        1.21 Flaw (incorrect, vague, or inexplicit formula)
        1.22 Hitch (incomplete procedure)
2. Abuse (act professed but hollow)
    2.1 Insincerity (lack of requisite feelings, thoughts, or intentions)
    2.2 Breach (failure to follow through)
    2.3 "Gloss" (procedures used to cover up problems)
    2.4 "Flop" (failure to produce appropriate mood or atmosphere)
3. "Ineffectuality" (act fails to precipitate anticipated empirical change)
4. "Violation" (act effective but demeaning)
5. "Contagion" (act leaps beyond proper boundaries)
6. "Opacity" (act unrecognizable or unintelligible)
7. "Defeat" (act discredits or invalidates acts of others)
8. "Omission" (act not performed)
9. "Misframe" (genre of act misconstrued)

RITUAL INFELICITY IN THE OLD TESTAMENT

I have selected examples to fit the typology, but, as anyone who has ever tried to apply and test some theory or scheme knows, all sorts of unanticipated problems appear as soon as one faces a specific tradition with that theory. When we engage in extended case studies rather than selecting examples, the lack of fit between theory and data begins to show. I am no biblical scholar and have neither the space nor training to pursue a case study here, but it might be helpful at least to suggest lines along which a study of performative infelicity in the Old Testament might proceed. I have indicated some of the more interesting examples in the epigraphs.

Beginning with biblical texts is basically, but not entirely, an inductive procedure. I have, after all, picked texts that appear to be relevant to the typology. For instance, the tale of the confrontation of Moses and Aaron with the Egyptian magicians seems to be, among others things, a story about magical combat. Comparative religion and symbolic anthropology are replete with similar stories about sorcerers and magicians who pit their rites against one another. This feature of the account appears to be a straightforward illustration of ritual "defeat" (#7). By itself this sort of labeling does not tell us very much; the work of interpretation has hardly begun when one categorizes the action. It begins to get interesting, however, when we inquire why these same magicians are said to have been successful in an earlier phase of competition. Like Moses and Aaron they too succeed in bringing frogs upon the land of Egypt by use of their "secret arts" (Ex. 8:7). An interpreter can account for the success of one attempt followed by the failure of a subsequent one by appealing to either narrative or ritual. It heightens suspense to have the magicians seem like real competition and then have them defeated—an argument in favor of the narrative explanation. But it may be that a symbolic, possibly ritualistic, issue is at stake when the magicians are successful in bringing frogs (amphibians associated with water) but fail with gnats (creatures of the air associated in the text with dust). Whether or not my speculations bear any fruit, the point is simply that categorizing the conflict as ritual defeat, a species of performative infelicity, precipitates an avenue of inquiry not entirely typical of biblical studies.

Consider a second biblical example, that of Cain's offering (Gen. 4). Popular interpretations of the story fill in the silence of the text by assuming that God rejects the offering because Cain hides some secret sin such as arrogance, or that he is insincere. Such an interpretation implies a classification of the problem as "insincerity" (#2.1), "lack of requisite feelings, thoughts, or intentions."

Modern scholarship, on the other hand, often reads the story as personifying a conflict between two ways of life: agricultural (symbolized by Cain and his vegetable/fruit offering) and nomadic (symbolized by Abel and his offering of livestock). Whereas the popular view treats Cain's failure as a form of "abuse" (#2), an act professed but hollow, the scholarly one treats it as a "misinvocation" (#1.1) of some sort; "the act is disallowed." Following speech act theory we would have to inquire whether it is disallowed because there is no accepted conventional procedure for such an offering, or whether the persons or circumstances are inappropriate. If the latter, then we would have to ask: inappropriate in what respects?

A third instance is Abraham's near sacrifice of Isaac, popularly regarded as a "test," but considered by some scholars as reflecting a cultural transition from child sacrifice to a more sublimated, more ethically sophisticated rite in which an animal is substituted. In the language of speech act theory we would say this is a "misapplication" (1.12), because it involves an inappropriate object: a person rather than an animal.

But from the point of view of Isaac, we might imagine, it is better regarded as an instance of ritual "violation" (#4)—or near violation since the act was not completed. From the point of view of the child-sacrificing culture (if there ever was one), Abraham's failure to follow through would have constituted a "breach" (2.2). But modern Jews and Christians might well question whether any sort of infelicity or failure has occurred at all. The story, they might insist, is about a successful ritual revision or a successful attempt to resist a temptation to use ritual to satisfy an infanticidal obsession. What this third example illustrates is that the typology does not answer questions so much as precipitate them by providing a vocabulary.

A final example is the short folktale of Hadab and Abihu, the son of Aaron (Leviticus 10). In one sense it parallels the Cain and Abel story: God is not happy with an offering. But instead of refusing it, he destroys the brothers with fire because they offered "unholy fire." The pun notwithstanding, the act is a "misfire" (#1), but of what sort? The only way to be precise is to know more about what constituted unholiness for the ancient Hebrews. Does the problem lie in intentions? In procedures? Or should we circumvent these alternatives altogether and classify the action according to its results? If the latter, we need a new category, say, "backfires," which we could make an independent category or a sub-category of "contagion" (#5), which is what occurs when a performance leaps beyond proper boundaries.

FURTHER RESEARCH ON RITUAL INFELICITY

I have raised far more questions than I have answered—deliberately so. My aim has not been to "apply" a theory of speech acts to biblical "data." Rather it has been to experiment with the theory, both extending its scope and exposing its limits, as well as teasing a few texts with some new questions. I have implied that the typology is incomplete, although I believe I have shown how one might begin to expand beyond Austin's original aims and to build on his vocabulary. The categories need much more testing by application to specific rites. For the moment, the most I expect of them is that they call attention to what is often ignored, namely, infelicitous performances, and that they provide a tentative glossary for beginning to assess them. Some obvious limitations of the typology are: (1) that it does not solve the problem of point of view. Who—participant or observer—is to decide whether procedures fail, and if they do, what sort of infelicity has been committed? Nor (2) does it indicate how kinds of infelicity transpire in relation to one another. For instance, one may "gloss" a rite, deliberately making it "opaque," thereby laying the grounds for a ritual "defeat." Something like this happened when Spanish conquistadors taught native people of the new world to venerate crosses without fully conveying their meaning. Later, the conquerors used this devotion as a means of discouraging rebellion among the conquered and of obtaining formal, ceremonial submission.

A third (3) unanswered question is one I mentioned in the beginning: What are the motives and mechanisms for evading the judgment that a rite does not work? One also might want to inquire whether the terms are ethnocentric. Austin's British, understated "infelicitous"/"happy" and my overstated, American "failure"/"success" might suggest that ritual criticism is inextricably bound up with national or even temperamental sensibilities.

A fourth (4) problem is that the typology does not systematically separate "failure in" and failure of" rituals. In some types the problem lies with the ritualists, in others with the rite itself, and in still others with the relation between the rite and surrounding religio-cultural processes.

Finally (5), there are undoubtedly other types and examples. What shall we call the rite that is so rigidified that it cannot change? How shall we name those that are so weak dramatically, conceptually, or socially that they simply have no effect? And what of annulments, e.g., of weddings? As the types and examples proliferate, we must, of course, begin to examine the logic of sub- and superordination of the categories. Are there "levels" of failure?

Among these five issues number one (the point of view problem) and number four (the failure-in / failure-of distinction) are in my estimation the most important and troublesome, so a few additional comments may be necessary, if only to encourage further reflection and research.

Put simply, there is no resolving the point of view problem if one imagines there is some universal, meta-ritualistic criterion which, like a meter stick, can be used to measure every rite cross-culturally. Even the exemplary meter stick lacks currency not only in the New Guinea bush, but in the U.S. I have deliberately refrained from referring to the categories as "criteria." They constitute a typology, an organized (perhaps in the future, systematized) phenomenology. Their worth consists of their ability to point to troublesome dynamics and to provide a vocabulary for recognition, debate, and discussion. They are useless as some kind of performative canon with which to prove failure or rebuke ritualists. Ritualists have so little difficulty evading ritual criticism that a set of a-cultural criteria would be of little practical use to anybody who is not already convinced that a problem exists.

Since rites, especially religious ones, function as paradigms, they themselves are often the idea-real by which the ordinary/semi-real is judged. Rites, like myths and dreams, resist criticism or, if you prefer, people resist having their rites, myths, and dreams subjected to criticism. The right to engage in it at all is probably either bought with membership and participation, or directly dependent upon the richness of one's observations and interpretations. Ritual criticism is but one phase—and not a privileged one either—of the hermeneutics of ritual. So if we are to speak of criteria at all, they are definitional not moral. Their weight comes from their ability to articulate, not their ability to prove or coerce. Consider, for instance, "violations," those ritual acts that demean. Demeaning may be defined as in bounds for an initiation rite. If one chooses to resist this definition, he or she will probably have the most success by appealing to one part of the rite as a basis for critcizing some other part. In the Abraham-Isaac story ritual infanticide is prevented not by a bare moral interdiction, but by a ritual substitute. The most effective ritual criticism is probably that which transpires on the basis of the ritual system itself, not on some heteronomous rule.

This brings me to the failure-in/failure-of distinction. Infelicity is often taken by participants to be the result of a failure in some detail of performance. They will blame themselves before impugning the rite, and will criticize some part of it before challenging the whole of it. Using a literary critical analogy, we might say that functional infelicity is likely to be translated into formal infelicity. Formally, a rite is a self-contained system; functionally, it achieves something in the environment, or does something to or for participants.

However, I must admit that I do not think a merely formal or morphological treatment of ritual failure will suffice, but neither will one that considers failure in purely functional, sociological terms. Furthermore, I believe it is a mistake always to blame persons rather than rituals—a tactic that prevents ritual criticism. I doubt that one can ever judge a rite as failed or flawed in any absolute way. It is always flawed from person or group X's point of view, or in relation to goal Y. If we learn to make such discriminations, we may become less susceptible to the wholesale waves of ritophobia and ritophilia that periodically sweep postprotestant Western cultures. Analyzing ritual failure involves more than defining terms, supplying examples, or applying labels. But learning to do so is a first step toward a useful ritual criticism.

REFERENCES

Apuleius
    1962   *The Golden Ass*. Trans. Jack Lindsay. Bloomington, Indiana: Indiana University Press.

Austin, J. L.
    1965   *How to do Things with Words*. New York: Oxford.

Cannizzo, Jeanne
    1983   "The Shit Devil: Pretense and Politics among West African Urban Children." In *The Celebration of Society: Perspectives on*

Contemporary Cultural Performance. Ed. Frank E. Manning. London, Canada: Congress of Social & Humanistic Studies.

Deren, Maya
    1970   *Divine Horsemen: Voodoo Gods of Haiti.* New York: Chelsea House.

Fenn, Richard K.
    1982   *Liturgies and Trials: The Secularization of Religious Language.* New York: Pilgrim.

Finnegan, Ruth
    1969   "How To Do Things with Words: Performative Utterances among the Limba of Sierra Leone." *Man* (N.S.) 4: 537-552.

Geertz, Clifford
    1973   *The Interpretation of Cultures.* New York: Basic Books.

Girard, René
    1977   *Violence and the Sacred.* Trans. Patrick Gregory. Baltimore: John Hopkins University Press.

Goffman, Erving
    1974   *Frame Analysis: An Essay on the Organization of Experience.* New York: Harper & Row.

Halifax, Joan, ed.
    1979   *Shamanic Voices: A Survey of Visionary Narratives.* New York: Dutton.

Leacock, Seth and Ruth
    1975   *Spirits of the Deep: A Study of an Afro-Brazilian Cult.* Garden City, NY: Anchor.

Levi-Strauss, Claude
    1967   *Structural Anthropology.* Trans. Claire Jacobson and Brooke G. Schoepf. Garden City, NY: Doubleday.

Myerhoff, Barbara
    1978   *Number Our Days.* New York: Simon and Schuster.

Norbeck, Edward
    1967   "African Rituals of Conflict." In *Gods and Rituals: Readings in Religious Beliefs and Practices.* Ed. John Middleton. Garden City, NY: Natural History Press.

Opler, Morris E.
    1969   *Apache Odyssey: A Journey Between Two Worlds.* New York: Holt, Rinehart and Winston.

Ray, Benjamin
    1973   "'Performative Utterances' in African Rituals." *History of Religions* 13: 16-35.

Roberts, William O., Jr.
    1982   *Initiation to Adulthood: An Ancient Rite of Passage in Contemporary Form.* New York: Pilgrim.

Searle, John
- 1969 *Speech Acts: An Essay in the Philosophy of Language.* Cambridge: Cambridge University Press.
- 1979 *Expression and Meaning: Studies in the Theory of Speech-Acts.* Cambridge: Cambridge University Press.

Tambiah, S.J.
- 1968 "The Magical Power of Words." *Man* (N.S.) 3: 175-208.

Vaillant, George C.
- 1962 *Aztecs of Mexico.* Rev. Suzannah B. Vaillant. Baltimore: Penguin.

White, Hugh C.
- 1979 "A Theory of the Surface Structure of the Biblical Narrative." *Union Seminary Quarterly Review* 34: 159-173.

Winquist, Charles
- 1983 "Theology, Deconstruction, and Ritual Process." *Zygon* 18: 295-309.

III.

Responses

POTENTIAL AND ACTUAL INTERACTIONS BETWEEN SPEECH ACT THEORY AND BIBLICAL STUDIES

Martin J. Buss
Emory University

The potential contribution of speech act theory can be viewed either in terms of a theoretical reconceptualization of the process of exegesis or in terms of a refinement of exegetical procedures in their application to specific passages. These two aspects cannot be strictly separated, of course, since the first-mentioned concerns questions which the interpreter asks (in this sense it is practical), and the second involves the providing of answers to these questions (so that it has a theoretical side).

Among those who discuss the speech act theory in the present volume, the two biblical scholars—Hugh White and Daniel Patte—approach the theoretical question. One might have liked to see a practical application, but it appears that they, like others in the field, are concerned about the need for a fundamental re-orientation of the discipline.

A fundamental question revolves around the relation of speech to life. As is well known, speech has relations to the speaker, to the addressee, and to the referent (real or hypothetical). Historical criticism has been concerned especially with the first and third of these dimensions (authorship and reference). These concerns can be, and to a larger extent have been, pursued on the assumption that speech is a reflection of the author or of the referent, so that the primary aim of textual analysis is to reconstruct either the thought of the author or the reality to which the text, more or less accurately, refers.[1] From this point of view, the aim of textual analysis is to recognize a world outside the text.

In the twentieth century there has been a considerable redirection of interest, namely toward the text itself. The reasons for this shift are numerous; they include at least the following considerations. To begin with, any aesthetic orientation tends to focus on the qualities of the text itself, just as it does on the qualities of visual art or music. (An observer can recognize a socially and even biologically useful function in this, but that is usually not an intention of the individual involved.) Secondly, it has been pointed out (sometimes with excessive stress) that human life hardly is human without language and that human perception of the world is always influenced by linguistically explained concepts, so that emphasis has shifted from thought to embodied communication. Thirdly, there has been a relative loss of interest in history.[2]

Any reaction easily leads to an overreaction. Thus Anglo-American "New Criticism," together with its German and French versions, went too far in cutting off a text from its social and psychological environment. Some phases of biblical study, sometimes influenced directly or indirectly by this approach, similarly weakened their connection with extralinguistic reality. These include the work now of some literary critics.[3] Daniel Patte's work, too, had heretofore leaned in that direction.

Patte rightly argues in his contribution to the present discussion that such an imbalance needs to be overcome. It is not necessary, of course, that every study must equally emphasize all aspects. Thus Patte's own earlier work, which in a very profound fashion emphasized the intrinsic aspect of biblical speech, remains important. Nevertheless, it is very much to Patte's credit that he recognizes the significance of additional dimensions. These include a role for subjectivity.

Some caveats, however, can be raised in regard to Patte's essay, even though they do not contradict its fundamental thrust. First of all, Patte's appropriation of speech act theory one-sidedly emphasizes its relation to the author's mental state, so that he considers its thrust more expressive than pragmatic. Certainly, human action (as distinguished from mere motion, which may be involuntary) involves some kind of subjective consciousness, but it is also oriented toward a goal, or likely consequence. A similar goal-directedness appears in phenomena that are not human; it is useful to describe plants and animals and even cybernetic machines and some physical processes in such terms. Speech act theory places language within the broader category of action, which in turn can be seen within a still wider perspective of movement. More or less conscious intention indeed plays an important role for speech acts, and this aspect properly receives attention from Searle and others (compare White in his introductory essay). The degree, however, to which deliberate purpose plays a role is a highly debated question, with political overtones. In particular, Grice's theory of individual intention is criticized by Jürgen Habermas (275) in a work, influenced in part by Karl Marx, which provides a possible perspective within which to see that of Austin (who had at least some interest in Marxism [Hampshire: 42; Berlin: 6-7]).

Perhaps related to this issue is another; namely, Patte's belief that "religious discourses are peculiar speech acts which cannot be assimilated to other kinds." Indeed, speech act theory may allow one to recognize the special nature of religious activities. At the same time, a part of the strength of that approach lies in enabling one to see the continuity between religious and other acts. For instance, biblical prayers, commands, promises, narrations (with their functions!), threats, and declarations all have correspondences in nonreligious life.

In short, a theory that considers action can cover continuities from the nonhuman to the human and from the secular to the sacred. In drawing such lines, it can also clarify the differences that obtain.

White's surveys of speech act theory and of approaches to language in biblical study are wide-ranging and very helpful. They pass over, however, the relation of this theory to biblical form criticism, a connection in which I have been interested for some time.[4] In recent years especially, biblical study going under the name of form cirticism has drawn quite close to speech act theory. The pattern outlined by Gene Tucker and followed in the commentary series, "The Forms of Old Testament Literature," edited by him together with Rolf Knierim, includes the following relevant facets: genre, setting, and intention. What constitutes a "genre" is not an easy question, but a number of the designations used under that heading—both in that series and in other form-critical work—appear, or logically can appear, in classifications by speech act theorists; to give just one example, "lament" occurs in Searle's taxonomy (1979 [see Patte]: 6). The rather broad term "setting" certainly includes the social context important for Austin. The term "intention," in the series mentioned, usually covers Austin's "illocution" (verbal force), more rarely his "perlocutionary object" (desired effect).

Can form criticism learn from speech act theory? Undoubtedly so. One general consideration can be mentioned briefly. Gunkel's concept of *Sitz im Leben* concentrated excessively on the original or customary location of a genre, so that this category often loses a direct relevance to a particular text and remains only as a historical background for the form. If the concept of human situation is applied to the context in which a text actually stands, it can strongly support a functional or operational view of the text, which is still greatly underrepresented in biblical study. Gunkel gave extensive notice to what Austin (104) called the "parasitic" uses of a speech act, when it is used in a manner and context not natural to it. That was appropriate, for this aspect is important for literature. For Gunkel, however, this abnormal use for the artful-literary aspect of the text not infrequently overshadowed its practical dimension (only oral expressions were, to him, truly "living"). His followers (such as Sigmund Mowinckel) have corrected this imbalance considerably, but further progress can be made toward a systematic sociopsychological analysis of biblical literature.

Very briefly, one may raise a historical question. It is not impossible that Austin was influenced, at least indirectly, by biblical form criticism.

It is known that Austin closely studied linguistics, especially, it seems, in the 1950's (Warnock: 16). His notion of "performative" predates the latter period, according to his own report (Warnock:5), but the analysis of illocution and perlocution and of the different kinds of verbal performances, as presented in a large part of his 1955 lectures, appears to have been relatively new at the time. Some aspects of his mature analysis had been sketched by the noted British linguist J. R. Firth, who outlined types of "verbal action" in relation to types of situation insofar as they are "relevant" (28, 31, 182 [originally published in 1935 and 1950]). Firth refers to stimulation in this regard by the Egyptologist A. H. Gardiner (7, 181). Gardiner was the author of a book on the theory of language, which discusses four basic types of speech and uses terminology—"act of speech" and "locution" (for the non-active part of speech)—that anticipate Austin's. Gardiner can hardly have avoided knowing about biblical form criticism (or absorbing some of its procedures indirectly through Adolf Erman's work); he may even have mentioned it in discussion. All this does not prove a linkage between biblical scholarship and Austin but only the possibility of such a one, although there was, most likely, a historical connection between biblical form criticism and one or two other streams of speech act theory.[5]

While a modern connection between speech act theory and form criticism (some of it lies simply in a common scholarly ethos) is in part speculative, a common background can be located in classical studies. Austin was very interested in Aristotle (Warnock: 4, 16); classical education had deeply affected Gunkel. In fact, one of the advantages of Austin's approach lies in its theoretical affinity with Aristotle's (although the latter has problems which need to be discussed in another context). Sophists before Aristotle had tended to look upon rhetorical patterns as merely or primarily conventional. Aristotle attempted to see their inherent and universal character. Similarly, Austin as a philosopher delineated general characteristics of speech acts, while stressing the role of conventions. Gunkel operated on both levels—sometimes emphasizing natural and universal elements, more often giving primary attention to local conventions. His followers, with some exceptions, have tended to carry on the latter dimension more fully than the former. The truth of the matter is that both aspects must be considered for an understanding of speech.

To set biblical study into a universal dynamic perspective may well constitute the most fundamental contribution of speech act theory. Only with such a vision can past and present, East and West, body and mind, faith and life as such be integrated, together with attention to their differences. Included in such an integration is a renewed appreciation for biblical study antedating the rise of historical criticism, for much of that was indebted to Greco-Roman analyses of speech acts.[6]

Now that the broader theoretical issues have been noted and reference has been made to biblical form criticism as a version of speech act theory, one can turn toward some specific procedures and applications. These are exemplified in contributions by Ronald Grimes, Michael Hancher, and Susan Lanser. None of the three are primarily biblical scholars; for this reason they have a good potential for bringing some new perspectives to the subject matter.

Ritual actions, described by Grimes, lie on the border between speech and nonlinguistic action. They include one or more of the following: speech, other symbolic actions, and still other habitual acts (just exactly what these include depends on the definition of "ritual"). Many, although not all, of them are believed by participants to have a direct effect upon reality greater than a modern scientific observer is likely to admit. Grimes discusses in a very useful manner how conditions creating the "happiness" of a speech act, as pointed out in part by Austin, apply to ritual action.

One small clarification may be needed, concerning the term "performative". It does not affect Grimes' argument, but may be useful for an understanding of speech act theory. According to Grimes, Benjamin Ray contends that ritual language is "performative in Austin's sense of the word." What Ray actually says, more strictly in line with Austin's terminology, is that "the Trobianders regard these spells as perlocutionary acts" (1973 [see Grimes]: 27); that is, they have an actual effect on reality, although without being understood by the recipient. As Austin developed his argument in his 1955 lectures, he came to the conclusion that all speech acts have a performative aspect (e.g., 133-134, since description, also, is a performance), so that the question becomes not whether they perform, but in what manner they perform. From this perspective, one needs to defend Charles Winquist's reported view that theology is performative and to question Grimes' statement that prophetic and kerygmatic speech is more performative than theology.

Grimes' biblical examples concern rituals, or ritual-like actions, as they are reported in biblical literature. They thus show the nature not of the biblical speech act itself—narration in each case—but of the act depicted by the narrator. The same situation holds true for the analyses presented by Hancher and Lanser. They discuss the force of statements attributed to God and Adam in Genesis 1-3. White, in his introduction, calls such quoted statements "internal" in relation to literature. Although this is not the place to analyze their roles in detail, it can be pointed out that (hypothetical) speech acts appearing within a narrative have in principle the same characteristics, including force and consequence, as have those not so reported.[7] Their context is, in general, the social world of the narrative and, in particular, the situation depicted. Their consequences within the narrative are dependent on the beliefs of the narrator or recipient or on the structure of the world projected in the story, just as consequences attributed to ritual actions reflect the beliefs of the one who set them forth. An analysis of speech within speech does involve an extra layer of complexity, since the two levels of speech interact and may even merge.

Following Searle, Hancher treats the statement, "Let there be light!" as a "declaration." One problem in dealing with this sentence is that one must enter into the world internal to the text—if one pleases, into the mind of the author. The writer stood within a culture which held to a belief in an automatic power of speech, even apart from understanding by the one affected. One must then ask the question, what kind of speech act is, "Let there be light," when viewed from within such a culture? Probably it is something like a command or an expressed wish (the normal use of the linguistic form in question), as part of an imaginative or story world in which words have automatic effects, with a power especially great since it is God's. One must rule out its classification as a declaration. "Declaration" names an illocution (what is done "in" a speech act), not a perlocution (what is done "by" a speech act, with a focus on what comes after the utterance has ceased). Examples of declaration are: naming, the pronouncement of legal guilt or innocence, and an umpire's call of a play. In the story of Genesis 1, the appearance of light occurs not "in" the words, but thereafter by means of them. Such an occurrence is part of the words' perlocution, as B. Ray observed for beliefs concerning rituals. Admittedly, the distinction between illocution and perlocution is not altogether precise and is denied by some language theorists (e.g., Ballmer and Brennenstuhl: 46) as an appropriate one.

While one can thus differ with Hancher at some points of his analysis (including his view that only some statements are performative), his general conclusion still holds, namely, that "sacred speech acts are heightened or idealized versions of the ordinary performative discourse that people have always encountered in everyday life." For instance, the belief that words have direct consequences in nature is, undoubtedly, in part based on the fact that human speech had social, and therefore natural, consequences; it already begins with a child's observations of the effectiveness of its utterances.

Lanser has presented important considerations for a feminist reading of Genesis 2-3. At least two kinds of feminist approaches have been made in relation to biblical texts. One is to show that the Bible is not as patriarchal as has sometimes appeared to be the case. Another is to expose those patriarchal elements that are present. The studies to which Lanser responds exhibit largely the first of these two approaches. She raises a question mark about some of their analyses, with the aid of categories derived from Austin, Searle, and Grice.

Most of Lanser's observations are very well made. For instance, she rightly points out that even written literature must be placed into a context. She further astutely notes how *hāʾādām* oscillates between designating humanity and referring to the (first) male. This oscillation creates a situation in which common humanity sometimes comes to the fore (this can be viewed as antipatriarchal) and the male is sometimes given preference, or at least precedence. Lanser may well be right that this expresses an inner ideological tension within the text.

A question can be raised about her discussion of the woman's being named. There is no doubt that Adam names Eve as an individual, after the "fall" (Gen 3:20). Yet there is an uncertainty about the force of an earlier statement in regard to the woman generically: "This one shall be called woman, because she was taken from man" (2:23b). Phyllis Trible has argued that this sentence does not constitute a naming, comparable to Adam's giving of (generic) names to animals, since the phrasing is different. Lanser rightly points out that the preceding naming of animals has set up an expectation in the reader that a naming would, or may, occur; in fact, the use of "this one" for the woman appears to imply a continuation in which woman stands in contrast to the animals. Yet caution is in order. To determine whether this is a naming, or is perceived as one, one needs to ask, what is the conventional form in which a naming is normally expressed. To answer this, one appropriately follows a procedure standard in form criticism, namely, to look for occasions in which such an act is narrated. Two such occasions appear in Gen 17:5 and 35:10. In these, the form is, in good declarative style: "your name [is] . . ." In the New Testament one finds: "his name is . . ." (Luke 1:63). Thus there is not a strong stylistic ground for considering Gen 2:23b a naming (unless one argues that a generic naming has a different form).

If one looks for other instances of the passive formula as it appears in Gen 2:23b, or of the virtually equivalent impersonal active form, one discovers that they occur in predictions and in aetiological reports.[8] The latter usage fits well with the content of Gen 2:23b, which is aetiological. By whom is this spoken? The statement is awkward on Adam's lips, because of a third-person reference to him; furthermore, it is followed by an aetiological verse about a man's clinging to his wife, generally attributed to the narrator. The oddity of 2:23b (including an unexpected appearance of the word *ʾîš* for "male," for Adam) can perhaps be explained historically.[9] As it stands in the text, however, it appears to exhibit a phenomenon that often occurs in literature (certainly, in the Bible), i.e., a merging of the perspectives of the narrator and of the story's character. The statement both is and is not made by Adam.

In short, there is an ambiguity in the text. The force and even the source of the statement are in doubt. Lanser's pointing to an anticipation that a naming would occur is correct, but literature thrives on frustrated anticipations. Here a reasonable expectation is only partially fulfilled. Thus Lanser's final conclusion about tensions within the text is supported.

The essays included in this volume show that speech act theory has much to contribute to biblical studies, both on the theoretical level and in regard to the subtle details of the text. One can hope that other studies will draw on the resources of that theory and on the observations contained in the fine individual contributions. The current response has attempted to continue the conversation.

NOTES

[1] Cf. M. H. Abrams (see listing by Patte) on the image of a "mirror" for such a reflection. As is well known in certain circles, V. Lenin insisted (one may judge him old-fashioned here) that human knowledge "reflects" the world, while as a Marxist he also, of course, believed that the purpose of philosophy is not to understand, but to change, the world.

[2] I have discussed this trend elsewhere (see bibliography of White's second essay).

[3] E.g., recent contributions by Brevard Childs, in part reflecting—intentionally or not—the approach of New Criticism.

[4] During 1958/59 I conversed as a colleague with a young philosopher, Nicholas Fotion, who had already absorbed much of Austin's outlook since that was becoming known through lectures, second-hand reports, and writings emanating from his circle. I was struck then by its similarity to form criticism (which, further, I saw in the light of perspectives current in anthropology, especially that of Bronislaw Malinowski, who in part stands behind J. R. Firth, to be mentioned). An early publication (1961) was in large part an attempt to join form criticism with philosophical language analysis, as practiced in a movement which included works by R. M. Hare (influenced by Austin; cf. my note 12 there) and the later Wittgenstein.

[5] In the 1940's, the notable American linguist Zellig Harris began the development of "discourse analysis," which included attention to types of speech and situation (greatly elaborated in later text-linguistic studies, such as in the German end of that movement). Harris, whose area specialty was Canaanite literature, knew, and to some extent had employed, form criticism in the Gunkel tradition; the wording of his project (1952: 3,19-30) makes a connection virtually certain. In the 1950's and beyond, Kenneth Pike (cf. Fotion: 635) constructed an elaborate speech act approach to linguistics that resembles biblical form criticism; he may have come to know this tradition through the theological training he had received or from his involvement in teaching Bible translators. (My autobiographical remarks in note 4, above, illustrate how difficult it can be to trace connections, since some of them are oral.)

[6] Details of these exegeses, in part closely similar to Austin, are to be presented in a forthcoming volume. Even a distinction closely approximating Austin's between illocution and perlocutionary object (using the respective labels *intentio* and *finis*) appears pervasively in medieval exegesis. The relevant classical background includes rhetoric, Stoic analysis of language, and pagan exegesis. Perhaps the earliest known speech act analysis is by Protagoras; as reported by Aristotle (*Poetics*, 1456b), he objected to Homer's "Sing of the wrath, Goddess" being phrased as a command although a request is intended. Apuleius' *Peri Hermeneias*, a Stoic work widely known in the Middle Ages, noted that speech includes not only argumentations, but also commands, praise, etc.

[7] Thus their rules can include both constitutive and regulative ones (assuming that such a distinction can be upheld), contrary to White's wondering whether internal speech acts are

governed only by regulative rules. It is true, however, that a culture may contain special conventions for reported speech acts.

⁸In all three cases in which the form "your [or: his] name [is] . . ." appears, the passive formula "your name [or: he] shall be called . . ." also occurs shortly before—in the first two cases in the negative (for the name to be dropped), in the last on the lips of the named person's mother (prior to the father's use of the other formula). This passive form can be viewed as one of prediction rather than of naming. (It is true that in biblical narratives, many a child's name is given by the mother, but in the Lucan account one does not get the impression that the mother's statement by itself was enough to determine the name.) In addition, the passive formula appears in predictions (Deut 25:10, as a penalty; Jer 19:6, negatively; Isa 35:8; 54:5; 56:7; 58:12; 61:3,6; 62:2,4,12) and in an aetiological report (Eze 20:29). The impersonal active form is used—apparently always—in aetiological reports (Gen 50:11; Josh 5:9, pointable as passive; Judg 2:5; 1 Sam 23:28; 1 Chron 11:7; 2 Chron 20:26; Esth 9:26).

⁹So, Coats: 53 (following Werner Schmidt). Coats: 58 also notes the aetiological use of the formula discussed, although (like most commentators known to me commenting on this) he characterizes the verse as a naming (50, 53).

WORKS CITED

Austin, J. L.
    1975   *How to Do Things With Words*, 2nd ed. Cambridge, MA: Harvard University Press.

Ballmer, Th., and Brennenstuhl, W.
    1981   *Speech Act Classification*. Berlin: Springer Verlag.

Berlin, Isaiah
    1973   *Essays on J. L. Austin*. Oxford: Clarendon Press.

Buss, Martin J.
    1961   "The Language of the Divine 'I'" *Journal of Bible and Religion* 29: 102-107.

Coats, George W.
    1983   *Genesis* (The Forms of Old Testament Literature, I). Grand Rapids, MI: Eerdmans.

Firth, J. R.
    1957   *Papers in Linguistics, 1934-1951*. London: Oxford University Press.

Fotion, N.
    1979   "Speech Activity and Language Use." *Philosophia* 8: 615-638.

Habermas, Jürgen
    1984   *The Theory of Communicative Action*, I. Boston: Beacon Press (German, 1981).

Hampshire, Stuart
    1969   "J. L. Austin, 1911-1960." Pp. 22-23 in *Symposium on J. L. Austin*. Ed. K. T. Fenn. London: Routledge and Kegan Paul.

Harris, Zellig
    1952   "Discourse Analysis," *Language* 28: 1-30.

Tucker, Gene M.
    1971   *Form Criticism of the Old Testament*. Philadelphia: Fortress Press.

Warnock, G. J.
    1969   "John Langshaw Austin, A Biographical Sketch." Pp. 3-21 in *Symposium on J. L. Austin*. Ed. K. T. Fenn. London: Routledge and Kegan Paul.

SPEAKING OF BELIEVING IN GENESIS 2-3

Robert Detweiler
Emory University

Susan S. Lanser is disturbed—and rightly so—that Phyllis Trible and Mieke Bal in treating "the Bible as literature" assume the formalist approach to be *the* literary approach, as if it were the only one, and wishes to show the possibility of a speech act approach to Genesis 2-3 as an alternative to their formalism, an alternative that could provide a more effective, non-sexist reading of that passage. I would like to extend Lanser's concern in a related yet somewhat different direction and argue that the choice of the approach to this passage should also be determined by an awareness of *what kind* of literature Genesis 2-3 is. There are, obviously, different kinds of literature just as there are different kinds of interpretive modes for the literature, and the kind of literature at hand can help to determine the kind of interpretation. I am calling attention to genre as part of the context in which language is used—literary language in this case—that makes a difference. I am particularly concerned with what Lanser articulates but does not elaborate on toward the end of her essay: "To some extent, in part according to the reader's own self-consciousness, everyone brings cultural and personal contexts to the act of reading—from the ways in which, say, I understand gender relations or the meanings of specific words to my conviction that the Bible can or cannot protray a sexist God. It is not that such assumptions and beliefs do anything so simple as to 'bias' the reader; rather, they operate as a kind of grid that obscures certain meanings and brings others to the foreground" (p. 77).

Deciding what kind of literature Genesis 2-3 is is not all that simple, and in describing why it is not we shall see why it matters to make the attempt. One can, for a start, identify the passage as a traditional sacred text, which immediately raises the question of how the present-day reader responds to it. Does she believe in it as a sacred text for herself, one that makes certain fiduciary demands on her and her interpretive community, or does she encounter it as a historical-cultural document with which she can deal more or less disinterestedly, although perhaps in terms of academic concerns that might translate indirectly into personal values? In speech act terms, does this text consist of locutionary, illocutionary, or even perlocutionary statements for the modern reader? It is not enough to characterize the text in terms of the performative, constative, or persuasive nature of its statements as these would have appeared to an "original" audience; one must also be aware of how these statements impress us as modern readers. Thus for Trible, for whom, as Lanser says, Genesis 2-3 has theological import, its statements are constative and performative. In fact, because she is a scholar with theological and feminist commitments and thus deals with the text in an intensely ideological way, it even has in some fashion perlocutionary resonance for her. The text seems to be less "crucial" for Bal, whose interest in it is feminist-semiotic, and as a result she employs it mainly for its locutionary qualities, interpreting its information to explain the evolution of female character in narrative and thus making it part of her illocutionary effort that exploits the text but does not necessarily make it a part of her ideology. Lanser herself has still more distance on Genesis 2-3 as a sacred text, employing it as the background for illustrating the flawed use of it by others and in order to suggest the need for greater hermeneutical sophistication.

My line of argument thus far may seem inconsequential, until one recognizes that Trible especially, but also Bal, in some sense borrow from or depend on the sacred textuality of Genesis 2-3 for their positions. To put it oversimply: if Trible did not believe in some sort of authority inherent in the Genesis text, why would she bother to argue against its real or attributed sexism? Or in other words, why would the text *matter* in a theological rhetoric of sexuality if it did not already function as a foundational (i.e., authoritative) text? This privileged status given to the Genesis text by Trible is accepted by Bal, at least to the degree that she takes it seriously as the source for the origin of an important narratological moment—the emergence of female character. Lanser, however, seems interested in the text mainly as the context for literary critical argument; one could not gather from her essay a reverence for the text that Trible displays and Bal reflects.

What difference does this attitude toward the text's ideological value make? I can respond by returning to genre. A sacred text that one does not believe in is often called a myth, and indeed, Genesis 2-3 as part of a narrative of cosmogany and anthropogany (and including elements of folktale and legend) can properly be called mythic. Although Trible focuses on the poetry of Genesis 2-3, she is clearly aware of the mythic status of the text (poetry and myth are not mutually exclusive generic forms). In what way then can she believe in this text and find interpreted meaning for our age? One answer is that this is *our* myth, a sacred story that we as a particular interpretive community may no longer literally believe yet still value as retaining a strong residue of meaning/truth value, versus the myths of others, which our interpretive community has never accepted as sacred stories and which we tend not to interpret for their "existential" meaning. Trible likely views Genesis 2-3 as *our* myth that has strong residual value. How does she construe her interpretive task as the nurturing or recovering of this value? She assumes a sufficient agreement by the rest of the interpretive community regarding the high status of the biblical text: we all (or most of us) confess that, although we do not read Genesis 2-3 as a factual/historical account, we nonetheless find in it elements of a belief system, an ideology, that has strongly informed our own, so that in the millenia-long dialogue with this text we locate a good part of our cultural identity. For Trible, as a Christian theologian, that attitude must have a more acute aspect. Genesis 2-3, although mythic, is still the start of salvation history, the record of a people's faith in a redemptive God that at some point merges with the documents and discourse of modern Christian faith. Thus for Trible her interpretation of Genesis 2-3 matters doubly. The test's actual or attributed sexism needs to be corrected in order to correct a distortion in our cultural heritage, and to encourage a more enlightened, balanced, and just Christian belief.

For Bal and for Lanser the authority of the Genesis text as source of cultural identify is—as far as we can tell from their writing—all that matters. That Genesis 2-3 is part of the cosmogany and anthropogany of Hebrew mythology poses no problems of belief for them, for they are not concerned about theological matters. In fact, their interpretations, in a way, "recuperate" the text for those uninterested in its theological dimension, Bal by showing its narratological import, and Lanser by demonstrating its utility for hermeneutical strategies. In other words, they suggest a cultural value of Genesis to a secular readership (or better said, non-readership) by placing it significantly in the context of literary-hermenetical study and, in the process, in the context of gender study. To learn that Genesis 2-3 has important mythic things to say about human sexual relationships, via narratological and hermeneutical grids, is to appreciate it, culturally, socially, and personally, anew.

But—to return to genre identification one more time—Genesis 2-3 is not only sacred text and myth. It is also narrative fiction. It has setting, plot, characterization, diegesis and mimesis (*qua* telling and showing), dialogue, and point of view. Trible's thorough, and often brilliant, treatment of the text in *God and the Rhetoric of Sexuality*, both exploits and—curiously—ignores its fictionality. Bal, of course, stresses the "genesis" of female character, but does not go on to show how this originary moment has significantly influenced the history of fiction. Neither Trible nor Bal makes explicit why this narrative featuring invented characters, actions, etc. should be taken so seriously for purposes of religious faith and cultural values, and it is at this point that I would locate the *aporia* of their reading, "the point that unravels the argument" (75). Lanser, on the other hand, sets the stage for an explanation of why this text as fiction remains meaningful to modern readers by engaging speech act theory, and I would like to follow through on her preview.

Actually, Lanser has gone much further in this effort in an appendix to her 1981 book, *The Narrative Act*, called, "Speech Act Theory and the Status of Fictional Discourse," and I will make extensive use of this text. Here Lanser corrects what she considers false assumptions of speech act theory, that "only historical or factual discourse is referential, that only referential discourse has illocutionary force, and that illocutionary action assumes a direct relationship between sender and receiver on which the force of the utterance is built. These assumptions have also involved a confusion between literature and fiction that must be untangled in order for the status of discourse that is both literary and fictional to be understood" (284). She goes on, following Mary Louise Pratt, to identify literary texts as "display texts" that function via "Cultural communication [that] operates through four codes: *instruction* (essay), *suggestion* (lyricism, association), *information* (history and biography), and *fiction* (example). Fiction is the reporting of events involving nonhistorical characters and alternative worlds" (284-5). Speech act theory has not adequately circumscribed fictional utterances, Lanser maintains, but has viewed them as deviant from some illocutionary norm. To John Searle's five categories of illocutionary activity (representatives, directives, commissives, expressives, and declaratives) she proposes adding a sixth class of speech acts, what she calls "hypotheticals." These are distinguishable by their context from other categories and can function "on a kind of 'semireferential' plane" (290). It is fictional speech acts, of course, that are hypotheticals and that guide us in constructing the "alternative worlds" of novel and story. In our erecting of these alternative worlds which parallel the real and historical one we are able to reflect on the real world and see it more clearly, and *because* we know that the author of the fictional text wants us to take his work seriously as "ideological instruction" (293), we apply the "lesson" of the alternative world, which we see clearly, to the murkiness of the real world in the hope of illuminating it. Just how this is done Lanser does not explain: "What remains to be explored, then, is the means by which we 'disbelieve' in order to 'believe,' the mechanisms that transform hypothetical speech acts into an alternative world with all the force and power of 'reality,' indeed, with perhaps more transformative potential than historical fact" (293-4).

Is Genesis 2-3 fictive utterance and a hypothetical? It is indeed, and one reason we know it is that we can build through it via a series of transformational relationships with the real world (what Lanser calls "formal realism" and "evaluative illocutions" 292) an alternative world that encourages us to understand and evaluate our historical existence.

Trible, Bal, and Lanser all do their interpretations on the basis of the assumption that the Genesis text is such an alternative world, but only Lanser deals self-consciously with this fictionality. Because Trible and Bal do not distinguish between the illocutionary acts *in* the text and those performed by the author(s) *of* the text, their arguments on the text's sexism conflict with each other and lose force. Making this distinction with the Genesis text is especially crucial because of its threefold nature as sacred text, myth, and fiction. Although we recognize it as a fiction, yet assign it high status as a sacred text with at least residual power in our secular world (as *our* myth, in other words), its authors and its ancient-world audience considered it to be "real"—direct, referential discourse—as indeed a good number of conservative Christians still do. This disharmony between what the text reveals itself to be and what its authors intended it to be (and what its ancient and some modern reponders thought/think it to be) ought to provoke a hermenutics of cultural communication. Because interpreters such as Trible do not take their interpretations through the process of disbelieving in order to believe, naive referentialty becomes conflated with ideology, and much of the text's subtle power is left unappreciated.

How can one then comprehend the process whereby we disbelieve in order to believe? Lanser projects "The expansion of speech act theory to encompass ficitional discourse and literary texts" (294) as one avenue. I would like to propose, briefly, another possibility that could be fairly easily joined to speech act theory: the work of "segmentation" undertaken on the "writerly text" as described by Kaja Silverman in *The Subject of Semiotics*. Silverman borrows the concepts of the "readerly" and "writerly" texts (*texte lisible* and *texte scriptible*) from Roland Barthes' S/Z and demonstrates, in her attention to the *texte scriptible*, how such a focus and attitude can explode a text and make it available to, among other things, the reader's subjectivity and cultural orientation.[1] The writerly text provides a concept of reading radically different from the traditional one. As Silverman puts it, it "comes into existence as an archaeological dig at the site of a classic text. It exhumes the cultural voices or codes responsible for the latter's enunciation, and in the process it discovers multiplicity instead of consistency, and signifying flux instead of stable meaning. The writerly text is one which the reader has obliged to reveal the terms of its own construction, one which has been made available as discourse instead of as a transparent poetic, novelistic, or cinematic fiction" (246). This reconstitution of the text as discourse undertakes energetically, it seems to me, what speech act theorists have proposed timidly. Its stress is precisely on how we disbelieve to believe by refusing empathy with the test's fictionality and instead relentlessly laying bare each device that attempts to provide referentiality. Barthes' strategy for exposing and demystifying these devices is to proceed via the intelligence of five "codes" (the semic, hermaneutic, proairetic, symbolic, and cultural) that constantly push the reader to a deeper and deeper awareness of the text's artifice—and of the artifice of our reconstitution of it. "The writerly text replaces the concepts of 'product' and 'structure' with those of 'process' and segmentation.' These substitutions effect a profound transformation in the experience of textuality. Whereas the notion of the text as product implies a reader or viewer who functions as a passive consumer, that of process suggests instead a reader or viewer who participates in an on-going manufacture of meaning, an activity without a final goal or resting place. Similarly, whereas the notion of structure implies a kind of seamlessness or transparency, that of segmentation draws attention not only to the seams which join together the pieces which make up the whole, but to the ways in which the former exceed the latter" (247). Segmentation produces a drastic fragmentation of the text that is systematized but not harmonized or unified by the codes. Rather, "The writerly text . . . draws attention to itself as a series of cultural utterances. It does this by permitting all of the voices on its premises to be heard, i.e., by tolerating a veritable Babel" (248).

That metaphor from Genesis may signal an apt point to conclude my commentary. I cannot illustrate here how Barthes' codes might be engaged to reread Genesis 2-3 as a writerly text and in a way that would disclose its "agendas," its subjectivity and cultural self-consciousness, the process of attempting which would reveal my own agendas. But I am confident that it could be done, and I think that it *should* be done with the contributions of speech act theory in mind, in order to show how our ideologies masquerading as fictions can be disclosed, and appreciated, as *real* fictions.

NOTES

[1] Lanser in *The Narrative Act* (114n) states her lack of confidence in the writerly text as a viable concept. Silverman (248) sees point of view (the study of which is the focus of Lanser's book) as a device that promotes closure—leaves the reader under the influence of the text's fictionality—rather than segmentation that would expose the fictionality. Nevertheless, I do not believe that Lanser and Silverman are very far apart in their research.

WORKS CITED

Barthes, Roland
    1974   *S/Z*. Tr. Richard Miller. New York: Hill and Wang.
Lanser, Susan S.
    1981   *The Narrative Act: Point of View in Prose Fiction*. Princeton: Princeton University Press

Pratt, Mary Louise
    1977   *Toward a Speech Act Theory of Literary Discourse.* Bloomington: Indiana University Press.

Searle, John
    1969   *Speech Acts: An Essay in the Philosophy of Language.* London: Cambridge University Press.

Silverman, Kaja
    1983   *The Subject of Semiotics.* New York and Oxford: Oxford University Press.

Trible, Phyllis
    1978   *God and the Rhetoric of Sexuality.* Philadelphia: Fortress Press.

PHILOSOPHY OF LANGUAGE IN THE SERVICE OF RELIGIOUS STUDIES

Charles E. Jarrett
Camden College of Arts and Sciences
Rutgers University

Introduction

The authors of these essays are involved in an exploration of new territory, and their aim is to shed light on religious speech and action by making use of relatively recent developments in the philosophy of language. They are also, for the most part, cautious in their claims about what can be expected from the application of philosophical work on language to religious studies, despite their conviction that something of significance, perhaps even a key, will be uncovered as the enterprise proceeds. None of them has, nor claims to have, a complete answer to the question of what is to be learned by putting philosophy to work in this way.

The philosophical developments on which the present enterprise depends have occurred over the past quarter century and have become known as "Speech Act Theory". J. L. Austin is rightly seen as the creator of the field, and virtually all subsequent work is indebted to his *How To Do Things With Words* (1962). The contributors to this volume rely almost exclusively on Austin's work (1961, 1962, 1962a), and on the modifications and extensions of it set out by John Searle (1969, 1974, 1985).

I share with the contributors the belief that speech act theory can be used to make significant advances in our understanding of religious discourse. It is my hope that by addressing the problems I raise, the principle theses set forth in this volume can be clarified and extended in important ways, and thus our understanding of speech in a religious context can be deepened.

My procedure here has been to provide separate comments on each author's contribution, although on one occasion I offer some ideas of my own. This yields the following divisions: (i) Hancher on Divine Illocutions; (ii) Grimes on Ritual Infelicities; (iii) External Infelicities and the

Diversity of Viewpoints; (iv) Lanser and Feminist Interpretations; (v) Patte on the Speech Act Approach; (vi) White on the Value of Speech Act Theory. Each section is relatively self-contained, and variation in their length is a reflection more of my interests than of a judgement of the merits of the papers reviewed.

(i) Hancher on Divine Illocutions

Michael Hancher's contribution begins with a question about the classification of divine utterances, such as "Fiat lux" in Genesis. What kind of illocutionary act is being reported here? Hancher's thesis is that this and similar pronouncements cannot be (Searlean) directives, taken as "attempts . . . to get the hearer to do something." For such attempts, unlike God's, might fail, and there are no hearers at the beginning of Genesis. We are thus invited to accept Searle's claim that "Fiat lux" is a declaration, where such utterances (by definition) ". . . bring about some alteration in the status or condition of the referred to object or objects solely in virtue of the fact that the declaration has been successfully performed."

Hancher's reasoning here is not completely transparent. Why is it that necessary as opposed to contingent 'obedience' disqualifies "Fiat lux" as a directive? And if this is so, why is an analogue of it not also true? For necessary as opposed to contingent truth *does* characterize some *statements*.

The absence of hearers is a stronger reason. But if we are to proceed this far, why not farther? Hancher does not address the question of how God can literally speak at all, nor whether, if He does, He must then have a body. And in what language could He have spoken? These, and a good many other questions, presumably help to motivate the traditional doctrine, according to which God's 'speech' in Genesis is actually a *thought* produced by a nonphysical being or substance. This would evidently be thought in no (human) language.

Various misunderstandings and inadequate criticisms of Austin's work by Barthes, Benveniste, and Derrida, are then pointed out by Hancher. There are two (very) small puzzles here. First, it is claimed that when Barthes wrote "The Death of the Author," (*published* in 1968), Austin had published relatively little about speech acts, although Barthes had read Benveniste's *Problems in General Linguistics* (1966). This is a puzzle because virtually everything of Austin's that is now in print was published by 1962. (Austin's *How to Do Things with Words* was published posthumously in 1962, as was *Sense and Sensibilia*, while *Philosophical Papers* appeared in 1961. "Performatif—Constatif", incidentally, was published in *Cahiers de Royaumont, Philosophie No. IV, La Philosophie Analytique* in 1962. This is the text of a lecture given at Royaumont in 1958.¹) Secondly, in showing that "self-reflexivity" is not a sufficient mark of performative utterances, Hancher considers "I whisper this to you" (whispered to you), and holds that "nobody would be tempted to call the act a performative utterance". This seems wrong primarily because (as noted by Hancher) the constative-performative distinction was replaced by the locutionary-illocutionary distinction. Hancher's point about "whispering" is correct, however: it indicates the manner in which an act is performed, not a special category of illocutionary act. But why the complications? "I was there yesterday" or "I am now speaking in English," would apparently suit his purposes just as well.

(iii) Grimes on Ritual Infelicities

Ronald Grimes extends Austin's classification of infelicities and applies it to religious rituals. Austin's discussion is found in Lectures II–IV of *How to Do Things with Words* and has, as Grimes notes, received little attention from those interested in the use of speech act theory in religious studies. According to both Austin and Grimes, however, the notion of infelicity developed by Austin is not limited to speech acts. "Infelicity is an ill to which *all* acts are heir which have the general character of ritual or ceremonial, all *conventional* acts . . ." Although Grimes makes an exception for "breaches" (maintaining that they are found only in speech acts), he seems mistaken in this.

Some misunderstanding of Searle and Austin is found in Grimes' paper, but this is not important, so far as I can see, for the main points that he makes. Thus Grimes writes, "Searle (1969: ch. 5) argues that predication ("saying") is also an act, thus softening Austin's contrast between constatives and performatives." But Austin himself 'softened', and indeed abandonded, the contrast between constatives and performatives (1965: 149), and Searle's notion of predication in Chapter 5 of *Speech Acts* is a notion of "saying or predicating something *of*" a thing, which is neutral between (certain) types of illocutionary force. Thus in *stating* that the cat is white and in *asking* if the cat is white, you predicate whiteness of the cat, according to Searle. Predication (like reference) is in his view an act that cannot occur alone; it ". . . can only occur as part of some illocutionary act" (1969: 124).

This slip, large as it might be in other contexts, does not in the least undermine the contribution made by Grimes in this paper. What he provides is a good start (with a wealth of examples) on the study of how religious rituals can in particular situations go wrong and of how whole procedures (not just their application in particular cases) can be criticized. The classificatory scheme he offers *is*, I think, a useful extension of Austin's work, although, as Grimes notes, the construction of a taxonomy will often enough raise more questions than it answers. Chief among these is what Grimes calls "the problem of the point of view. Who—participant or observer—is to decide whether procedures fail, and if they do, what sort of infelicity has been committed?" Of course participants and observers *will* decide, no doubt in conflicting ways, as when the participant is an aborigine engaged in a rain dance, and the observer is an ivy-league sociologist. Grimes denies that a solution to this problem is possible ("if one imagines there is some universal, meta-ritualistic criterion which . . . can be used to measure every rite cross-culturally"), but he does not, I presume, imply by this that rain dances sometimes cause rain. The question he then addresses is what sort of criticism is "most effective".

But what acts or 'procedures' *are* subject to infelicity? Austin spoke of acts that "have the general character of ritual or ceremonial—that is, all conventional acts," but he provided almost no further elucidation. Similarly Grimes speaks of "rites" and "rituals" with little more said than that this is an 'impure' genre (like opera) and a 'multifold phenomenon'. He thus leaves it open whether, for example, a tennis match, the passing of the collection plate, or the reshelving of library books are rituals.

(iv) External Infelicities and the Diversity of Viewpoints

At least three different distinctions are relevant to the notion of "ritual criticism", although all of them cut across the ritual–non-ritual distinction. There is, first, a distinction between acts that are communicative and those that are not. When you put Aristotle's collected works back on the shelf, you are no doubt doing something with words, but you are not performing a speech act, and you are not communicating with anyone. Even so, there may of course be a 'conventional' way of doing it, a 'conventional' place to put it, and a prescribed procedure to follow. If, in contrast, you say to someone, "Aristotle goes on the top shelf," or if you make gestures to indicate that this book is to go there, then you have (when all goes right) communicated. So too, presumably, if you take the collection plate around during church services, you are making a request (and communicating), whether you say anthing or not.

A second distinction is between acts that are, as we might put it, 'symbolic' and those that are not. Thus the setting up of a manger scene at Christmas might for Christians symbolize the birth of Christ and various events that occurred long ago, while the same manger set, discovered in an attic by atheists or children, might be arranged with no such meaning. So also the gestures made in a dance might or might not depict some event or ancient story, as a Porsche might or might not be purchased for its 'symbolic value'.

There is, finally, a distinction between acts that can, and those that cannot, be performed in the absence of some relatively closed and discrete framework, such as (paradigmatically) a system of rules. Kicking a ball and kicking a fieldgoal illustrate the difference, as do moving a wooden figure to a certain square and checkmating your opponent. In these examples, as in others where highly structured games are involved, a specialized concept or description is in effect defined by the rules. There are at least two reasons why Searle's distinction between constitutive and regulative rules (1965:33–42) is important for a study of ritual. First a concept (or act-description) that is *defined* in relation to a system of rules can only be correctly applied when the actors conceive of themselves as following those rules. You can't hit a triple (in the relevant sense) unless you are playing ball, and you aren't playing ball unless you (and others) are (consciously) acting in accordance with the rules. Secondly, the system of rules, or what I would prefer to call the 'framework' of the activity, standardly sets out a specialized notion of assessment, or of success and failure, and hence provides an 'internal' concept of infelicity. A strike-out is (from one team's viewpoint) an infelicity, but it is one that can be found only within this specialized, rule-governed activity.

The three distinctions that are (very roughly) outlined here are related, no doubt in complex ways, to each other and to the notion of a ritual. It seems, clear, for example, that communicative acts might or might not be symbolic, in the intended sense, and that many non-symbolic acts are non-communicative. It is less clear, however, whether all symbolic acts are communicative. However this may be, it seems important to draw these distinctions (or similar ones), because of the connections between them and the ways in which 'ritual acts' can go wrong. In addition, the question whether an act is communicative or symbolic at all must surely be answered in large measure by reference to the intentions and beliefs of the actor (and, we must add, of fellow participants and 'intended audiences', if there are any). For these concepts are an essential part, if not the whole, of the bridge between an outstretched arm and a left-turn signal, and between an Austinian rheme and pheme. (This is so even if the bridge must also proceed via some notion of convention.[2]) In addition, the 'rule dependent' classification of an act requires, as we have seen, a more or less complex set of beliefs and intentions on the part of the actor or actors. However detailed your description of the game in terms of "mere motions", you will have omitted an essential element of "what is going on" if you fail to note how the players themselves conceive of their acts and if you fail to characterize their acts as 'rule-governed.'

It *seems* evident (although even this has been disputed[3]) that an act can be classified in different ways and that these descriptions are often hierarchically related. There are different 'levels' of description. You are putting marks on paper, writing a name, signing a check, and paying a bill all at once, and within this hierarchy there are different types of 'infelicity'. You cannot, in a fairly natural sense, misspell marks, although you can misspell your name, for example. Explicit development of the concept of different 'levels' of description can be expected, I think, to advance our understanding of ritual infelcitiy.

I indicated above that systems of rules, or 'frameworks', can be more or less 'discrete' or isolated from each other, and from other activities. In baseball, chess, and other highly structured games, there is a relatively high degree of 'autonomy' or 'isolation' found in the special concepts defined by the constitutive rules of the game. In other activities, such as travelling somewhere, swimming in a pool, or improvising something on the piano, a relatively small role is played in our description by concepts whose meaning is tied to constitutive rules. The activity itself does not consist essentially in following rules. But even for activities whose very being (or conception) is brought into existence by rules, the isolation is never complete. For we have concepts (one of the most important of which is that of causality) that invariably connect, or can connect, rule-defined acts with those that are not. In hitting a homer, for example, you may well injure a fan, even if doing so constitutes no official part of baseball.

It is partly *because of* these connections between the 'officially' recognized acts (that is, those characterized in the special 'rule-defined' terms) and more mundane events that no sphere of activity can immunize itself against external criticism or evaluation. Thus aside from the set of purposes, and hence types of failure, that arise with a rule-defined activity such as tennis, and aside from the 'internally defined' infelicities (such as "service faults" and shots that are "out"), 'external' infelicities are always possible. A rain dance or a sacrifice may be regarded as a successful appeal to the gods, as a backhand volley may be regarded as 'in', but there can be no guarantee—from within officialdom—that this is really so or really good.

The distinction between 'internal' and 'external' infelicities, and between an interna'. and external point of view, has received a good deal of attention in recent years in the philosophy of law. The latter distinction, in particular, has been put to extensive use by H. L. A. Hart (1961; also 1948–49), whose work is largely within (and is a partial progenitor of) 'ordinary language philosophy'.

We can perhaps illuminate the 'problem of the point of view' in understanding religious rituals by considering the legal analogue. The concept of a 'valid law', for example, seems clearly relative to a given time and place. That the laws of a given jurisdiction change and that there are different jurisdictions is unproblematic, since the laws that were valid in the U.S. in 1840 are not the same as those that are now valid, nor are they the same as those recognized in the Soviet Union. Now Hart has stressed the idea that different legal systems have different 'criteria of validity', found in the standards to which the officials of the system appeal. These standards, called 'secondary rules', are used by the officials to determine what the 'primary rules of obligation' actually are. Hart maintains further that for a legal system to exist, the officials of the system must *accept*, or take the *internal point of view* toward, the secondary rules, even if ordinary citizens, for their part, merely obey (without 'accepting') the primary rules.

Hart thus thinks of a legal system as a relatively closed (two-tiered) system of rules, where each system contains within itself the criteria for determining which rules the populace will be required to obey. In his view, there is no necessary connection between the laws recognized as valid in some system and the requirements of (true) morality. The concept of a legal obligation is not a species of, nor is it necessarily connected with, the concept of what is morally required.

A legal system thus defines a notion of infelicity within itself, as when the U.S. Supreme Court decided that Texas' abortion statute violated the Constitution, and hence was not 'valid law'. But in addition to this, there are 'external' standards—provided by the ideals of a universal moral code—by which law can be criticized on non-legal grounds.

A similar position could of course be taken concerning religious ritual. Catholic rites will be regarded as 'valid' or 'invalid', successful or infelicitous, from the standpoint of the church, which provides its own standards and thus its own concept of infelicity. But these rites will be looked upon by Hindus much as U.S. law is seen by the Soviets.

There is a sense in which you cannot fully understand a religious rite unless you see it as the participants do. But this does not require that you actually accept their rules; it requires only that you grasp what they are, and see the participants' behavior as governed by them. So too the understanding of a baseball game requires an understanding of the rules of *that* game, and the understanding of the behavior of Americans requires (sometimes) the understanding of U.S. law. Of course, 'Catholic validity' and 'Hindu validity' are distinct, as U.S. law and Soviet law are distinct. But Soviet citizens *can* state (but not *decide* or *determine*) what is required of someone by U.S. law, as well as Americans can, and Hindus as well as Catholics can state what is required of Catholics, and what, according to the Catholic Church, is 'infelicitous'. What, then, is 'the problem of the point of view'?

Part of the problem, no doubt, is that religious rites are engaged in by people with radically different ideas about what really exists, and about what causes what. The ivy-league sociologist criticizes the aborigines on the grounds that their dance could not cause rain. Insofar as that is the point of the dance, it cannot succeed. This is 'external' criticism of course, but the sociologist is quite right. Furthermore, problems of this sort are in principle resolvable.

Another part of the problem, however, arises from the fact that religious traditions, like legal systems, do not merely provide a framework for abstract beliefs about the world. They provide a framework for action, and for attitudes and emotions, and they purport to specify or stipulate what should, and what should not, be done. On what grounds could this part of the problem of divergent viewpoints be irresolvable? Moral scepticism or relativism, we might note, would presumably entail the irresolvability thesis, and indeed it is doubtful that in their absence the thesis could be supported at all.

Note that Hart's position on the relation between legal and moral obligation contains a serious problem. He holds that these are conceptually distinct, although what is morally required and what is required by a given legal system are (often) partially coextensive. The implications of holding that there are *two* conceptually distinct (and conceptually unrelated) notions of obligation, however, are quite unattractive. It is analogous to holding that there are *two* (temporally unrelated) temporal systems or *two* space-times (with no spatio-temporal relation between them). In a similar way, the thesis that we are subject to *two* normative systems would entail that when one enjoins what the other forbids, no resolution is possible. Without a unitary concept of obligation, we would have to think of ourselves, in such cases, as *two* beings rather than one—a 'legal' being, in this case, and a 'moral' one.

A similar thesis regarding the evalution of religious rituals would likewise be unattractive. The thesis would maintain in effect that Catholic rites are 'catholically required', but of course not 'Hindu-required', and that there is no unitary standpoint from which you can determine whether performance of the rite is, simply, *required* (or good or effective). Without a unitary normative standpoint, however, it seems impossible to think of ourselves as unified beings. That the official's call or the aboriginal description must in some sense be 'valid from its point of view', while the real story (if we could ascertain it) is somehow unable to provide 'legitimate' criticism thus seems to me to require an incoherent conception of ourselves. No specialized arena (such as law and religion) can immunize itself from external assessment; if it were to try do so, it must deny the legitimacy or relevance of 'non-official' evaluative criteria, or else promote a non-unitary conception of ourselves (with irresolvable conflicts contained in our very being).

(iv) Lanser and Feminist Interpretations

The contribution by Susan Lanser contrasts 'formalist' and 'use' theories of language, and traces the inadequacies of some recent feminist interpretations of Genesis 2–3 to the former. Her stalking horse is an interpretation set out recently by Phyllis Trible and Mieke Bal, according to which (1) Adam and Eve were created simultaneously (from a neuter being), (2) Eve (or 'woman') is the 'culmination of creation', (3) "woman is treated less severely than the man for disobeying", and (4) the inequality of man and woman arises "as a consequence of disobedience, but not as punishment."

As presented by Lanser, the arguments of Trible and Bal proceed largely from premises about the general properties of the text's language. They point out, for example, that "$hā^{\,\prime}ādām$", which is used to refer to God's first human creation, is a masculine noun, and that grammatical gender is not a certain guide to the actual gender, if any, of the referent. Lanser, in contrast, appeals to speech act theory to explain that the use of a masculine noun (and of masculine pronouns) to refer to a person would naturally be taken to refer to a male, and thus to explain why it was not just a mistake, *pace* Bal, for readers or hearers to infer that the first human being was a man.

A similar argumentative strategy is used by Trible in support of the thesis that the utterance of "she shall be called woman" at 2:23 is not an act of naming. Lanser explains,

> "Her reason is that this verse (2:2), unlike 2:19–20, does not join the verb $qr^{\,\prime}$ (call) with the noun $šēm$ (name), into the phrase "to call the name of." Instead, 2:23 merely uses the verb "to call" . . ."

Appealing again to speech act theory, Lanser correctly points out that the surface structure is an insufficient guide to the type of illocutionary act performed. She also maintains that the difference between "to call" and "to call the name of" is here inconsequential.

Although some readers will think that Lanser's account ascribes one *non-sequitur* after another to Bal and Trible, Lanser's own diagnosis is that the 'formalist' approach to language is itself defective and has mistakenly come to be seen as *the* literary approach. It is as if the understanding of a text could proceed without consideration of a context, and in the absence of context-dependent inferences. I have no quarrel with her main thesis here, nor with her portrayal of the crucial differences between formalist and speech act approaches. These are said to be, in outline, differences in the type of context, and in the extent to which any context, is explicitly used by the interpreter. 'Formalists' have more to say, however, and much of it concerns the utility of the concept of the "zero" or "null-context". Although this dispute is sure to continue, Lanser seems to me to make a good start here in establishing the value of a speech act approach to biblical interpretation.

(v) Patte on the Speech Act Approach

Daniel Patte's contribution to this volume raises a number of important questions about "speech act exegesis", and goes on to list the steps necessary for its development. Although initially skeptical of the speech act approach, he has come to hold that this approach is promising, and indeed necessary.

Patte's exploration of "the interface of speech act theory and biblical exegesis" contains many useful points, only a few of which I will mention here. (i) The mere appropriation of speech act theory (including taxonomies of illocutionary acts) by those who pursue 'traditional exegetical goals' is likely to be much less fruitful than a reconsideration of those goals themselves in light of the 'conceptual framework' of speech act theory. (This lesson is taught from experience with the impact of structural semiotics on exegesis.) (ii) The conceptual framework of speech act theory is the reverse of that of structuralism and semiotics. The latter takes language as a model for understanding the non-linguistic realm, while the former takes non-linguistic phenomena (primarily actions) as a model for understanding linguistic phenomena. (iii) The conceptual shift required by a speech act approach is from viewing "linguistic sequences . . . as expressing actions" to viewing them "in and of themselves as actions", and this approach requires an emphasis on intentionality and subjectivity. (iv) A speech act approach requires that the production and reading of religious texts be viewed as *religious* acts.

Patte's final comments raise an additional important issue. He maintains

> ". . . *religious discourses are peculiar speech acts* which cannot be assimilated to other kinds of speech acts. . . . it might be that what makes a discourse a religious discourse is its characteristic illocutionary points and forces and its characteristic intentionality."

I doubt very much that this is so, however, at least concerning illocutionary forces. Prayers, for example, characteristically contain statements, requests, apologies, expressions of thanks, and so on. And surely an utterance of "God exists" is best regarded as a statement, and is intended to be true (or false), even when the utterance is itself a religious act. I would suggest, then, that while *some* religious utterances may have a unique illocutionary point, not all of them do.

This issue is a large and important one, however, and demands greater consideration than it has yet received. Like the 'logical status' of fictional discourse (Searle, 1979: Ch. 3), the status of religious discourse promises to yield continuing controversy. Patte has advanced matters by raising this and other important issues, and we can hope that a more extensive treatment of them will be forthcoming in the near future.

(vi) White on the Value of Speech Act Theory

Hugh White's contribution begins with an explication of the central problem (and, indeed, apparent dilemma) that has arisen in Biblical studies, especially as encountered within the "New Hermeneutics". His suggestion is that speech act theory offers a promising way of resolving this problem. What is the problem and how can speech act theory help to resolve it? White claims that ". . . the central problem of the new hermeneutics was the relation of literary-historical criticism to theological interpretation." Expressions of this (or a similar) problem by Westermann and Funk are set out, followed by his own exposition:

> "Historical criticism detaches the past from present concerns in order to prevent the distinctive, unique, and even alien features of previous historical periods from being ignored or distorted by the passion to make the past relevant to present circumstances. But the gap that is left between the present and past becomes so immense that the significance of both is threatened by the sea of relativity. Theology, on the other hand, tends to seek either eternal truths, or significance for the present within the transitory events of the past to the extent that the historical uniqueness of the past is eroded."

Here the problem is presented as at least partly a conflict or tension that arises between two apparently distinct enterprises; one of these is sociological or historical, while the other is theological. Elsewhere the difficulty is presented somewhat differently:

> "At the root of the hermeneutical problem lies the practice of historical criticism which attempted to sever the text from the presuppositions and ideology of the critic in order to grant the text its right to historical uniqueness. This method viewed the language of the text as referents of ideas and facts that were peculiar to the world and time of its authorship, and its truth or meaning could only be established . . . through reconstructing the extra-textual historical milieux that provides the referential context which discloses the original meaning of the text and intentions of the author.
> On the other extreme, reflecting the turn away from history toward epistemological primacy of language in text analysis, are the formalist approaches which assume the meaning of the text arises from the internal linguistic/semantic structure of the text itself. Here the view of truth and meaning of the text is the same as in the historical approach; it is the referential content of the text's language which determines its meaning."

The central problem seems here to arise from the conflict or tension between models of textual interpretation that rely primarily on universal or timeless features, and those that rely primarily on particular and variable features, of the text.

There is surely no doubt that the examination of a text will miss a great deal if it relies exclusively on the (general) meaning of the words, along with the syntax, of the language employed. Indexicals, to take one very simple example, must be fleshed out, to say nothing about irony, ambiguity, tacit premises, or speech acts. On the other hand, it is equally impossible to ignore the timeless features of a text, such as the (standard) meaning of a given word in a certain language. The distinction, labelled by Grice (1968) as that between "utterer's meaning" and "timeless meaning" cannot be ignored, despite the difficulties in interpretation to which it gives rise.

Divergences between what a speaker said and what he meant, and (what is not the same) between what his words mean and what he means by them, are commonplace, and create or help to create conflicting interpretations of a text. (Readers will have their own favorite examples, but one of mine is "tanquam", as used by Spinoza in the *Ethica*, Part I, definition 4. This may mean "as" or "as if" and thus the famous 'problem of the attributes' continues to plague contemporary Spinoza scholarship.) Conflicting interpretations are also bound to arise when interpreters are at 'cross-purposes'. A philosopher who reads Kant may do so largely to make use, for his own constructions, of what he finds there, and may well wind up with an interpretation that contains 'slippage'. Kant didn't quite say this, perhaps, but we make better sense of the passage to suppose that this is what it expresses. A 'pure' historian (if such there be) will have little sympathy for such slippage, and will be found typically to focus more closely on variant earlier drafts of the passage, the date of composition, and so on. (The best interpreters combine these interests.) Philosophers standardly read others with a constant concern for evaluation ("Is it true? Is the argument any good? Is it 'philosophically' important?), while historians are for the most part interested in different questions. Of course everyone's account must be accurate, and so when pressed, the philosopher must fall back a bit: this is a 'reconstruction' or, worse yet, this is (merely) what he should have said or meant. If the 'slippage' is too great, and we refuse to say this, we confuse 'interpretation' with our own fantasies.

A theologian who looks at the sacred texts of a different religious tradition is like a Neo-Platonist reading Aristotle. He or she can afford, so to speak, to let the sociologists and historians have their say about what the writer meant, at least up to the point at which the writer *must*—on the basis of theological premises—have said something true or (less ambitiously) believed. The account provided by one writer of another's divinely inspired text or speech can always be regarded as inaccurate, rough, or even false; but if divinity is incompatible with the utterance of falsity or lies, and the speaker is taken to have this status, there is a clear constraint on the attribution of meaning to an utterance. As a last resort, perhaps, it must have been metaphorical.

The situation is significantly different when a theologian examines the sacred texts of his or her own tradition. This is much more like asking a federal judge (informally) what "the establishment of religion" in the First Amendment means than asking a philosopher what Kant meant in a certain passage by "transcendental idealism". For there is no 'official' philosophical answer (even if there is something like that), but there is an 'official' (legal) reading of the First Amendment. When there is, as in law, an authoritative interpretive tradition, the original meaning and intent of the author is only *one* of the factors to be considered in determining "what the text means". This is especially so with texts that are used as a source of norms, for, as often remarked, changing conditions give rise to questions that could not have been envisaged by earlier writers. A standard example of this concerns the 4th Amendment—for the Founding Fathers were not in a position to consider whether, or under what conditions, a wiretap is an unreasonable search.

The interpretation of such ('normative') texts is not so much the search for the original meaning and intent of the author as the construction of meaning for the present. This is one situation in which Barthes' view, quoted by White, is nearly right. But it is not because "there is no factual, historical situation" which can be reconstructed (sometimes) by the historian. It is just that our aim in interpretation is not merely to discover this. Neither law nor theology is history. (Nor, Barthes tells us, is literary criticism.)

The problem that speech act theory is called upon to solve looks initially like the problem of finding a metaphysically neutral description of religious writings. This can be illustrated, somewhat crudely, by asking of a given text whether it contains the word of God or rather the words and beliefs of certain people at a particular stage of history. (Of course there is nothing, in the abstract, to prevent it from doing both.) It is, surely, *sometimes* possible to do this, but it seems to me quite doubtful that a theologian, working on the sacred texts of his own religious tradition, would wish to do this. For it would not, I think, be an attractive position for a theologian to hold what seems to be required by such metaphysically neutral descriptions, namely, a non-cognitivist conception of religious language. Metaphysical neutrality is not, I would think, a theological virtue.

Whether this is so or not, however, what seems to me most to be in need of elucidation in Hugh White's paper is just how speech act theory is to provide the resolution. White writes that the notions of illocutionary force and felicity provide a starting point for a non-metaphysical theory of language and a non-correspondence theory of truth.[5] I do not myself see how a non-metaphysical theory of language is possible, if that means a theory of language that does not elucidate relations between language (or speech) and 'the real world', nor do I see how the theorist is to avoid all committments to the (real) existence of objects (and/or 'stuff') in the world. Even a formal semantics for an artificial language carries 'ontological committments' (via set theory). More to the point, however, we will find in practice, I believe, that the classification of religious speech acts carries metaphysics in its train.

It is important to note, however, that my use of "metaphysical" is much broader than Hugh White's. He has in mind a notion or style of metaphysics that is associated with the later Heidigger, while I use the term to cover nearly any question concerned with what is 'real' or existent, and especially with what is most fundamental.[6]

White also writes,

> ". . .because of the importance of felicity conditions, a speech act theory of literature would have to place biblical literature in its social and even historical context thereby eliminating the dichotomy between literary interpretation, and historical critical analysis. By treating language itself as an act, the dichotomy between literary word, and historical fact is eliminated. . . ."

But thus far it is unclear *how* speech act theory, by placing biblical literature in its social and historical context, is to avoid the criticisms to which the historical-critical analysis has been subjected. To say that language itself is treated as an act does not seem of much help. For there is nothing within speech act theory itself to prevent a language from being regarded as a set of abstract sounds or marks (distinguished from others by a syntax and phonology) with which 'meanings' are associated. A first order logic, with standard syntax and (set-theoretical) semantics, for example, could be taken as a language by speech act theorists. So too, the English word, "dog", can be taken as an abstract object, a type, whose tokens are the various occurrences of a certain sound as used by a population.

It must again be noted, however, that while speech act theory itself does not require a language to be an act, as opposed to a system of abstract objects, one theorist (who, roughly, is within this tradition) has set out a position that is quite congenial to White's program. This is Paul Grice, who has suggested that the concept of utterer's meaning is more basic than that of 'timeless meaning' (1957; 1968). The latter, indeed, is dependent on the former. We can perhaps put this by saying that the concept of what a word in a language means is a construction from what speakers mean when they use the word. This, I suppose, would imply that the notion of a (synchronic, 'timeless') semantics for a language is, in the end, a concept within pragmatics (to use vague, but fashionable, jargon).

Concluding Remarks

Philosophical work on language has had an important and beneficial influence on several fields, including, most notably, linguistics. Indeed, the central issues in pragmatics have arisen largely under the influence of philosophy, as a recent textbook on the subject indicates (Levinson: 1983). Although the suggestion has been made that speech act theory may be superseded by more 'empirically based' studies, and while this is worthy of sustained consideration, present work of this sort does not inspire much confidence. The insights of Austin and Grice are likely to remain with us for a very long time.

Other developments in linguistics and philosophy of language may of course prove useful to those concerned with religious texts and utterances. It is difficult, however, to see what could be more promising than the Austinian framework of locutionary, illocutionary, and perlocutionary acts, and the Gricean notion of a conversational 'maxim' (*Logic and Conversation*), which sets speech within a framework of rational action.

The attempt to put philosophical work to use in religious studies no doubt has a long way to go. These papers stride forth in the most promising direction, and if they do not reach the final destination, they nevertheless take the first crucial steps. We can thus hope that by their efforts the insights of Austin, Searle, and Grice will have as salutary an effect on religious studies as they have already had on linguistics.

NOTES

[1] See the Forward written in 1969 by J. O. Urmson, and G. J. Warnock to Austin (1961).

[2] It is crucial (here and elsewhere) to emphasize the type-token distinction, and the distinction between a general procedure and its use or invocation on a particular occasion. After the convention has been established, an individual who extends his arm may correctly be regarded as having given a left-turn signal, even when no intention to signal is present. But this would not be possible in the absence of the general procedure (or a special arrangement), and the general procedure could not be said to exist if people (generally) did not intend to 'communicate their intention' to turn by extending their arms.

Thus "intention constitutes the bridge" between extended arms and left-turn signals in the sense that the former could not be the latter, without the general use of the gesture to express an intention (and without the recognition of this intention by others). Thus I do not mean to say that Jones, say, gives a left-turn signal when extending his arm if and only if he intends, by extending his arm, to communicate his intention to turn left.

In a similar way, that "dog" means what it does in English, is presumably a reflection of the fact that (some) people have certain intentions rather than others when they use this sound (or these marks). This makes the semantic relations of a language partially dependent on the intentions of speakers (generally), and provides, apparently, the only possible account of semantic change. It does not make the word "dog", as uttered by Jones on this occasion, refer to whatever Jones intends by it, nor does it deny that a given speaker can express a certain intention only because there is an accepted ('conventional') device available to him for this purpose.

[3] See especially Alvin I. Goldman (1976: Ch. 1). For a contrary view, see Donald Davidson (1963). Goldman's position is discussed and rejected by Charles Jarrett (1982). Some issues within speech act theory turn on more general questions concerning action; it might thus be

profitable, for those interested in the speech act approach to religious discourse, to turn next to recent philosophical work on action (and mind).

[4] The dispute between Lanser and these 'formalist' interpreters of Genesis is in some respects not unlike that between Spinoza and Maimonides. Spinoza, one of the founders of modern biblical scholarship, maintained that knowledge of the original language used is crucial. He also held, in agreement with the speech act approach, that a correct interpretation must take into account the identity of the authors, their purposes in writing, their intended audience, and generally the 'occasion' of writing. Maimonides in contrast supposed that you must first know whether it is true before determining whether the bible asserts it. (Cf. Leo Strauss: "In our time scholars generally study the bible in the manner in which they study any other book. As is generally admitted, Spinoza more than any other man laid the foundation for this kind of Biblical study" [Straus, 1965: 35]). Spinoza's general position and his discussion of Maimonides on Biblical interpretation is found in Chapter VII of the *Tractatus Theologico-Politicus* (1951: 98–119). Various questions (such as the authorship of the Pentateuch) are taken up in Chapter VIII, IX, X and XI.

[5] Austin's words may suggest that he did not hold a 'correspondence theory of truth' in *How to do This with Words* but this is at best misleading as a characterization of his view. Truth, according to him, may not be a simple relation, but it does attach to statements in virtue of facts to which, he says at one place, they 'refer.' See p. 148 of *How to Do Things with Words* (1965) and compare "Truth" and "Unfair to Facts" in *Philosophical Papers* (1961).

[6] I am endebted to Hugh White for this clarification.

WORKS CONSULTED

Austin, John L.
    1961   *Philosophical Papers*. Oxford: Oxford University Press.
    1962   *Sense and Sensibilia*. Oxford: Oxford University Press.
    1962a   *How to do Things With Words*. Cambridge, Mass.: Harvard University Press.

Cole, Peter
    1981   *Radical Pragmatics*. New York: Academic Press.

Cole, Peter, ed.
    1975   *Syntax and Semantics 9: Pragmatics*. New York: Academic Press.

Cole, Peter, and Jerry L. Morgan, eds.
    1975   *Syntax and Semantics 3: Speech Acts*. New York: Academic Press.

Davidson, Donald.
    1963   "Actions, Reasons, and Causes." *The Journal of Philosophy* 60: 685–700.

Grice, H. P.
    1957   "Meaning." *The Philosophical Review* 67: 377–388.
    1968   "Utterer's Meaning, Sentence-Meaning and Word-Meaning." *Foundations of Language* 4: 1–18.

           Logic and Conversation. Unpublished manuscript of the William James Lectures, Harvard University. Portions appear in P. Cole and J. L. Morgan (1975), and P. Cole (1981).

Hart, H. L. A.
  1949　"The Ascription of Responsibility and Rights." Pp. 171–194 in *Proceedings of the Aristotelian Society*.
  1961　*The Concept of Law*. Oxford: Oxford University Press.
Goldmann, Alvin I.
  1976　*A Theory of Human Action*. Princeton: Princeton University Press.
Jarrett, Charles E.
  1982　"Materialism." *Philosophy Research Archives* 8: 457–497.
Levinson, Stephen C.
  1983　*Pragmatics*. Cambridge: Cambridge University Press.
Searle, John R.
  1969　*Speech Acts. An Essay in the Philosophy of Language*. Cambridge: Cambridge University Press.
  1979　*Expression and Meaning*. Cambridge: Cambridge University Press.
  1983　*Intentionality*. Cambridge: Cambridge University Press.
Spinoza
  1951　*The Chief Works of Spinoza*. Trans. by R. H. M. Elwes. New York: Dover Publications.
Straus, Leo
  1965　*Spinoza's Critique of Religion*. Trans. by E. M. Sinclair. New York: Schocken Books; original edition Akadamie-Verlag, 1930.

IV.

Bibliographies

ANNOTATED INTRODUCTORY BIBLIOGRAPHY ON SPEECH ACT THEORY

Altieri, Charles
- 1976   "Wittgenstein on Consciousness: A Challenge to the Derriderean Literary Theory." *Modern Language Notes* 91: 1397–1423. Considers the relationship of speech act theory to the philosophy of Wittgenstein.
- 1981   *Act and Quality: A Theory of Literary Meaning and Humanistic Understanding.* Amherst: The University of Massachusetts Press. A wide ranging constructive work of literary theory heavily influenced by Grice, incorporating previous articles on Grice and Wittgenstein.

Austin, J. L.
- 1975   *How to do Things with Words.* 2nd edition. Ed. J. O. Urmson and Marina Sbisa. Cambridge, Mass.: Harvard University Press, 1962, 1975. This is the prime source for the theory of speech acts.
- 1979   *Philosophical Papers.* 3rd edition. Ed. J. O. Urmson, and G. J. Warnock. Oxford: Clarendon Press. Includes important early essay on "Performative Utterances" (1956), "Truth" (1950), and "A Plea for Excuses" (1956–57).

Bach, Kent and Robert M. Harnish
- 1979   *Linguistic Communication and Speech Acts.* Cambridge, Mass." The MIT Press. An authoritative development of speech act theory for application to linguistics.

Benveniste, Émile
- 1966   *Problems in General Linguistics.* Trans. by Mary E. Meek. Coral Gables, Fla.: University of Miami Press. Seminal work in linguistics which has had extensive influence on semiotics and speech act theory in France. The work on pronouns has been especially important.

Bruns, Gerald L.
- 1984   "Hermeneutics." *diacritics* (spring): 22–23. Criticizes Derrida's deconstruction of Austin as "an argument against the tenability of positions as such."

Culler, Jonathan
- 1982   *On Deconstruction: Theory and Criticism after Structuralism.*

Ithica, N.Y.: Cornell University Press. Extensive discussion of the debate between Searle and Derrida, pp. 110–134.

1984   "Problems in the Theory of Fiction." *diacritics*, pp. 2–11. This is a critical review of Pratt (1977) and Lanser (1981) from a deconstructionist viewpoint.

Derrida, Jacques

1977   "Signature Event Context." *Glyph One,* pp. 172–197. Also in *Margins of Philosophy,* by Jacques Derrida. Tr. with notes by Alan Bass. Chicago: The University of Chicago Press; Brighton, Sussex: The Harvester Press Ltd., 1982. Derrida's first major response to the thought of J. L. Austin.

1977a   "Limited Inc a b c . . ." *Glyph Two* (1977); 162–254. Derrida's lengthy and polemical response to Searle's defense of Austin in *Glyph One*.

Ducrot, Oswald

1978   "Structuralisme, énonciation et sémantique." *Poétique* 33: 107–128. Argues as a semanticist for the primacy of the *énonciation* in the production of meaning, and concludes that, "the illocutory aspect of the activity of parole confers on it a necessary reference to itself and permits already the recognition of itself as the indispensible 'primacy' to its structural study."

1980   *Les Mots du Discours.* Paris : Les Éditions de Minuit. Denies that signification is based on the literal sense of statements, but rather on the concrete, context-related occurrance of the word (enunciation), which he ultimately grounds upon illocutory force.

1980   *Dire et ne pas dire: Principles de sémantique linguistique.* Paris: Herman. Uses speech act theory to find a middle position between the Saussurian concept of *langue* and language use by speakers. Analzes the performative function of presupposition, implicit codes, etc. in conversation (esp. p. 70).

Eaton, Marcia

1976   "Speech Acts: A Bibliography." *Centrum* 2 (1976): 57–72. Excellent source of references for the discussion of speech act theory in the field of literary criticism.

Evans, Donald D.

1963   *The Logic of Self-Involvement: A Philosophical Study of Everyday Language with Special Reference to the Christian Use of Language about God as Creator.* London: SCM Press. Argues that the divine Word in the Bible cannot be understood as a propositional statement, but rather as a self-involving act which he understands in terms of Austin theory of illocutionary language. This work has been of seminal importance in the subsequent development of speech act approaches to theology and hermeneutics.

1974   "Faith and Belief." *Religious Studies* 10 (March, June); also in *Faith and Contemporary Epistemologies*, ed. by M. F. Duchesneau. Ottawa: University of Ottawa Press, 1977. He proposes to supplement speech act theory with a theory of analogy.

Fann, K. T., ed.
1969   *Symposium on J. L. Austin*. London: Routledge and Kegan Paul. Biographical essays along with critical responses to Austin's writings by Warnock, Urmson, Searle, Ayer, Strawson and others.

Felman, Shoshana
1983   *The Literary Speech Act: Don Juan with J. L. Austin, or Seduction in Two Languages*. Trans. from the French by Catherine Porter. Ithaca, N.Y.: Cornell University Press, 1980, 1983. A study of Cervantes' *Don Juan* from an Austinian point of view, and a deconstructive use of Austin to analyze his own work, *How to do Things with Words*.

Fish, Stanley E.
1976   "How to do Things with Austin and Searle: Speech Act Theory and Literary Criticism." *Modern Language Notes* 91: 983–1025. Excellent example of the application of speech act theory to a major piece of literature (*Coriolanus*), and critical discussion of theories of Iser, Ohmann, and Searle.

1976a   "Structuralist Homiletics." *Modern Language Notes* 91: 1186–1207. Shows the tension between the syntagmatic and paradigmatic axes. The syntagmatic comes to embody and manifest the paradigmatic: "the meaning it offers is found not at the end of it, in the *fullness* of time, but at every point in its temporal succession." The performative dimensions of the text are thereby brought to light.

1982   "With the Compliments of the Author: Reflections on Austin and Derrida." *Critical Inquiry* 8: 693–721. An in-depth analysis of the issues at stake in the Derrida/Searle debate.

Flahault, Francois
1978   *La parole intermédiare*. Paris: de Seuil. Analyzes the "effect of place" in communication in terms of a system of implicit illocutionary acts. Arguments rely on Ducrot, Benveniste, Austin and Searle.

Fraser, Bruce
1973   "On Accounting for Illocutionary Forces." *Festschrift for Morris Halle*. Eds. Stephen R. Anderson, and P. Kiparsky. N.Y.: Holt

Rinehart and Winston. Uses Grice to develop formal definition of illocutionary force.

Fowler, Roger
1981 *Literature as Social Discourse: The Practice of Linguistic Criticism*. Bloomington: University of Indiana Press. Uses speech act theory to analyze the "interpersonal-interactional-discursive dimensions of literary texts" especially with reference to the verbal creation of the ideal reader and the function of pronouns (esp. pp. 80–90.) Proposes a form of modal analysis of narratives based on a "unified modal-illocutionary theory" (see p. 124).

Fuessel, K.
1982 *Sprache, Religion, Ideologie: Von einer sprachanalytischen zu einer materialischen theologie*. Frankfort am Maine. Bern: Peter Lang Verlag. One chapter deals with theories of language use, and the philosophy of J. L. Austin.

Gasché, Rodolphe
1981 "'Setzung' and 'Übersetzung': Notes on Paul de Man." *Diacritics* 11: 36–57. Argues for the self-reflexivity of speech acts, and explicates the use de Man has made of speech act theory in his *Allegories of Reading*.

Grabner-Haider, Anton
1975 *Glaubensprache: Ihre Struktur und Anwendbarkeit in Verkundigung und Theologie*. Basel, Wien, Frieburg: Herder. Pp. 82–92 deals with the logic of speech acts. Austin, Wittgenstein and others are utilized.

Gottfried, Gabriel
1975 *Fiktion und Wahrheit: Eine Semantische Theorie de Literatur*. Stuttgart-Bad Cannstat: Friedrich Fromman Verlag. Analyzes the fictional narrative using speech act theory to define more precisely the intentional and conventional character of language as opposed to ontological views of language (Fregge). He denies that there must be particular sets of objects called 'fictional objects' to account for non-referential language, and proposes a typology of speech according to language use, grounding truth claims ultimately in the intentions of the primary speaker.

Graff, Gerald
1979 *Literature Against Itself: Literary Ideas in Modern Society*. Chicago: University of Chicago Press. Offers a critique of literary applications of speech act theory.

Grice, H. Paul
1975 "Logic and Conversation." In Cole, Peter and Jerry L. Morgan. *Speech Acts. Syntax and Semantics* 3: 41–58. A work of fundamental importance to the present discussion of speech act the-

ory and literature. The theories of Austin are modified and extended to illuminate a broad range of phenomena which account for the movement of ordinary conversation.

Hancher, Michael
- 1977 "Beyond a Speech-Act Theory of Literary Discourse." *Modern Language Notes* 92: 1081–1098. An important critique of Mary Louise Pratt's work, *Toward a Speech Act theory of Literary Discourse*.
- 1983 "Pragmatics in Wonderland." In *Rhetoric, Literature, and Interpretation*. Ed. by Steven Mailloux. *Bucknell Review* 28: 165–184. The theories of Austin and Searle are expanded by more recent investigations in pragmatics which illuminate the witty dialogue of *Alice in Wonderland*.

Iser, Wolfgang
- 1971 "Indeterminacy and the Reader's Response." Pp. 1–47 in *Prose Fiction: Aspects of Narrative*. Ed. J. Hillis Miller. N.Y. and London: Columbia University Press. The literary text falls into Austin's category of performative utterance since it does not intend to describe something which is outside of itself, but through an element of indeterminacy, to evoke a response from the reader. Discusses Thackery, Fielding, Joyce and Beckett.

Johnson, Barbara.
- 1980 *The Critical Difference: Essays in the Contemporary Rhetoric of Reading*. Baltimore: Johns Hopkins University Press. Rev. *Modern Language Notes* 96 (1981): 1163–1168. Essays on a number of critical (Barthes) and fictional works, e.g. a study of the homology in *Billy Budd* between the incompatibility of being and doing and of constative and performative language.

Just, Wolf-Dieter
- 1975 *Religioese Sprache and analytische Philosophie: Sinn und Unsinn religioeser Aussagen*. Stuttgart: W. Kohlhammer. A Comprehensive discussion of ordinary language philosophers, Braithwaite, Hare, Wittgenstein, Wisdom, Ramsey and Austin written from the viewpoint of logical positivism.

Kerbrat-Orecchioni, Catherine.
- 1977 *La Connotation*. Lyon: Presses Universitaires de Lyon. A careful linguistic study of connotation from the viewpoint of the centrality of the enunciation; she ultimately relates connotation to implicit illocutory values which are grafted onto the explicit meanings.

Lanser, Susan Sniader
- 1981 *The Narrative Act: Point of View in Prose Fiction*. Princeton: Princeton University Press. She creates a conception of the

literary act in which the literary form and the social and ideological context of the writer are brought together by a theory of point of view which makes use of Jacobson's communication model to analyze the context, and speech act theory (especially Grice's theory of conversational implicature) to connect the novelistic discourse to this context.

Larson, Gerald J.
1978 "Prolegomenon to a Theory of Religion." *Journal of the American Academy of Religion* 46: 443–465. Utilizes Wittgenstein, Austin and Umberto Eco to develop definitions of religion, religious studies and religions.

Lentricchia, Frank
1980 *After the New Criticism*. Chicago: The University of Chicago Press. Excellent survey of literary theory from existentialism through post-structuralism, focusing particularly on Frye, Hirsch, de Man and Bloom. Concludes with sympathy for Foucault's position.

Lecointre, Simone and Jean Le Galliot
1973 "le Je(u) de L'énonciation." *Langages* 31: 64–79. Beginning with Benveniste's study of pronouns, proposes a method of narrative analysis which hinges upon the performative functions of allocutions within the text and between the text and the reader.

Man, Paul de
1977 "The Purloined Ribbon" *Glyph One* (1977): 28–49. Brings to light the tension between the cognitive character of guilt, and the performative character of the excuse in Rousseau's confession.

Manley, Lawrence
1981 "Concepts of Convention and Models of Critical Discourse." *New Literary History* 13: 31–52. The tension between nature and convention is parallelled by the tension between the literary system and the individual work. So formalisms either seek to extract the universal and natural from the relative and conventional, or to seek the signs of the individual uniqueness which diverges from the conventional.

Margolis, Joseph
1979 "Literature and Speech Acts." *Philosophy and Literature* 3: 39–52. Astute philosophical criticism of Pratt and Ohmann regarding the definitions of the various literary speech acts, and the lack of genuine constraints surrounding them which would qualify them as illocutionary acts.

Marin, Louis
1976 "Remarques Critiques sur l'énonciation: La Question du Pré-

sent dans le discours." *Modern Language Notes* 91: 939–951. Amplifies Benveniste's concept of pronouns. The I is the point of meeting between the coherent system of discourse (*la langue*) and the act of speech (*la parole*) and this conjunction is effectuated dialogically.

Morse, Christopher
1979 *The Logic of Promise in Moltmann's Theology.* Philadelphia: Fortress Press. Morse applies the perspectives of Evans, Searle and others to the concept of the promise in J. Moltmann's theology in order to clarify the relation of revelation to ordinary language and to narration. "Revelatory narrative is promissory narration." Narration is treated only in terms of the general features of historical narrative writing.

Ohmann, Richard
1973 "Literature as Act." Pp. 81–108 in *Approaches to Poetics*, Selected Papers from the English Institute, ed. by S. Chatman. N.Y., London: Columbia University Press. Groundbreaking study which applies speech act theory to literature, relying upon the concept of mimesis.

Ortigues, Edmund
1978 *Le Discours et le Symbole.* New edition. Aubier: Éditions Montaigne. Fundamental study of the constitutive function of language. "Language, inasmuch as it is constitutive of properly human society, is the mediating form between expression and signification."

Polk, Timothy
1984 *The Prophetic Persona: Jeremiah and the Language of the Self. Journal for the Study of the Old Testament: Supplement Series* 32. Sheffield, England: JSOT Press. Applies the general concept of performative language as developed by Austin and Donald Evans to the language of the confessions of Jeremiah.

Porter, Joseph A.
1986 Pragmatics for Criticism: Two Generations of Speech Act Theory." *Poetics* 15: 243–257. Concise treatment of both first and second generation of speech act theorists with illustrative material taken from Shakespeare.

Pratt, Mary Louise
1977 *Toward a Speech Act Theory of Discourse.* Bloomington: Indiana University Press, 1977; rev. in *Journal of Literary Semantics* 8 (1979): 45–47; *Journal of Pragmatics* 4 (1980): 61–64; *Style* 12 (1978): 404–407; *Language* 55 (1979): 475–476; *Sewanee Review* 87 (1979): 635–636; *Journal of Aesthetics and art Criticism* 36 (1977): 225–228; *Philosophy and Rhetoric* 11 (1979):

134–138. The first major systematic attempt to develop a comprehensive speech act theory of literature.

Prince, Gerald
    1973   "On Presupposition and Narrative Strategy." *Centrum* 1: 23–31. Examines the way in which presupposition functions as a semantic level which imposes a universe of discourse, controls distance, and manipulates point of view. Similar in viewpoint to the semanticist Oswald Ducrot.

Ravenhill, Philip L.
    1976   "Religious Utterances and the Theory of Speech Acts." Pp. 26–39 in *Language in Religious Practice*. Ed. by William J. Samarin. Rowley Mass: Newbury House. The question of religious illocutionary acts is considered.

Schmachtenberg, Reinhard
    1982   *Sprechakttheorie und dramatischer Dialog: Ein Methodenansatz zur Drameninterpretation*. Tübingen: Max Niemeyer Verlag. Criticizes the notion that literary speech acts are mimetic, and poses instead the thesis that fictive speech acts in drama differ from ordinary speech acts because of the unusual nature of the relation of the viewer (or reader) to them. The author or playwrite must provide "deiktischen Ordnungsschemata" to create the fictional world, and this then breaks down the conventional context of speech acts and requires a psychological and sociological "rezeptionsaesthetik."

Schneider, Monique
    1980   "The Promise of Truth—The Promise of Love." *Diacritics* 11 (1981): 27–38. This is a review of Felman (1980).

Searle, John R.
    1969   *Speech Acts*. Cambridge: Cambridge Univ. Press. Major exposition and development of Austin's philosophy of language.
    1971   "What is a Speech Act?" Pp. 39–53 in *The Philosophy of Language*. London: Oxford Univ. Press. Defines constitutive and regulative rules, and distinguishes between the illocutionary act and the propositional content.
    1975   "The Logical Status of Fictional Discourse." *New Literary History* 6: 319–332. Also pp. 58–75 in *Expression and Meaning*. N.Y., London: Cambridge University Press, 1979. Rev. *Philosophy* 56 (1981): 270–271; rev. Philosophy 56 (1981): 270–271. Argues that literary speech acts are mimetic or pretended speech acts. Distinguishes between fictive and non-fictive discourse within the work of fiction.
    1977   "Reiterating the Differences: A Reply to Derrida." *Glyph One*. Pp. 198–208. Response to Derrida's deconstruction of Austin by

arguing that Austin's view of literary discourse as 'parasitic' is simply a way of referring to "a relation of logical dependence" which bears no moral connotations.

1982   "The Word Turned Upside Down." *New York Review of Books* (October 27): 74–79. An extensive review of Jonothan Culler's *On Deconstruction*. Continues the debate with Derrida began in *Glyph 1*.

Sinclair, J. M. and R. M. Coulthard
1975   *Towards an Analysis of Discourse*. London: Oxford Univ. Press. Proposes to use speech act theory to develop categories for discourse analysis which go beyond the level of sentence grammar.

Strawson, P. F.
1971   "Intention and Convention in Speech Acts." Pp. 23–38 in *The Philosophy of Language*. Ed. J. R. Searle. London: Oxford Univ. Press. Fundamental critique of Austin's view of conventionality with the aim of giving primacy to intentionality.

Thiemann, Ronald F.
1985   *Revelation and Theology*. Notre Dame, Ind.: University of Notre Dame Press. Attempts to go beyond the subject/object split of modern epistemological thinking to recast revelation and the doctrine of God in terms of a theory of narrated promise based on Austin and Searle. His emphasis falls upon the significance of God's identity as an intentional agent disclosed through the promissory gospel narratives with *Matthew* used as an example.

van Dijk, Teun A.
1972   *Some Aspects of Text Grammars: A Study in Theoretical Linguistics and Poetics*. The Hague: Mouton. The last chapter includes reference to speech act theory.

Woodmansee, Martha
1981   "Speech-Act Theory and the Perpetuation of the Dogma of Literary Autonomy." *Centrum* 6; 75–89. Criticizes the recent attempts to develop a speech act theory of literature by considering literary speech acts as mimetic, with no trustworthy propositional or referential content. She refutes this by citing a poem by a Nazi who obviously maintained the propositional truth of his poetic utterence.

SELECTED GENERAL BIBLIOGRAPHY ON SPEECH ACT THEORY

Altieri, Charles
    1978   "What Grice Offers Literary Theory: A Proposal for 'Expressive Implicature'." *Centrum* 6: 90–103.

Amante, David J.
    1981   "The Theory of Ironic Speech Acts." *Poetics Today* 2: 77–96.

Beardsley, Monroe
    1970   *The Possibility of Criticism*. Detroit: Wayne State University Press.
    1973   "The Concept of Literature." Pp. 23–39 in *Literary Theory and Structure: Essays in Honor of William K. Wimsatt*, eds. F. Brady, J. Palmer, M. Price. New Haven: Yale University Press.

Benjamin, James
    1976   "Preformatives as a Rhetorical Construct." *Philosophy and Rhetoric* 9: 84–95.

Brinkman, B. R.
    1972   "Sacramental Man and Speech Acts Again." *Heythrop Journal* 16: 371–401; also 13 (1972): 371–401; 14 (1973): 5–34, 162–189; 280–306; 396–416.

Bruns, Gerald L.
    1980   "Intention, Authority, and Meaning." *Critical Inquiry* 7: 297–309.

Burke, Kenneth
    1975   "Words as Deeds." *Centrum* 3: 147–168.

Campbell, B. G.
    1975   "Toward a Workable Taxonomy of Illocutionary Forces, and its Implication to Works of Imaginative Literature." *Language and Style*, 8: 3–20.

Campbell, Gordon J.
    1972   "Are All Speech Acts Self-involving?" *Religious Studies* 8: 161–164.

Cellard, Jacques, Shoshana Felman, Phillipe Sollers, Viviane Forrester, and Monique Schneider
    1981   "Don Juan ou la promesse d'amour." *Tel Quel* 87: 16–36.

Cicourel, Aaron V.
    1980   "Language and Social Interaction: Philosophical and Empirical Issues." *Sociological Inquiry* 50: 1–30.

Cohen, L. Jonothan
    1964   "Do Illocutionary Forces Exist?" *Philosophical Quarterly* 14: 118–137.

Cooper, Marilyn M.
    1981   "Implicature, Convention, and 'The Taming of the Shrew.'" *Poetics* 10: 1–14.
    1982   "Context as Vehicle: Implications in Writing." Pp. 105–128 in Martin Nystrand, ed. *What Writers Know: The Language, Process and Structure of Written Discourse*. New York: Academic Press.

Culler, Jonathan
    1981   "Convention and Meaning." *New Literary History* 13: 15–30.

Dalferth, Ingolf
    1979   "Religiöse Sprechakte als Kriterien des Religiosität? Kritique eines Confusion." *Linguistica Biblica* 44: 101–118.

Davidson, Donald
    1984   "Communication and Convention," *Synthèse* 59: 3–18.

Derrida, Jacques
    1981   *Dissemination*. Tr. from the French by Barbara Johnson. Chicago: The University of Chicago Press; London: The Athlone Press.

Finnegan, Ruth
    1969   "How to do Things with Words: Performative Utterances Among the Lumba of Sierra Leone." *Man* 4: 537–552.

Fish, Stanley
    1973–74   "How Ordinary is Ordinary Language?" *New Literary History* 5: 41–54.
    1978   "Normal Circumstances, Literary Language, Direct Speech Acts, the Ordinary, the Everyday, the Obvious, What Goes Without Saying, and Other Special Cases." *Critical Inquiry* 4: 625–644.
    1979   "A Reply to John Reichert; or, How to Stop Worrying and Learn to Love Interpretation." *Critical Inquiry* 6: 173–178.
    1980   *Is There a Text in This Class?: The Authority of Interpretive Communities*. Cambridge, Mass.: Harvard University Press, 1980. Rev. *Modern Language Notes* 96 (1981): 1168–1171.

Foucault, Michel
    1979   "What is an Author?" in *Textual Strategies*, ed. Josue V. Harari. Ithaca: Cornell University Press. Pp. 141–160.

Gill, Sam D.
- 1977 "Prayer as a Person: The Performative Force in Navajo Prayer Acts." *History of Religions* 17: 143–157.

Halliday, M. A. K.
- 1974 "The Context of Linguistics." *Georgetown University Round Table on Languages and Linguistics,*. Pp. 179–197.

Hancher, Michael
- 1972 "Three Kinds of Intention." *Modern Language Notes* 87: 837–851.
- 1975 "Understanding Poetic Speech Acts." *College English* 36: 632–639. Rpt. in *Linguistic Perspectives on Literature* ed. Marvin L. K. Ching, Michael C. Haley, and Ronald S. Lundsford. London: Routledge, 1980, Pp. 295–304.
- 1978 "Describing and Interpreting as Speech Acts." *Journal of Aesthetics and Art Criticism* 36 (1978): 483–485.
- 1980 "How to Play Games With Words: Speech-Act Jokes." *Journal of Literary Semantics* 9: 20–29.
- 1981 "Humpty Dumpty and Verbal Meaning." *Journal of Aesthetics and Art Criticism* 40: 49–58.
- 1981a "What Kind of Speech Act is Interpretation?" *Poetics* 10: 263–282.
- 1982 "Dead Letters: Wills and Poems." *Texas Law Review* 60: 507–525.

Hermeren, Goeran
- 1975 "Intention and Interpretation in Literary Criticism." *New Literary History* 7: 57–62.

Hernadi, Paul
- 1981 "Literary Theory." Pp. 98–115. In *Introduction to Scholarship in Modern Languages and Literatures,* ed. Joseph Gibaldi. New York: Modern Language Association of America.

Hirsch, Eric Donald, Jr.
- 1976 *The Aims of Interpretation.* Chicago, London: University of Chicago Press.
- 1975 "What's the Use of Speech Act Theory?" *Centrum* 3: 121–146.
- 1975a "Current Issues in the Theory of Interpretation." *Journal of Religion* 55: 298–312.
- 1975b "Stylistics and Synonymity." *Critical Inquiry* 1: 559–580.

Holland, Norman
- 1980 "Re-Covering 'The Purloined Letter': Reading as a Personal Transaction." Pp. 50–370 in *The Reader in the Text: Essays on Audience and Interpretation.* Edited by Susan R. Suleiman and Inge Crosman. Princeton: Princeton University Press.

Huttar, George L.
    1980   "Metaphorical Speech Acts." *Poetics* 9: 383–401.

Iser, Wolfgang
    1978   *The Act of Reading: A Theory of Aesthetic Response*. Baltimore, London: Johns Hopkins Press.

Johnson, Barbara
    1977   "Poetry and Performative Language." *Yale French Studies* 54 (1977): 52–66.

Kasher, Asa
    1984   "Are Speech Acts Conventional?" *Journal of Pragmatics* 8: 65–70.

Kuhns, Richard, David Halliburton, Martin Steinmann,Jr., and T. R. Martland
    1972   "Discussion: Literature as Performative." *Centrum* 6: 113–172.

Leonardi, Paolo, ed.
    1984   *Speech Acts after Speech Act Theory*. Special issue of the *Journal of Pragmatics* 8:1.

Mack, Dorothy
    1975   "Metaphoring as Speech Act: Some Happiness Conditions for Implicit Similes and Simple Metaphors." *Poetics* 4: 221–256.

Man, Paul de
    1976   "Political Allegory in Rousseau." *Critical Inquiry* 2: 649–675.

Margolis, Joseph
    1957   "Meaning, Speakers' Intentions, and Speech Acts." *Philosophical Review* 66: 377–388.

Martinich, A. P.
    1975   "Sacraments and Speech Acts." *Heythrop Journal* 16: 289–303 (on baptism); 17 (1975): 405–417 (other sacraments).

McGuire, R. R.
    1977   "Speech Acts, Communicative Competence, and the Paradox of Authority." *Philosophy and Rhetoric* 10: 30–45.

Meiland, Jack W.
    1978   "Interpretation as a Cognitive Discipline." *Philosophy and Literature* 2: 23–45.

Nohrenberg, James
    1974   "On Literature and the Bible." *Centrum* 2: 5–43.

Ohmann, Richard
    1971   "Speech, Action, Style." Pp. 241–262 in *Literary Style: A Symposium*. London, New York: Oxford Univ. Press.
    1971a   "Speech Acts and the Definition of Literature." *Philosophy and Rhetoric* 4: 1–19.
    1972   "Speech, Literature, and the Space Between," *New Literary*

Prince, Gerald
- 1982 "Narrative Analysis and Narratology." *New Literary History* 13: 179–188.

Putnam, Hilary
- 1981 "Convention: A Theme in Philosophy." *New Literary History* 13: 1–14.

Randsell, J.
- 1971 "Constitutive Rules and Speech Act Analysis." *Journal of Philosophy* 13: 385–400.

Ray, Benjamin
- 1973–74 "'Performative Utterances' in African Rituals." *History of Religions* 13: 16–35.

Reichert, John
- 1977 *Making Sense of Literature*. Chicago: Univ. of Chicago Press.
- 1979 "But That Was in Another Ball Park: A Reply to Stanley Fish." *Critical Inquiry* 6: 164–171.

Rosaldo, M. Z.
- 1982 "The Things We Do With Words: Ilongot Speech Acts and Speech Act Theory in Philosophy." *Language and Society* 11: 203–237.

Sadock, Jerrold, M.
- 1974 *Toward a Linguistic Theory of Speech Acts*. New York: Academic Press. Reviews found in the *Linguistic Reporter* 19 (Nov. 7, 1976); *General Linguistics* 16 (1976): 236–242.

Sanders, Robert E.
- 1976 "In Defense of Speech Acts." *Philosophy and Rhetoric* 9: 112–122.

Schleusener, J.
- 1980 "Convention and the Context of Reading." *Critical Inquiry* 6: 669–680.

Searle, John R.
- 1971 Ed. *The Philosophy of Language*. London: Oxford University Press.
- 1973 "Austin on Locutionary and Illocutionary Acts". Pp. 141–159 in *Essays on J. L. Austin*, ed. G. J. Warnock. Oxford: Clarendon Press.
- 1983 With Daniel Vanderveken. *Foundations of Illocutionary Logic*. Cambridge: Cambridge University Press, 1983.

Shirley, Edward S.
- 1975 "The Impossibility of a Speech Act Theory of Meaning." *Philosophy and Rhetoric* 8: 114–122. The rebuttal to this argument

is given by Robert E. Sanders, "In Defense of Speech Acts." *Philosophy and Rhetoric* 9 (1976): 110–115.

Skinner, Quentin
    1971   "Conventions and the Understanding of Speech Acts." *Philosophical Quarterly* 20: 118–138.

Smith, Barbara Herrnstein
    1978   *On the Margins of Discourse*. Chicago, London: University of Chicago Press, 1978.

Spivak, Gayatri Chakravorty
    1980   "Revolutions That as yet Have No Model: Derrida's *Limited Inc*." *Diacritics* 10: 29–49.

Steinmann, Martin, Jr.
    1973–74   "Cumulation, Revolution and Progress." *New Literary History* 5: 477–490.

Vendler, Z.
    1970   "Les Performatifs en Perspective." *Langages* 17: 73–90.

Verschueren, Jeffry
    1981   "The Pragmatics of Text Acts." *Journal of Literary Semantics* 10: 10–19.

Warnock, G. J.
    1973   "Some Types of Performative Utterance." In *Essays on J. L. Austin*. Ed. Isaiah Berlin, G. J. Warnock, et al. Oxford: Clarendon Press.

Weber, Samuel
    1978   "It." *Glyph* 4: 1–31.

Wildekamp, Ada, Ineke van Montfoort, and Willem van Ruiswijk.
    1980   "Fictionality and Convention." *Poetics* 9: 547–567.

Wright, Edmund
    1982   "Derrida, Searle, Contexts, Games, Riddle" *New Literary History* 13: 463–477.

Wunderlich, Dieter
    1976   *Studien zur Sprechakttheorie*. Frankfort am Main: Suhrkamp Verlag.

www.ingramcontent.com/pod-product-compliance
Lightning Source LLC
Chambersburg PA
CBHW032256150426
43195CB00008BA/471